BLOOM'S

HOW TO WRITE ABOUT

F. Scott Fitzgerald

KIM E. BECNEL

BLOOM'S
LITERARY CRITICISM
An imprint of Infobase Publishing

Bloom's How to Write about F. Scott Fitzgerald

Bloom's Literary Criticism
An imprint of Infobase Publishing
132 West 31st Street
New York NY 10001

Library of Congress Cataloging-in-Publication Data

Becnel, Kim E.
    Bloom's how to write about F. Scott Fitzgerald / Kim E. Becnel ; introduction by Harold Bloom.
        p. cm.
    Includes bibliographical references (p.) and index.
    ISBN 978-0-7910-9482-2 (hc : alk. paper) 1. Fitzgerald, F. Scott (Francis Scott), 1896–1940—Criticism and interpretation. 2. Criticism—Authorship. 3. Report writing. I. Bloom, Harold. II. Title. III. Title: How to write about F. Scott Fitzgerald.

    PS3511.I9Z55773 2008
    813'.52—dc22   2006101321

Bloom's Literary Criticism books are available at special discounts when purchased in bulk quantities for businesses, associations, institutions, or sales promotions. Please call our Special Sales Department in New York at (212) 967-8800 or (800) 322-8755.

You can find Bloom's Literary Criticism on the World Wide Web at http://www.chelseahouse.com

Text design by Annie O'Donnell
Cover design by Ben Peterson

Printed in the United States of America

Bang MSRF 10 9 8 7 6 5 4 3 2 1

This book is printed on acid-free paper.

CONTENTS

SERIES
INTRODUCTION

BLOOM's How to Write about Literature series is designed to inspire students to write fine essays on great writers and their works. Each volume in the series begins with an introduction by Harold Bloom, meditating on the challenges and rewards of writing about the volume's subject author. The first chapter then provides detailed instructions on how to write a good essay, including how to find a thesis; how to develop an outline; how to write a good introduction, body text, and conclusions; how to cite sources; and more. The second chapter provides a brief overview of the issues involved in writing about the subject author and then a number of suggestions for paper topics, with accompanying strategies for addressing each topic. Succeeding chapters cover the author's major works.

The paper topics suggested within this book are open-ended, and the brief strategies provided are designed to give students a push forward on the writing process rather than a road map to success. The aim of the book is to pose questions, not answer them. Many different kinds of papers could result from each topic. As always, the success of each paper will depend completely on the writer's skill and imagination.

HOW TO WRITE ABOUT
F. SCOTT FITZGERALD

Introduction by Harold Bloom

BY GENERAL consent of what Samuel Johnson and Virginia Woolf termed "the common reader," *The Great Gatsby* (1925) constitutes F. Scott Fitzgerald's masterwork, though *Tender Is the Night* (1934) was his most ambitious novel. One of his short stories, "Babylon Revisited," is a splendor comparable to the best of Henry James in that genre, though the fantasy "The Diamond as Big as the Ritz" is more famous among Fitzgerald's shorter fictions.

Still, when one thinks of F. Scott Fitzgerald, Gatsby rises before one, doubtless looking like Robert Redford playing the role in Jack Clayton's rather inadequate film (1974), only partly redeemed by Sam Waterston's Nick Carraway. Waterston was good enough to make me reflect upon Joseph Conrad's Marlow as the principal narrative influence upon Faulkner, Hemingway, and Fitzgerald alike. In Faulkner, Conrad merges with the influences of Melville and of Mark Twain, while Twain fuses with Conrad in Hemingway's way of telling a story. Fitzgerald, a higher romantic even than Faulkner and Hemingway, mixed much of the stance and sensibility of John Keats with the Conradian-Jamesian way of storytelling.

There are many ways to write usefully about Fitzgerald, but his lifelong love of Keats provides one of the good places to begin. Like Keats, Fitzgerald loved the richness of sensation that the world affords us, when we are young, ambitious, and fecund with hope. Keats died of tuberculosis before he was 26, and Fitzgerald had not turned 44 before an alcohol-induced heart attack ended him. Each, though, left permanent works, despite the terrible sadness of their final years.

Tender Is the Night not only takes its title from Fitzgerald's favorite poem, "Ode to a Nightingale," but also can be read as structuring itself through an elaboration on Keats's themes and procedures in that astonishing lyric. But much of *The Great Gatsby* is also Keatsian. I recall once observing that Jay Gatsby himself is a splendidly improbable and yet persuasive amalgam of John Keats and an American "front-man" gangster of the Roaring Twenties. Daisy is a pathetic substitute for Keats's muse, Fanny Brawne, but for different reasons both women are unattainable.

Writing about the Keatsian Scott Fitzgerald would emphasize his oxymoronic style, as replete with unresolved contradictions as Keats's own rich diction. The style in each instance was both the man and the author. Beyond any other American master of prose narrative, Fitzgerald was a lyrical storyteller. In his finest work, he is as disenchanted as Keats, while preserving also Keats's capacity of being open to the possibility of enchantment. Like Henry James, Fitzgerald was an exquisite artist, fully in control of his intended effects. Yet unlike James and Conrad, Fitzgerald gratifies our inner ear, ravished by his Keatsian harmonies.

HOW TO WRITE
A GOOD ESSAY
by Laurie A. Sterling and Kim E. Becnel

WHILE THERE are many ways to write about literature, most assignments for high school and college English classes call for analytical papers. In these assignments, you are presenting your interpretation of a text to your reader. Your objective is to interpret the text's meaning in order to enhance your reader's understanding and enjoyment of the work. Without exception, strong papers about the meaning of a literary work are built upon a careful, close reading of the text or texts. Careful, analytical reading should always be the first step in your writing process. This volume provides models of such close, analytical reading, and these should help you develop your own skills as a reader and as a writer.

As the examples throughout this book demonstrate, attentive reading entails thinking about and evaluating the formal (textual) aspects of the author's works: theme, character, form, and language. In addition, when writing about a work, many readers choose to move beyond the text itself to consider the work's cultural context. In these instances, writers might explore the historical circumstances of the time period in which the work was written. Alternatively, they might examine the philosophies and ideas that a work addresses. Even in cases where writers explore a work's cultural context, though, papers must still address the more formal aspects of the work itself. A good interpretative essay that evaluates Charles Dickens's use of the philosophy of utilitarianism in his novel *Hard Times*, for example, cannot adequately address the author's treatment of the philosophy without firmly grounding this discussion in the book itself. In other words, any

1

analytical paper about a text, even one that seeks to evaluate the work's cultural context, must also have a firm handle on the work's themes, characters, and language. You must look for and evaluate these aspects of a work, then, as you read a text and as you prepare to write about it.

WRITING ABOUT THEMES

Literary themes are more than just topics or subjects treated in a work; they are attitudes or points about these topics that often structure other elements in a work. Writing about theme therefore requires that you not just identify a topic that a literary work addresses but also discuss what that work says about that topic. For example, if you were writing about the culture of the American South in William Faulkner's famous story "A Rose for Emily," you would need to discuss what Faulkner says, argues, or implies about that culture and its passing.

When you prepare to write about thematic concerns in a work of literature, you will probably discover that, like most works of literature, your text touches upon other themes in addition to its central theme. These secondary themes also provide rich ground for paper topics. A thematic paper on "A Rose for Emily" might consider gender or race in the story. While neither of these could be said to be the central theme of the story, they are clearly related to the passing of the "old South" and could provide plenty of good material for papers.

As you prepare to write about themes in literature, you might find a number of strategies helpful. After you identify a theme or themes in the story, you should begin by evaluating how other elements of the story—such as character, point of view, imagery, and symbolism—help develop the theme. You might ask yourself what your own responses are to the author's treatment of the subject matter. Do not neglect the obvious, either: What expectations does the title set up? How does the title help develop thematic concerns? Clearly, the title "A Rose for Emily" says something about the narrator's attitude toward the title character, Emily Grierson, and all she represents.

WRITING ABOUT CHARACTER

Generally, characters are essential components of fiction and drama. (This is not always the case, though; Ray Bradbury's "August 2026: There

Will Come Soft Rains" is technically a story without characters, at least any human characters.) Often, you can discuss character in poetry, as in T. S. Eliot's "The Love Song of J. Alfred Prufrock" or Robert Browning's "My Last Duchess." Many writers find that analyzing character is one of the most interesting and engaging ways to work with a piece of literature and to shape a paper. After all, characters generally are human, and we all know something about being human and living in the world. While it is always important to remember that these figures are not real people but creations of the writer's imagination, it can be fruitful to begin evaluating them as you might evaluate a real person. Often you can start with your own response to a character. Did you like or dislike the character? Did you sympathize with the character? Why or why not?

Keep in mind, though, that emotional responses like these are just starting places. To truly explore and evaluate literary characters, you need to return to the formal aspects of the text and evaluate how the author has drawn these characters. The 20th-century writer E. M. Forster coined the terms *flat* characters and *round* characters. Flat characters are static, one-dimensional characters who frequently represent a particular concept or idea. In contrast, round characters are fully drawn and much more realistic characters who frequently change and develop over the course of a work. Are the characters you are studying flat or round? What elements of the characters lead you to this conclusion? Why might the author have drawn characters like this? How does their development affect the meaning of the work? Similarly, you should explore the techniques the author uses to develop characters. Do we hear a character's own words, or do we hear only other characters' assessments of him or her? Or does the author use an omniscient or limited omniscient narrator to allow us access to the workings of the characters' minds? If so, how does that help develop the characterization? Often you can even evaluate the narrator as a character. How trustworthy are the opinions and assessments of the narrator? You should also think about characters' names. Do they mean anything? If you encounter a hero named Sophia or Sophie, you should probably think about her wisdom (or lack thereof), since *Sophia* means "wisdom" in Greek. Similarly, since the name *Sylvia* is derived from the word *sylvan*, meaning "of the wood," you might want to evaluate that character's relationship with nature. Once again, you might look to the title of the work. Does Herman Melville's "Bartleby, the Scrivener" signal anything about Bartleby himself? Is Bartleby adequately defined by his job as scrivener?

Is this part of Melville's point? Pursuing questions like these can help you develop thorough papers about characters from psychological, sociological, or more formalistic perspectives.

WRITING ABOUT FORM AND GENRE

Genre, a word derived from French, means "type" or "class." Literary genres are distinctive classes or categories of literary composition. On the most general level, literary works can be divided into the genres of drama, poetry, fiction, and essays, yet within those genres there are classifications that are also referred to as genres. Tragedy and comedy, for example, are genres of drama. Epic, lyric, and pastoral are genres of poetry. *Form,* on the other hand, generally refers to the shape or structure of a work. There are many clearly defined forms of poetry that follow specific patterns of meter, rhyme, and stanza. Sonnets, for example, are poems that follow a fixed form of 14 lines. Sonnets generally follow one of two basic sonnet forms, each with its own distinct rhyme scheme. Haiku is another example of poetic form, traditionally consisting of three unrhymed lines of five, seven, and five syllables.

While you might think that writing about form or genre might leave little room for argument, many of these forms and genres are very fluid. Remember that literature is evolving and ever changing, and so are its forms. As you study poetry, you may find that poets, especially more modern poets, play with traditional poetic forms, bringing about new effects. Similarly, dramatic tragedy was once quite narrowly defined, but over the centuries playwrights have broadened and challenged traditional definitions, changing the shape of tragedy. When Arthur Miller wrote *Death of a Salesman,* many critics challenged the idea that tragic drama could encompass a common man like Willy Loman.

Evaluating how a work of literature fits into or challenges the boundaries of its form or genre can provide you with fruitful avenues of investigation. You might find it helpful to ask why the work does or does not fit into traditional categories. Why might Miller have thought it fitting to write a tragedy of the common man? Similarly, you might compare the content or theme of a work with its form. How well do they work together? Many of Emily Dickinson's poems, for instance, follow the meter of traditional hymns. While some of her poems seem to express traditional religious doctrines, many seem to challenge or strain against traditional conceptions of God and theology. What is the effect, then, of her use of traditional hymn meter?

WRITING ABOUT LANGUAGE, SYMBOLS, AND IMAGERY

No matter what the genre, writers use words as their most basic tool. Language is the most fundamental building block of literature. It is essential that you pay careful attention to the author's language and word choice as you read, reread, and analyze a text. Imagery is language that appeals to the senses. Most commonly, imagery appeals to our sense of vision, creating a mental picture, but authors also use language that appeals to our other senses. Images can be literal or figurative. Literal images use sensory language to describe an actual thing. In the broadest terms, figurative language uses one thing to speak about something else. For example, if I call my boss a snake, I am not saying that he is literally a reptile. Instead, I am using figurative language to communicate my opinions about him. Since we think of snakes as sneaky, slimy, and sinister, I am using the concrete image of a snake to communicate these abstract opinions and impressions.

The two most common figures of speech are similes and metaphors. Both are comparisons between two apparently dissimilar things. Similes are explicit comparisons using the words *like* or *as;* metaphors are implicit comparisons. To return to the previous example, if I say, "My boss, Bob, was waiting for me when I showed up to work five minutes late today—the snake!" I have constructed a metaphor.

Writing about his experiences fighting in World War I, Wilfred Owen begins his poem "Dulce et decorum est" with a string of similes: "Bent double, like old beggars under sacks, / Knock-kneed, coughing like hags, we cursed through sludge." Owen's goal was to undercut clichéd notions that war and dying in battle were glorious. Certainly, comparing soldiers to coughing hags and to beggars underscores his point.

"Fog," a short poem by Carl Sandburg, provides a clear example of a metaphor. Sandburg's poem reads:

> The fog comes
> on little cat feet.

> It sits looking
> over harbor and city
> on silent haunches
> and then moves on.

Notice how effectively Sandburg conveys surprising impressions of the fog by comparing two seemingly disparate things—the fog and a cat.

Symbols, by contrast, are things that stand for, or represent, other things. Often they represent something intangible, such as concepts or ideas. In everyday life we use and understand symbols easily. Babies at christenings and brides at weddings wear white to represent purity. Think, too, of a dollar bill. The paper itself has no value in and of itself. Instead, that paper bill is a symbol of something else, the precious metal in a nation's coffers. Symbols in literature work similarly. Authors use symbols to evoke more than a simple, straightforward, literal meaning. Characters, objects, and places can all function as symbols. Famous literary examples of symbols include Moby-Dick, the white whale of Herman Melville's novel, and the scarlet *A* of Nathaniel Hawthorne's *The Scarlet Letter.* As both of these symbols suggest, a literary symbol cannot be adequately defined or explained by any one meaning. Hester Prynne's Puritan community clearly intends her scarlet *A* as a symbol of her adultery, but as the novel progresses, even her own community reads the letter as representing not just *adultery,* but *able, angel,* and a host of other meanings.

Writing about imagery and symbols requires close attention to the author's language. To prepare a paper on symbolism or imagery in a work, identify and trace the images and symbols and then try to draw some conclusions about how they function. Ask yourself how any symbols or images help contribute to the themes or meanings of the work. What connotations do they carry? How do they affect your reception of the work? Do they shed light on characters or settings? A strong paper on imagery or symbolism will thoroughly consider the use of figures in the text and will try to reach some conclusions about how or why the author uses them.

WRITING ABOUT HISTORY AND CONTEXT

As noted above, it is possible to write an analytical paper that also considers the work's context. After all, the text was not created in a vacuum. The author lived and wrote in a specific time period and in a specific cultural context and, like all of us, was shaped by that environment. Learning more about the historical and cultural circumstances that surround the author and the work can help illuminate a text and provide you with productive material for a paper. Remember, though, that when you write analytical papers, you should use the context to illuminate the text. Do not lose sight of your goal—to interpret the meaning of the literary work. Use historical or philosophical research as a tool to develop your textual evaluation.

Thoughtful readers often consider how history and culture affected the author's choice and treatment of his or her subject matter. Investigations into the history and context of a work could examine the work's relation to specific historical events, such as the Salem witch trials in 17th-century Massachusetts or the restoration of Charles to the British throne in 1660. Bear in mind that historical context is not limited to politics and world events. While knowing about the Vietnam War is certainly helpful in interpreting much of Tim O'Brien's fiction, and some knowledge of the French Revolution clearly illuminates the dynamics of Charles Dickens's *A Tale of Two Cities,* historical context also entails the fabric of daily life. Examining a text in light of gender roles, race relations, class boundaries, or working conditions can give rise to thoughtful and compelling papers. Exploring the conditions of the working class in 19th-century England, for example, can provide a particularly effective avenue for writing about Dickens's *Hard Times.*

You can begin thinking about these issues by asking broad questions at first. What do you know about the time period and about the author? What does the editorial apparatus in your text tell you? These might be starting places. Similarly, when specific historical events or dynamics are particularly important to understanding a work but might be somewhat obscure to modern readers, textbooks usually provide notes to explain historical background. These are a good place to start. With this information, ask yourself how these historical facts and circumstances might have affected the author, the presentation of theme, and the presentation of character. How does knowing more about the work's specific historical context illuminate the work? To take a well-known example, understanding the complex attitudes toward slavery during the time Mark Twain wrote *Adventures of Huckleberry Finn* should help you begin to examine issues of race in the text. Additionally, you might compare these attitudes to those of the time in which the novel was set. How might this comparison affect your interpretation of a work written after the abolition of slavery but set before the Civil War?

WRITING ABOUT PHILOSOPHY AND IDEAS

Philosophical concerns are closely related to both historical context and thematic issues. Like historical investigation, philosophical research can provide a useful tool as you analyze a text. For example, an investigation into the working class in Dickens's England might lead you to a topic on the philosophical doctrine of utilitarianism in *Hard Times.* Many other works explore philosophies and ideas quite explicitly. Mary Shelley's famous novel *Frankenstein,* for example, explores John Locke's tabula rasa theory of human knowledge as she portrays the intellectual and emotional development of Victor Frankenstein's creature. As this example indicates, philosophical issues are somewhat more abstract than investigations of theme or historical context. Some other examples of philosophical issues include human free will, the formation of human identity, the nature of sin, or questions of ethics.

Writing about philosophy and ideas might require some outside research, but usually the notes or other material in your text will provide you with basic information, and often footnotes and bibliographies suggest places you can go to read further about the subject. If you have identified a philosophical theme that runs through a text, you might ask yourself how the author develops this theme. Look at character development and the interactions of characters, for example. Similarly, you might examine whether the narrative voice in a work of fiction addresses the philosophical concerns of the text.

WRITING COMPARISON AND CONTRAST ESSAYS

Finally, you might find that comparing and contrasting the works or techniques of an author provide a useful tool for literary analysis. A comparison and contrast essay might compare two characters or themes in a single work, or it might compare the author's treatment of a theme in two works. It might also contrast methods of character development or analyze an author's differing treatment of a philosophical concern in two works. Writing comparison and contrast essays, though, requires some special consideration. While they generally provide you with plenty of material to use, they also come with a built-in trap: the laundry list. These papers often become mere lists of connections between the works. As this chapter will discuss, a strong thesis must make an assertion that you want to prove or validate. A strong comparison/contrast thesis, then, needs to comment on the significance of the similarities and differences you observe. It is not enough merely to assert that the works contain similarities and differences. You might, for example, assert why the similarities and differences are important and explain how they illuminate the works' treatment of theme. Remember, too, that a thesis should not be a statement of the obvious. A comparison/contrast paper that focuses only on very obvious similarities or differences does little to illuminate the connections between the works. Often, an effective method of shaping a strong thesis and argument is to begin your paper by noting the similarities between the works but then to develop a thesis that asserts how these apparently similar elements are different. If, for example, you observe that Emily Dickinson wrote a number of poems about spiders, you might analyze how she uses spider imagery differently in two poems. Similarly, many scholars have noted that Hawthorne created many "mad scientist" characters, men who are so devoted to their science or their art that they lose perspective on all else. A good thesis comparing two of these characters—Aylmer of "The Birthmark" and Dr. Rappaccini of "Rappaccini's Daughter," for example—might initially identify both characters as examples of Hawthorne's mad scientist type but then argue that their motivations for scientific experimentation differ. If you strive to analyze the similarities or differences, discuss significances, and move beyond the obvious, your paper should move beyond the laundry list trap.

PREPARING TO WRITE

Armed with a clear sense of your task—illuminating the text—and with an understanding of theme, character, language, history, and philosophy, you are ready to approach the writing process. Remember that good writing is grounded in good reading and that close reading takes time, attention, and more than one reading of your text. Read for comprehension first. As you go back and review the work, mark the text to chart the details of the work as well as your reactions. Highlight important passages, repeated words, and image patterns. "Converse" with the text through marginal notes. Mark turns in the plot, ask questions, and make observations about characters, themes, and language. If you are reading from a book that does not belong to you, keep a record of your reactions in a journal or notebook. If you have read a work of literature carefully, paying attention to both the text and the context of the work, you have a leg up on the writing process. Admittedly, at this point, your ideas are probably very broad and undefined, but you have taken an important first step toward writing a strong paper.

Your next step is to focus, to take a broad, perhaps fuzzy, topic and define it more clearly. Even a topic provided by your instructor will need to be focused appropriately. Remember that good writers make the topic their own. There are a number of strategies—often called "invention"—that you can use to develop your own focus. In one such strategy, *freewriting*, you spend 10 minutes or so just writing about your topic without referring back to the text or your notes. Write whatever comes to mind; the important thing is that you just keep writing. Often this process allows you to develop fresh ideas or approaches to your subject matter. You could also try *brainstorming:* Write down your topic and then list all the related points or ideas you can think of. Include questions, comments, words, important passages or events, and anything else that comes to mind. Let one idea lead to another. In the related technique of *clustering*, or *mapping*, write your topic on a sheet of paper and write related ideas around it. Then list related subpoints under each of these main ideas. Many people then draw arrows to show connections between points. This technique helps you narrow your topic and can also help you organize your ideas. Similarly, asking journalistic questions—Who? What? Where? When? Why? and How?—can generate ideas for topic development.

THESIS STATEMENTS

Once you have developed a focused topic, you can begin to think about your thesis statement, the main point or purpose of your paper. It is imperative that you craft a strong thesis; otherwise, your paper will likely be little more than random, disorganized observations about the text. Think of your thesis statement as a kind of road map for your paper. It tells your reader where you are going and how you are going to get there.

To craft a good thesis, you must keep a number of things in mind. First, as the title of this subsection indicates, your paper's thesis should be a statement, an assertion about the text that you want to prove or validate. Beginning writers often formulate a question that they attempt to use as a thesis. For example, a writer exploring the contrasting ideas of womanhood held by Marjorie and Bernice in Fitzgerald's "Bernice Bobs Her Hair," might ask, Whose version of womanhood wins out in the end and is it really a better one? While a question like this is a good strategy to use in the invention process to help narrow your topic and find your thesis, it cannot serve as the thesis statement because it does not tell your reader what you want to assert about these characters and their idea of womanhood. You might shape this question into a thesis by instead proposing an answer to that question: Marjorie indoctrinates Bernice into new ideas of womanhood, helping her move from a belief that women are timid, sentimental creatures to a belief that women should be cheerful, lively, and witty. Although Marjorie's ideas are supposed to be progressive, they share the same central flaw as Bernice's—they imply that the supreme goal of women is to please men—while introducing a troubling new one: ruthless competition. Notice that this thesis provides an initial plan or structure for the rest of the paper, and notice, too, that the thesis statement does not necessarily have to fit into one sentence. After establishing Bernice's and Marjorie's ideas of womanhood, the writer can then compare and contrast these ideas, demonstrating their similarities and their differences.

Second, remember that a good thesis makes an assertion that you need to support. In other words, a good thesis does not state the obvious. If you tried to formulate a thesis about Bernice and Marjorie by simply saying, In Fitzgerald's "Bernice Bobs Her Hair," Marjorie and Bernice have different ideas about what it means to be a woman, you have done nothing but rephrase the obvious. Since the story makes this clear, there would be no point in spending three to five pages to support that assertion. You might try to develop a thesis from that point by asking yourself some further questions: What exactly are Bernice's and Marjorie's ideas? Where do they come from? How are they similar and different? Which one wins out in this story? Does the new idea of womanhood seem better or worse than the old one? Such a line of questioning might lead you to a more viable thesis, like the one in the preceding paragraph.

As the comparison with the road map also suggests, your thesis should appear near the beginning of the paper. In relatively short papers (three to six pages) the thesis almost always appears in the first paragraph. Some writers fall into the trap of saving their thesis for the end, trying to provide a surprise or a big moment of revelation, as if to say, "TA-DA! I've just proved that despite appearances to the contrary, Honoria, in Fitzgerald's 'Babylon Revisited' would be better off with her father, who is a more open, positive, and optimistic character than her bitter, envious aunt." Placing a thesis at the end of an essay can seriously mar the essay's effectiveness. If you fail to define your essay's point and purpose clearly at the beginning, your reader will find it difficult to assess the clarity of your argument and understand the points you are making. When your argument comes as a surprise at the end, you force your reader to reread your essay in order to assess its logic and effectiveness.

Finally, you should avoid using the first person ("I") as you present your thesis. Though it is not strictly wrong to write in the first person, it is difficult to do so gracefully. While writing in the first person, beginning writers often fall into the trap of writing self-reflexive prose (writing *about* their paper *in* their paper). Often this leads to the most dreaded of opening lines: "In this paper I am going to discuss. . . ." Not only does this self-reflexive voice make for very awkward prose, it frequently allows writers to boldly announce a topic while completely avoiding a thesis statement. An example might be a paper that begins as follows: `The Great Gatsby, Fitzgerald's most critically acclaimed novel, tells the story of Jay Gatz, a poor boy who became rich and invented a new identity for himself in order to win back the woman he once loved. In this paper, I am going to discuss the meaning of the American Dream in this novel.` The author of this paper has done little more than announce a topic for the paper (the significance of the American Dream). While the last sentence might be intended as a thesis, the writer fails to present an opinion about the significance of the American Dream. To improve this "thesis," the writer would need to back up a couple of steps. First, the announced topic of the paper is too broad; literary scholars have long discussed the meaning of the American Dream in *The Great Gatsby*. The writer should first think about what the novel is saying about the American Dream. The writer might want to decide whether the novel is portraying the American Dream in a negative or positive light and to what end. From there, the writer can begin to craft a specific thesis. A writer who chooses to argue that *The Great Gatsby* portrays a negative view of the American Dream, for example, might craft a thesis that reads, F. Scott Fitzgerald's *The Great Gatsby* illustrates that because the American Dream focuses on material success, people like Gatsby who spend their lives striving for it may reach their goal yet end up disappointed nonetheless because they remain spiritually and emotionally unfulfilled.

OUTLINES

While developing a strong, thoughtful thesis early in your writing process should help focus your paper, outlining provides an essential tool for logically shaping that paper. A good outline helps you see—and develop—the relationships among the points in your argument and assures you that your paper flows logically and coherently. Outlining not only helps place your points in a logical order but also helps you subordinate supporting points, weed out any irrelevant points, and decide if there are any necessary points that are missing from your argument. Most of us are familiar with formal outlines that use numerical and letter designations for each point. However, there are different types of outlines; you may find that an informal outline is a more useful tool for you. What is important, though, is that you spend the time to develop some sort of outline—formal or informal.

Remember that an outline is a tool to help you shape and write a strong paper. If you do not spend sufficient time planning your supporting points and shaping the arrangement of those points, you will most likely construct a vague, unfocused outline that provides little, if any, help with the writing of the paper. Consider the following example.

Thesis: F. Scott Fitzgerald's *The Great Gatsby* illustrates that because the American Dream focuses on material success, people like Gatsby who spend their lives striving for it may reach their goal and end up disappointed nonetheless because they remain spiritually and emotionally unfulfilled.

```
  I. Introduction and thesis

 II. The hard road to success
     A. Earning money

III. What Gatsby really wants and does not achieve
     A. Daisy
     B. To repeat the past

 IV. What success looks like—rewards of Gatsby's
     hard work
     A. Parties
     B. Possessions
     C. Making up stories about his life

  V. Conclusion
     A. Despite material success, Gatsby is
        unfulfilled
```

This outline has a number of flaws. First, the major topics labeled with the Roman numerals are not arranged in a logical order. It would make more sense, for example, to discuss the rewards of the American Dream after the paragraph on what Gatsby had to do to achieve the American Dream. Secondly, in section IV, the writer includes making up stories about his life as one of the rewards of Gatsby's hard work. This would fit much better under section II, which describes what Gatsby had to do to achieve success. A third problem is the inclusion of a letter A in sections II and V. An outline should not include an A without a B, a 1 without a 2, and so forth. The final problem with this outline is the overall lack of detail. None of the sections provides much information about the content of the argument, and it seems likely that the writer has not given sufficient thought to the content of the paper.

A better start to this outline might be the following:

```
Thesis: F. Scott Fitzgerald's The Great Gatsby illustrates
that because the American Dream focuses on material
success, those like Gatsby who spend their lives striving
for it may reach their goal and end up disappointed
```

nonetheless because they remain spiritually and emotionally unfulfilled.

    I. Introduction and thesis

   II. The hard road to success: the transformation
        from James Gatz to Jay Gatsby
        A. Earning money
        B. Inventing stories about himself
        C. Breaking away from his family

  III. What success looks like—rewards of Gatsby's
        hard work
        A. Parties—elaborate affairs that demon-
            strate conspicuous consumption
        B. Possessions—his mansion, his wardrobe

   IV. What Gatsby really wants
        A. Daisy
        B. To repeat the past

    V. Conclusion
        A. Despite material success, Gatsby is
            unfulfilled
        B. Perhaps we too readily celebrate the
            American Dream without really thinking
            about what it means, whether we really
            want to define success and happiness in
            terms of money and material goods.

This new outline would prove much more helpful when it came time to write the paper.

An outline like this could be shaped into an even more useful tool if the writer fleshed out the argument by providing specific examples from the text to support each point. Once you have listed your main point and your supporting ideas, develop this raw material by listing related support-ing ideas and material under each of those main headings. From there, arrange the material in subsections and order the material logically.

For example, you might begin with one of the theses cited above, Marjorie indoctrinates Bernice into new ideas of womanhood, helping her move from a belief that women are timid, sentimental creatures to a belief that women should be cheerful, lively, and witty. Although Marjorie's ideas are supposed to be progressive, they share the same central flaw as Bernice's—they imply that the supreme goal of women is to please men—while introducing a troubling new one: ruthless competition. As noted above, this thesis already gives you the beginning of an organization: Start by identifying and describing Marjorie's and Bernice's ideas of womanhood, show that Bernice's is connected to older notions of womanhood while Marjorie's represents the new, and then compare and contrast them. You might begin your outline, then, with the following topic headings: (1) Bernice's versus Marjorie's ideas of womanhood, (2) Bernice's ideas linked to past and Marjorie's ideas linked to present/future, (3) similarities between Marjorie's and Bernice's ideas, and (4) differences between Marjorie's and Bernice's ideas. Under each of those headings you could list ideas that support the particular point. Be sure to include references to parts of the text that help build your case.

An informal outline might look like this:

Thesis: Marjorie indoctrinates Bernice into new ideas of womanhood, helping her move from a belief that women are timid, sentimental creatures to a belief that women should be cheerful, lively, and witty. Although Marjorie's ideas are supposed to be progressive, they share the same central flaw as Bernice's—they imply that the supreme goal of women is to please men—while introducing a troubling new one: ruthless competition.

    1. Bernice's versus Marjorie's idea of womanhood
- Bernice's idea of womanhood
  - involves sentiment and emotion
  - involves forming close emotional attachments to other women
  - involves being warm and selfless
- Marjorie's idea of womanhood

○ Rejects Bernice's ideas as outdated and old-fashioned

○ Women should be lively, cheerful, and witty instead of timid and quiet

○ Marriages should be colorful partnerships instead of relationships of dominance and submission

2. Bernice's ideas linked to past, Marjorie's to present and future
   - Marjorie's mother is sympathetic to Bernice
   - Marjorie and her mother have different opinions of Marjorie's friends
     ○ Roberta Dillon—Mother says she is too thin; Marjorie says she is a marvelous dancer
     ○ Martha Carey—Mother says she is loud and stout; Marjorie says she is witty

3. Similarities between Bernice's and Marjorie's perceptions of women
   - Both require looks and charm
   - Both boil down to entertaining men
     ○ Marjorie's idea requires cheer and wit
     ○ Although this makes women more active, activities are all geared toward entertaining and impressing men

4. Significant difference between Bernice's and Marjorie's perceptions
   - Bernice expects there to be bonds between women
   - Marjorie believes it's "every girl for herself"
     ○ Marjorie gets upset that Bernice stole her beau

    ○ She gets revenge on Bernice, making her cut her hair so that she will lose popularity

Conclusion:
- The ruthless competition of the "new woman" does not seem like progress
- The story suggests that not all change is good

You would set about writing a formal outline with a similar process, though in the final stages you would label the headings differently. A formal outline for a paper on Fitzgerald's "Babylon Revisited" might look like this:

Thesis: While it might appear that the young heroine of F. Scott Fitzgerald's "Babylon Revisited," Honoria, would be better off remaining with her aunt Marion's family, the young girl would actually have a greater chance to prosper with her father, whose losses and hardships have made him a more open, positive, and compassionate character than Marion.

    I. Introduction and thesis

   II. It looks at first that Honoria should stay with her aunt Marion and her family
      A. They seem to be a loving family with a father and mother
      B. They have provided Honoria with a stable home
      C. Honoria's own father has not been good for her in the past
        1. He is an alcoholic
        2. He lost a great deal of money in the stock market crash
        3. He locked her mother out of the house, which ultimately caused her death

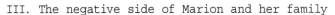

   III. The negative side of Marion and her family

      1. Marion is angry and bitter at Charlie for wasting money and for hurting her sister

      2. Marion seems mired in the past

      3. Marion is negative and pessimistic

   IV. The positive aspects of Charlie

      1. Losing his wife and his money has made him more appreciative of things

      2. He has reformed and has his alcoholism under control

      3. He has a more open, hopeful, loving manner than Marion does

   V. Conclusion

      1. Honoria would learn more about love and forgiveness with her father than with her aunt

      2. Fitzgerald chooses to have Marion refuse to grant Charlie custody

        A. Charlie determines to keep trying

        B. This reinforces the message that although past mistakes can help shape us into better people, others may still want to define us by them

As in the previous example, the thesis provided the seeds of a structure, and the writer was careful to arrange the supporting points in a logical manner, showing the relationships among the ideas in the paper.

BODY PARAGRAPHS

Once your outline is complete, you can begin drafting your paper. Paragraphs, units of related sentences, are the building blocks of a good paper, and as you draft you should keep in mind both the function and the qualities of good paragraphs. Paragraphs help you chart and control the shape and content of your essay, and they help the reader see your organization and your logic. You should begin a new paragraph whenever you move from one major point to another. In longer, more complex essays you might use a group of related paragraphs to support major points. Remember that in addition to being adequately developed, a good paragraph is both unified and coherent.

Unified Paragraphs

Each paragraph must be centralized around one idea or point, and a unified paragraph carefully focuses on and develops this central idea without including extraneous ideas or tangents. For beginning writers, the best way to ensure that you are constructing unified paragraphs is to include a topic sentence in each paragraph. This topic sentence should convey the main point of the paragraph, and every sentence in the paragraph should relate to that topic sentence. Any sentence that strays from the central topic does not belong in the paragraph and needs to be revised or deleted. Consider the following paragraph about Bernice's and Marjorie's ideas of womanhood. Notice how the paragraph veers away from the main point:

> After a few weeks of visiting, it becomes clear that Marjorie and Bernice have very different ideas of femininity and womanhood. Bernice finds her cousin "rather cold" and feels "the same difficulty in talking to her that she had in talking to men. Marjorie never giggled, was never frightened, seldom embarrassed, and in fact had very few of the qualities which Bernice considered appropriately and blessedly feminine." In Bernice's estimation, Marjorie lacks those traditionally integral feminine characteristics, warmth and feeling. Her complaints boil down to the fact that femininity, for Bernice, is about emotion and sentiment, particularly expressed between women. She longs to share giggles and tears with her cousin, while Marjorie, we are told, "had no female intimates," as she "considered girls stupid." Bernice is upset because not only does Marjorie refuse to be her friend but she has also lost the popularity

she enjoyed back home in Eau Claire. Bernice's mother threw frequent, lavish parties for her daughter and gave her a car, and these advantages helped Bernice be at the center of the social scene in her hometown.

Although the paragraph begins solidly and the first sentence provides the central theme, the author soon goes on a tangent. If the purpose of the paragraph is to demonstrate what Bernice and Marjorie think of womanhood, the sentences about Bernice's lack of popularity and her life back home in Eau Claire are tangential here. They may find a place later in the paper, but they should be deleted from this paragraph.

Coherent Paragraphs

In addition to shaping unified paragraphs, you must also craft coherent paragraphs, paragraphs that develop their points logically with sentences that flow smoothly into one another. Coherence depends on the order of your sentences, but it is not strictly the order of the sentences that is important to paragraph coherence. You also need to craft your prose to help the reader see the relationships among the sentences.

Consider the following paragraph about Bernice's and Marjorie's view of women. Notice how the writer uses the same ideas as in the paragraph above yet fails to help the reader see the relationships among the points:

After a few weeks of visiting, it becomes clear that Marjorie and Bernice have very different ideas of femininity and womanhood. Bernice finds her cousin "rather cold" and feels "the same difficulty in talking to her that she had in talking to men. Marjorie never giggled, was never frightened, seldom embarrassed, and in fact had very few of the qualities which Bernice considered appropriately and blessedly feminine." Bernice longs to share giggles and tears with her cousin, but Marjorie, we are told, "had no female intimates," as she "considered girls stupid." Bernice exclaims to Marjorie, "I think you're hard and selfish, and you haven't a feminine quality in you." Marjorie replies: "You little nut! Girls like you are responsible for all the tiresome colorless marriages; all those ghastly inefficiencies

that pass as feminine qualities. What a blow it must
be when a man with imagination marries the beautiful
bundle of clothing that he's been building ideals round,
and finds that she's just a weak, whining, cowardly
mass of affectations!" Marjorie completely rejects the
identification of womanhood with sentiment, which she
equates with affectation.

This paragraph demonstrates that unity alone does not guarantee paragraph effectiveness. The argument is hard to follow because the author fails both to show connections between the sentences and to indicate how they work to support the overall point.

A number of techniques are available to aid paragraph coherence. Careful use of transitional words and phrases is essential. You can use transitional flags to introduce an example or an illustration (*for example, for instance*), to amplify a point or add another phase of the same idea (*additionally, furthermore, next, similarly, finally, then*), to indicate a conclusion or result (*therefore, as a result, thus, in other words*), to signal a contrast or a qualification (*on the other hand, nevertheless, despite this, on the contrary, still, however, conversely*), to signal a comparison (*likewise, in comparison, similarly*), and to indicate a movement in time (*afterward, earlier, eventually, finally, later, subsequently, until*).

In addition to transitional flags, careful use of pronouns aids coherence and flow. If you were writing about *The Wizard of Oz*, you would not want to keep repeating the phrase *the witch* or the name *Dorothy*. Careful substitution of the pronoun *she* in these instances can aid coherence. A word of warning, though: When you substitute pronouns for proper names, always be sure that your pronoun reference is clear. In a paragraph that discusses both Dorothy and the witch, substituting *she* could lead to confusion. Make sure that it is clear to whom the pronoun refers. Generally, the pronoun refers to the last proper noun you have used.

While repeating the same name over and over again can lead to awkward, boring prose, it is possible to use repetition to help your paragraph's coherence. Careful repetition of important words or phrases can lend coherence to your paragraph by reminding readers of your key points. Admittedly, it takes some practice to use this technique effectively. You may find that reading your prose aloud can help you develop an ear for effective use of repetition.

To see how helpful transitional aids are, compare the paragraph below to the preceding paragraph about Bernice's and Marjorie's views of womanhood. Notice how the author works with the same ideas and quotations but shapes them into a much more coherent paragraph whose point is clearer and easier to follow.

> After a few weeks of visiting, it becomes clear that Marjorie and Bernice have very different ideas of femininity and womanhood. Bernice finds her cousin "rather cold" and feels "the same difficulty in talking to her that she had in talking to men. Marjorie never giggled, was never frightened, seldom embarrassed, and in fact had very few of the qualities which Bernice considered appropriately and blessedly feminine." Bernice's criticism of Marjorie lets us know that Bernice believes women should exhibit warmth and feeling. Not surprisingly, then, Bernice longs to share giggles and tears with her cousin, to develop an emotional connection to her; however, Marjorie, we are told, "had no female intimates," as she "considered girls stupid." When Bernice and Marjorie confront each other, Marjorie makes it clear that she is well aware that her definition of womanhood is decidedly different from Bernice's. When Bernice exclaims to Marjorie, "I think you're hard and selfish, and you haven't a feminine quality in you," Marjorie replies, "Girls like you are responsible for all the tiresome colorless marriages. . . . What a blow it must be when a man with imagination marries the beautiful bundle of clothing that he's been building ideals round, and finds that she's just a weak, whining, cowardly mass of affectations!" Marjorie completely rejects the identification of womanhood with sentiment, which she equates with affectation. Further, her comments suggest that she believes a woman should have more substance and strength than is traditionally considered good for her.

Similarly, the following paragraph from a paper on Fitzgerald's "Babylon Revisited" demonstrates both unity and coherence. In it, the author argues that, on the surface, it appears that Honoria would be better off with her Aunt Marion's family than with her father, who is trying to obtain custody.

> Initially, it appears that Honoria would be better off with her aunt Marion and the Peters family than with her father, Charlie. With the Peters, Honoria has both a mother and a father figure as well as siblings with whom she gets along quite well. If her father were to regain custody, she would have only him and perhaps his sister to care for her. Additionally, while the Peters family is by no means wealthy, the parents have provided Honoria with a safe, comfortable, stable home where she seems to be prospering. When Charlie goes to see her, he finds a cozy family scene: "The three children moved intimately about, playing through the yellow oblongs that led to other rooms; the cheer of six o'clock spoke in the eager smacks of the fire and the sounds of French activity in the kitchen." In contrast, judging from Charlie's past behavior, it does not seem as though he would provide a good home for his daughter. Charlie is an alcoholic; the reason Honoria is with the Peters at all is that Charlie was in a sanatorium when her mother died. Further, Charlie's irresponsible behavior contributed both to his financial ruin and the death of his wife, Honoria's mother.

INTRODUCTIONS

Introductions present particular challenges for writers. Generally, your introduction should do two things: capture your reader's attention and explain the main point of your essay. In other words, while your introduction should contain your thesis, it needs to do a bit more work than that. You are likely to find that starting that first paragraph is one of the most difficult parts of the paper. It is hard to face that blank page or screen, and as a result, many beginning writers, in desperation to start somewhere, start with overly broad, general statements. While it is often a good strategy to start with more general subject matter and narrow your focus, do not begin with broad sweeping statements such as Everyone needs a place to call home or Throughout the history of literature, many authors have examined what makes a good family. Such sentences are nothing but empty filler. They begin to fill the blank page, but they do nothing to advance your argument. Instead, you might try to gain your readers' interest. Some writers like to begin with a pertinent quotation or with a relevant question. Or you might begin with an introduction of the topic you will discuss. If you are writing about family and home in Fitzgerald's "Babylon Revisited," for instance, you might begin by talking about what is generally considered necessary for a good home and family in Western culture. Another common trap to avoid is depending on your title to introduce the author and the text you are writing about. Always include the work's author and title in your opening paragraph.

Compare the effectiveness of the following introductions:

1. Throughout history, family and home have been central to people's lives. Having a good family might be defined as having a mother, father, and siblings, while having a good home might be defined as having a safe place to live and enough to eat. In this story, while it might appear that Honoria would be better off remaining with her aunt Marion's family, the young girl would actually have a greater chance to prosper with her father, whose losses and hardships have made him a more open, positive, and compassionate character than Marion.

2. Traditionally and very basically, a good family has consisted of an attentive mother and father and preferably some siblings for companionship, and a good home has consisted of a safe place to live and enough to eat. However, there are other factors that are equally, if not more, important to a growing child. A truly good family and home need to provide not only shelter, food, and companionship but love, nurturing, and compassion as well. Therefore, while

> it might appear that the young heroine of F. Scott
> Fitzgerald's "Babylon Revisited," Honoria, would
> be better off remaining with her aunt Marion's
> family, the young girl would actually have a greater
> chance to prosper with her father, whose losses and
> hardships have made him a more open, positive, and
> compassionate character than Marion.

The first introduction begins with a boring, overly broad sentence; cites unclear, undeveloped examples; and then moves abruptly to the thesis. Notice, too, how a reader deprived of the paper's title does not know the title of the story that the paper will analyze. The second introduction works with the same material and thesis but provides more detail and is consequently much more interesting. It begins by offering a traditional definition of a good home and family and then offers a new definition based on the story to be analyzed. The paragraph ends with the thesis, which includes both the author and the title of the work to be discussed.

The paragraph below provides another example of an opening strategy. It begins by introducing the author and the text it will analyze, and then it moves on by briefly introducing relevant details of the story in order to set up its thesis.

> In F. Scott Fitzgerald's "Babylon Revisited," we are
> introduced to the Peters family, Lincoln and Marion
> Peters, their children Richard and Elsie, and Marion's
> niece Honoria, of whom the Peters have custody. The
> family seems to be living in harmony until Honoria's
> father, Charlie, comes along and wants to regain custody
> of his daughter. As Charlie's past comes to light,
> we learn that he is an alcoholic whose irresponsible
> behavior contributed to his financial ruin and the death
> of Honoria's mother. Charlie endeavors to prove to the
> Peters that he has reformed and can now offer Honoria a
> good home. While it might appear that the young heroine
> of "Babylon Revisited," Honoria, would be better off
> remaining with her aunt Marion's family, the young girl

would actually have a greater chance to prosper with her father, whose losses and hardships have made him a more open, positive, and compassionate character than Marion.

CONCLUSIONS

Conclusions present another series of challenges for writers. No doubt you have heard the old adage about writing papers: "Tell us what you are going to say, say it, and then tell us what you've said." While this formula does not necessarily result in bad papers, it does not necessarily result in good ones, either. It will almost certainly result in boring papers (especially boring conclusions). If you have done a good job establishing your points in the body of the paper, the reader already knows and understands your argument. There is no need to merely reiterate. Do not just summarize your main points in your conclusion. Such a boring and mechanical conclusion does nothing to advance your argument or interest your reader. Consider the following conclusion to the paper about family in "Babylon Revisited."

> In conclusion, love, compassion, and nurturing are necessary for a good family life. Charlie demonstrates these characteristics to a greater degree than Marion does. Thus, even though Marion could offer Honoria a more dependable, stable environment, the girl would do better growing up in the care of her father.

Besides starting with a mechanical and obvious transitional device, this conclusion does little more than summarize the main points of the outline (and it does not even touch on all of them). It is incomplete and uninteresting.

Instead, your conclusion should add something to your paper. A good tactic is to build upon the points you have been arguing. Asking "why?" often helps you draw further conclusions. Another method of successfully concluding a paper is to speculate on other directions in which to take your topic by tying it into larger issues. You might do this by envisioning your paper as just one section of a larger paper. Having established your points in this paper, how would you build upon this argument? Where would you go next? In the following conclusion to the paper on "Babylon Revisited," the author reiterates the main point of the paper but goes on to connect that point to forgiveness and the consequences of past mistakes.

> Although it is fairly clear that Honoria would be better off with her father, as he is a more compassionate and loving person than Marion, Fitzgerald chooses to have Marion refuse to grant Charlie custody of his daughter. Charlie's determination to keep trying only reinforces the idea that he is truly reformed and would now make a good father to Honoria. Fitzgerald's decision to have Marion refuse to grant Charlie custody, even though "part of her saw that Charlie's feet were planted on the earth now, and her own maternal feeling recognized the naturalness of his desire," highlights the fact that it is her own grudge against Charlie and her inability to forgive that is preventing Charlie from enjoying the second chance he has earned. Fitzgerald emphasizes here that even if we have learned from our past mistakes, they can continue to haunt us, especially if other people continue to define us by them.

Similarly, in the following conclusion to the paper on Marjorie's and Bernice's perceptions of femininity and womanhood, the author connects the story to the larger issues of developing gender roles and equality.

> While, by story's end, it is clear that Bernice has internalized the new model of femininity, this is not an entirely positive development. While exerting her own will and building confidence are positive results of her time with Marjorie, Bernice has, for the most part, only learned social skills designed to make her more appealing to men, and she has become competitive and selfish. The story emphasizes that not all change

is progress. It implicitly criticizes the fact that in an attempt to achieve equality, women were, in a way, attempting to become more like the stereotypical male: self-absorbed, calculating, and competitive, suggesting that perhaps women should develop their own strengths and demand equality on their own terms instead.

CITATIONS AND FORMATTING
Using Primary Sources

As the examples included in this chapter indicate, strong papers on literary texts incorporate quotations from the text in order to support their points. It is not enough for you to assert your interpretation without providing support or evidence from the text. Without well-chosen quotations to support your argument you are, in effect, saying to the reader, "Take my word for it." It is important to use quotations thoughtfully and selectively. Remember that the paper presents *your* argument, so choose quotations that support *your* assertions. Do not let the author's voice overwhelm your own. With that caution in mind, there are some guidelines you should follow to ensure that you use quotations clearly and effectively.

Integrate Quotations:

Quotations should always be integrated into your own prose. Do not just drop them into your paper without introduction or comment. Otherwise, it is unlikely that your reader will see their function. You can integrate textual support easily and clearly with identifying tags, short phrases that identify the speaker. For example:

> According to the narrator, "Her very aggressiveness gave him an advantage, and he knew enough to wait."

While this tag appears before the quotation, you can also use tags after or in the middle of the quoted text, as the following examples demonstrate:

> "I don't really need much taking care of anymore. I do everything for myself," claims Honoria.

"Please leave Helen out of it," Marion tells Charlie. "I can't bear to hear you talk about her like that."

You can also use a colon to formally introduce a quotation:

Charlie tries desperately to explain Lorraine and Duncan's appearance at the Peters' home: "I didn't tell them to come here. They wormed your name out of somebody."

When you quote brief sections of poems (three lines or fewer), use slash marks to indicate the line breaks in the poem:

As the poem ends, Dickinson speaks of the power of the imagination: "The revery alone will do, / If bees are few."

Longer quotations (more than four lines of prose or three lines of poetry) should be set off from the rest of your paper in a block quotation. Double-space before you begin the passage, indent it 10 spaces from your left-hand margin, and double-space the passage itself. Because the indentation signals the inclusion of a quotation, do not use quotation marks around the cited passage. Use a colon to introduce the passage:

Charlie comes to terms with his past, irresponsible behavior:

> He remembered thousand-franc notes given to an orchestra for playing a single number, hundred-franc notes tossed to a doorman for calling a cab. But it hadn't been given for nothing. It had been given, even the most wildly squandered sum, as an offering to destiny that he might not remember the things most worth remembering, the things that now he would always remember—his child taken from his control, his wife escaped to a grave in Vermont.

It is obvious that Charlie has come to understand the psychological motivations behind his behavior.

The whole of Dickinson's poem speaks of the imagination:

> To make a prairie it takes a clover and one bee,
> One clover, and a bee,
> And revery.
> The revery alone will do,
> If bees are few.

Clearly, she argues for the creative power of the mind.

It is also important to interpret quotations after you introduce them and explain how they help advance your point. You cannot assume that your reader will interpret the quotations the same way that you do.

Quote Accurately:

Always quote accurately. Anything within quotations marks must be the author's *exact* words. There are, however, some rules to follow if you need to modify the quotation to fit into your prose.

1. Use brackets to indicate any material that might have been added to the author's exact wording. For example, if you need to add any words to the quotation or alter it grammatically to allow it to fit into your prose, indicate your changes in brackets:

   > Bernice tells Marjorie's friends that she is "[g]oing down to the Sevier Hotel barber-shop, [to] sit in the first chair, and get [her] hair bobbed."

2. Conversely, if you choose to omit any words from the quotation, use ellipses (three spaced periods) to indicate missing words or phrases:

> Charlie found that remembering the night he had
> locked her out of the apartment "brought Helen
> nearer, and . . . he found himself talking to
> her again."

3. If you delete a sentence or more, use the ellipses after a period:

> Marjorie explains to her mother what a difficult
> time she has had with her boring, self-righteous
> cousin: "no girl can permanently bolster up a
> lame-duck visitor, because these days it's every
> girl for herself. . . . I'll bet she consoles
> herself by thinking that she's very virtuous and
> that I'm too gay and fickle and will come to a
> bad end."

4. If you omit a line or more of poetry, or more than one paragraph of prose, use a single line of spaced periods to indicate the omission:

> To make a prairie it takes a clover and one bee,
> . . . .
> And revery.
> The revery alone will do,
> If bees are few.

Punctuate Properly:

Punctuation of quotations often causes more trouble than it should. Once again, you just need to keep these simple rules in mind.

1. Periods and commas should be placed inside quotation marks, even if they are not part of the original quotation:

> According to the narrator, "Her very
> aggressiveness gave him an advantage, and he
> knew enough to wait."

The only exception to this rule is when the quotation is followed by a parenthetical reference. In this case, the period or comma goes after the citation (more on these later in this chapter):

```
According    to    the    narrator,    "Her    very
aggressiveness gave him an advantage, and he
knew enough to wait" (619).
```

2. Other marks of punctuation—colons, semicolons, question marks, and exclamation points—go outside the quotation marks unless they are part of the original quotation:

```
What does Charlie mean when he says, "We were a
sort of royalty"?
```

```
Marion asks pointedly, "Well, how do you find
Honoria?"
```

Documenting Primary Sources:

Unless you are instructed otherwise, you should provide sufficient information for your reader to locate material you quote. Generally, literature papers follow the rules set forth by the Modern Language Association (MLA). These can be found in the *MLA Handbook for Writers of Research Papers* (sixth edition). You should be able to find this book in the reference section of your library. Additionally, its rules for citing both primary and secondary sources are widely available from reputable online sources. One of these is the Online Writing Lab (OWL) at Purdue University. OWL's guide to MLA style is available at http://owl.english.purdue. edu/owl/resource/557/01/. The Modern Language Association also offers answers to frequently asked questions about MLA style on this helpful Web page: http://www.mla.org/style_faq. Generally, when you are citing from literary works in papers, you should keep a few guidelines in mind.

Parenthetical Citations:

MLA asks for parenthetical references in your text after quotations. When you are working with prose (short stories, novels, or essays) include page numbers in the parentheses:

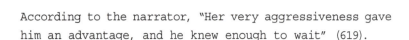

According to the narrator, "Her very aggressiveness gave him an advantage, and he knew enough to wait" (619).

When you are quoting poetry, include line numbers:

Dickinson's speaker tells of the arrival of a fly: "There interposed a Fly— / With Blue—uncertain stumbling Buzz— / Between the light—and Me—" (12–14).

Works Cited Page:

These parenthetical citations are linked to a separate works cited page at the end of the paper. The works cited page lists works alphabetically by the authors' last names. An entry for the above reference to Fitzgerald's "Babylon Revisited" would read:

Fitzgerald, F. Scott. "Babylon Revisited." *The Short Stories of F. Scott Fitzgerald: A New Collection*. New York: Scribner's, 1989. 616–33.

The *MLA Handbook* includes a full listing of sample entries, as do many of the online explanations of MLA style.

Documenting Secondary Sources:

To ensure that your paper is built entirely upon your own ideas and analysis, instructors often ask that you write interpretative papers without any outside research. If, on the other hand, your paper requires research, you must document any secondary sources you use. You need to document direct quotations, summaries or paraphrases of others' ideas, and factual information that is not common knowledge. Follow the guidelines above for quoting primary sources when you use direct quotations from secondary sources. Keep in mind that MLA style also includes specific guidelines for citing electronic sources. OWL's Web site provides a good summary: http://owl.english.purdue.edu/owl/resource/557/09/.

Parenthetical Citations:

As with the documentation of primary sources, described above, MLA guidelines require in-text parenthetical references to your secondary sources. Unlike the research papers you might write for a history class, literary research papers following MLA style do not use footnotes as a means of documenting sources. Instead, after a quotation, you should cite the author's last name and the page number:

> "Paradoxically, therefore, being a flapper or vamp in Fitzgerald's day—with all the preoccupation with beauty, fun, charm, and sexuality that such terms imply—can in actuality be equated with work in the female tradition" (Fryer 9).

If you include the name of the author in your prose, then you would include only the page number in your citation. For example:

> According to Fryer, "Paradoxically, therefore, being a flapper or vamp in Fitzgerald's day—with all the preoccupation with beauty, fun, charm, and sexuality that such terms imply—can in actuality be equated with work in the female tradition" (9).

If you are including more than one work by the same author, the parenthetical citation should include a shortened yet identifiable version of the title in order to indicate which of the author's works you cite. For example:

> Fitzgerald writes that "[a]t eighteen our convictions are hills from which we look; at forty-five they are caves in which we hide" ("Bernice" 31).

Similarly, and just as important, if you summarize or paraphrase the particular ideas of your source, you must provide documentation:

> According to Linda Pelzer, although most of Fitzgerald's stories are unremarkable, some of them are masterpieces and demonstrate great artistry. "Babylon Revisited" is perhaps the best of these (26).

Works Cited Page:

Like the primary sources discussed above, the parenthetical references to secondary sources are keyed to a separate works cited page at the end of your paper. Here is an example of a works cited page that uses the examples cited above. Note that when two or more works by the same author are listed, you should use three hyphens followed by a period in the subsequent entries. You can find a complete list of sample entries in the *MLA Handbook* or from a reputable online summary of MLA style.

WORKS CITED

Fitzgerald, F. Scott. "Babylon Revisited." *The Short Stories of F. Scott Fitzgerald: A New Collection.* New York: Scribner's, 1989. 616–33.

———. "Bernice Bobs Her Hair." *The Short Stories of F. Scott Fitzgerald: A New Collection.* New York: Scribner's, 1989. 25–47.

Fryer, Sarah Beebe. *Fitzgerald's New Women: Harbingers of Change.* Ann Arbor: UMI Research, 1988.

Pelzer, Linda C. *Student Companion to F. Scott Fitzgerald.* Westport, CT: Greenwood, 2000.

Plagiarism

Failure to document carefully and thoroughly can leave you open to charges of stealing the ideas of others, which is known as plagiarism, and this is a very serious matter. Remember that it is important to use quotation marks when you use language used by your source, even if you use just one or two words. For example, if you wrote, Being a flapper in Fitzgerald's day can be equated with work in the female tradition, you would be guilty of plagiarism, since you used distinct language without acknowledging Fryer as the source. Instead, you should write: "Being a flapper in Fitzgerald's time can be equated with work in the female tradition" (Fryer 9). In this case, you have properly credited Fryer.

Similarly, neither summarizing the ideas of an author nor changing or omitting just a few words means that you can omit a citation. Sarah Beebe Fryer's study of women contains the following passage:

In Fitzgerald's novels, which are accurate accounts of his moment in history, "the job"—for most women, at least—remains primarily in the realm of "possibility," not reality. Yet several principal female characters hint at their interest in the notion of economic independence. In *This Side of Paradise,* Rosalind cynically describes her social life as a business enterprise, with marriage as the ultimate deal she expects to close; Clara intimates to Amory that she is intensely relieved to have inherited enough money not to be obliged to remarry following the death of her husband; and Eleanor is outraged to the brink of self-destruction over her misfortune of being a "girl" and consequently destined to spend her lifetime married to a man almost certain to patronize her despite her superior intelligence. (9)

Below are two examples of plagiarized passages:

Rosalind, Clara, and Eleanor in Fitzgerald's *This Side of Paradise* all display a desire to be financially independent and a realization that in most cases women have to marry in order to be financially secure.

Fitzgerald's novels reflect the period he lived in. At this time, it was increasingly possible, at least in theory, for women to work outside the home. Rosalind, Clara, and Eleanor in *This Side of Paradise* all indicate interest in the notion of economic independence.

While the first passage does not use Fryer's exact language, it rephrases and summarizes her ideas. Since it does so without citing her work, this constitutes plagiarism. The second passage has changed some wording, but some of the phrasing is Fryer's. The first passage could be fixed with a parenthetical citation. Because some of the wording remains the same, though, the second would require the use of quotation marks in addition to a parenthetical citation. The passage below represents an honestly and adequately documented use of the original passage:

According to Sarah Beebe Fryer, in Fitzgerald's era, it was becoming increasingly possible, at least in theory, for women to work outside the home. His novel *This Side of Paradise* reflects the social changes in the atmosphere. Many of the novel's major female characters, including Rosalind, Clara, and Eleanor, "hint at their interest in the notion of economic independence" (9).

This passage acknowledges that the idea is derived from Fryer while appropriately using quotations to indicate her precise language.

While it is not necessary to document well-known facts, often referred to as "common knowledge," any ideas or language that you take from someone else must be properly documented. Common knowledge generally includes the birth and death dates of authors or other well-documented facts of their lives. An often-cited guideline is that if you can find the information in three sources, it is common knowledge. Despite this guideline, it is, admittedly, often difficult to know if the facts you uncover are common knowledge or not. When in doubt, document your source.

Sample Essay

Jodee Brown
Ms. Sterling
English 160
May 23, 2006

The "New Woman" in Fitzgerald's
"Bernice Bobs Her Hair"

F. Scott Fitzgerald's "Bernice Bobs Her Hair" is set in the early 20th century, a time in which gender roles were undergoing great change. Because of the "increase in women's leisure time afforded by the mechanization of many traditional domestic chores (washing, ironing, cleaning) and the accessibility of mass-produced food items like bread," women in the 1920s "suddenly had fewer taxing, routine demands on their time" (Fryer 8). This introduced the possibility of women working outside the home. Additionally, women had just achieved the right to vote. Clearly, there were major social changes under way, and Fitzgerald's "Bernice Bobs Her Hair" describes and comments on these changes. Marjorie, one of the story's principal female characters, represents the new model of femininity, while her cousin Bernice remains connected to the older values of her parents' generation. Marjorie indoctrinates Bernice into new ideas of womanhood, helping her move from a belief that women are timid, sentimental creatures to a belief that women should be cheerful, lively, and witty. Although Marjorie's ideas are supposed to be progressive, they share the same central flaw as Bernice's—they imply that the supreme goal of women is to please men—while introducing a troubling new one: ruthless competition.

After a few weeks of visiting, it becomes clear that Marjorie and Bernice have very different ideas of femininity and womanhood. Bernice finds her cousin "rather cold" and feels "the same difficulty in talking to her that she had in talking to men. Marjorie never giggled, was never frightened, seldom embarrassed, and in fact had very few of the qualities which Bernice considered appropriately and blessedly feminine" (29). Bernice's criticism of Marjorie lets us know that Bernice believes women should exhibit warmth and feeling. Not surprisingly, then, Bernice longs to share giggles and tears with her cousin, to develop an emotional connection to her; however, Marjorie, we are told, "had no female intimates," as she "considered girls stupid" (29). When Bernice and Marjorie confront each other, Marjorie makes it clear that she is well aware that her definition of womanhood is decidedly different from Bernice's. When Bernice exclaims to Marjorie, "I think you're hard and selfish, and you haven't a feminine quality in you," Marjorie replies, "Girls like you are responsible for all the tiresome colorless marriages. . . . What a blow it must be when a man with imagination marries the beautiful bundle of clothing that he's been building ideals round, and finds that she's just a weak, whining, cowardly mass of affectations!" (34). Marjorie completely rejects the identification of womanhood with sentiment, which she equates with affectation. Further, her comments suggest that she believes a woman should have more substance and strength than is traditionally considered good for her.

This difference in Marjorie's and Bernice's ideas about femininity reflects evolving social norms; Bernice's idea of womanhood is connected to that of the generation before her, while Marjorie is more in tune with the new ideas just coming into the mainstream. When Marjorie complains to her mother about Bernice, she already knows what her mother will say, down to the very arguments she will use to say that Bernice is a good example of womanhood. Marjorie states, "Oh, I know what you're going to say! So many people have told you how pretty and sweet she is, and how she can cook! What of it? She has a bum time. Men don't like her" (30). Marjorie can predict what her mother will say because she realizes that her mother approves of Bernice since Bernice fits her generation's idea of a good woman; she is pretty, sweet, and domestic.

These characteristics are not all that is necessary in Marjorie's world. And while it seems promising at first that popularity in Marjorie's generation is not judged by looks, social standing, or domestic ability alone, we soon begin to wonder if the characteristics valued by Marjorie's generation are really any more substantial than those valued by her mother's. When her mother complains that "other girls not half so sweet and attractive [as Bernice] get partners," such as Martha Carey, who is "stout and loud" and whose "mother is distinctly common," and Roberta Dillon, who "is so thin this year," Marjorie counters that "Martha is cheerful and awfully witty and an awfully slick girl, and Roberta's a marvelous dancer" (31). The substance and strength that Marjorie hinted at to Bernice seem ultimately to be nothing more than wit and charm. Women are now expected to be more active, but their actions are not an expression of their own desire or will. They are expressly designed to entertain men. Therefore, although Bernice tries to behave in as demure a fashion as possible, while Marjorie and her friends attempt to be as lively and entertaining as they can be, the goals of both groups are actually the same—to attract men. Marjorie's most dramatic statement regarding Bernice's failure is that "[m]en don't like her" (30).

When Marjorie explains to Bernice how to be successful—how to make men like her—according to the fashion of the day—we become even more suspicious that the new model of womanhood is not much more substantial or progressive than the old. First, Marjorie explains to a bewildered Bernice that although she despises "[d]ainty feminine things," "a girl has to be dainty in person. If she looks like a million dollars she can talk about Russia, ping-pong, or the League of Nations and get away with it" (35). She continues, informing Bernice that she must not neglect the "sad birds" at a party, because if a girl can make enough of the unpopular boys like her, then she will appear more popular, which will then attract a more desirable group of suitors. Besides, one can at least get in some good practice at one's dancing and conversational skill with even the saddest of birds. Bernice learns well. She does not talk about her hometown, cars, or her school but learns to confine "her conversation to me, you, and us" (39). She feigns delight when a not very interesting boy cuts in on the dance floor for the eighth time. In summary, what Bernice learns is that the new woman has to look attractive enough in order to "get away with" talking about politics or sports. She learns also, from the very person who had faulted her for affectation, to pretend enchantment and delight when she does not feel it.

Sadly, Bernice also learns that the giggling conspiratorial conversations that she expects between female friends have been replaced with ruthless competition. Marjorie may have helped her cousin gain popularity, but she will not be bested at her own game. When Marjorie's best beau, Warren, begins to court

Bernice, Marjorie tricks Bernice into getting her hair bobbed, although both young women know that this will be a disaster. According to Linda Pelzer, "[t]he clever twist of the story's ending certainly demonstrates the truth of Marjorie's assertion to her mother that 'these day's it's every girl for herself' and underscores the competitiveness of social success" (26). In her room the night of the fateful trip to the barber, Bernice wears "a new look" which "carried consequences" (46). Acting in a way that might be considered "selfish and hard," qualities she had once condemned in Marjorie, Bernice lops off Marjorie's braids and deposits them on Warren's front porch on her way out of town.

Bernice has internalized the new model of femininity, but it is not an entirely positive development. While exerting her own will and building confidence are positive results of her time with Marjorie, Bernice has, for the most part, only learned social skills designed to make her more appealing to men, and she has become competitive and selfish. The story emphasizes that not all change is progress. In fact, it implicitly criticizes the fact that in an attempt to achieve equality, women were, in a way, attempting to become more like the stereotypical male—self-absorbed, calculating, and competitive—and suggests that perhaps women should develop their own strengths and demand equality on their own terms instead.

Works Cited

Fitzgerald, F. Scott. "Bernice Bobs Her Hair." *The Short Stories of F. Scott Fitzgerald: A New Collection*. New York: Scribner's, 1989. 25–47.

Fryer, Sarah Beebe. *Fitzgerald's New Women: Harbingers of Change*. Ann Arbor, MI: UMI Research, 1988.

Pelzer, Linda C. *Student Companion to F. Scott Fitzgerald*. Westport, CT: Greenwood, 2000.

HOW TO WRITE ABOUT FITZGERALD

WRITING ABOUT FITZGERALD: AN OVERVIEW

THOUGH NOW firmly entrenched in the canon of great American authors, F. Scott Fitzgerald, during his lifetime, saw very little sign of the eventual upward trajectory of his literary reputation. It is true that he met with great successes during his career, but just as often, they were overshadowed by even greater failures and tragedies. Fitzgerald's fast-paced life and his perennial struggles with the vagaries of fortune make for a compelling story in and of themselves, so much so that it is tempting to become caught up in the biographical details of Fitzgerald's life, merely pointing out similarities between his life and his fictional worlds. However, Fitzgerald produced fiction, not memoirs, so you must be careful to approach the texts on their own terms.

That is not to say, however, that research into Fitzgerald's life and the times during which he lived and wrote is unnecessary or unhelpful. Quite the contrary. Even more so than that of many other writers, Fitzgerald's work is intimately connected to the time and place in which he lived. The more you know about the context in which Fitzgerald wrote, the more astute your comments and evaluations of his writing will be. And while merely matching certain characters and happenings in Fitzgerald's works to the historical counterparts in his life does little to further your understanding of the texts, discovering some of the broader patterns and themes in Fitzgerald's life and in American history and society during his life can aid you in discovering similar themes and patterns in the fiction.

For instance, a little research reveals some of the broad details of Fitzgerald's life and how Fitzgerald's fiction was influenced by those details. He was born Francis Scott Key Fitzgerald in St. Paul, Minnesota, on September 24, 1896. His father, Edward, was from Maryland, a state that never seceded from the Union during the Civil War but which had strong sympathies with the Old South. On the other hand, his mother, Mary McQuillan, was from Minnesota and was the daughter of an Irish immigrant. After attending St. Paul Academy and then the Newman School in New Jersey, Fitzgerald entered Princeton University. Before graduating, however, he joined the army and in 1918 was assigned to Camp Sheridan, near Montgomery, Alabama. While stationed there, he met his future wife, a popular southern belle named Zelda Sayre. Though she initially spurned him because of his lack of money, Zelda did eventually marry Fitzgerald, shortly after the successful publication in 1920 of his first novel, *This Side of Paradise.*

One thing that might strike you at this point is the way that the regional component of Fitzgerald's marriage mirrors—though with the gender roles reversed—that of his parents. Born, raised, and educated in Minnesota and New Jersey, Fitzgerald was undeniably a northerner. Zelda, on the other hand, came from the Deep South and therefore possessed a very different set of cultural values than did Fitzgerald. It is likely that Fitzgerald's childhood was shaped by the conflicts and negotiations between his parents and their differing cultural assumptions, and he and Zelda must have done much negotiating to find common ground despite their divergent backgrounds. We certainly may expect that some of this might be reflected in the fiction. In fact, one of Fitzgerald's stories, "The Ice Palace," seems to present as its central question whether it is possible at all for northerners and southerners to find any middle ground. Quite a few of Fitzgerald's other works tackle questions of regional differences in more subtle but important ways. In "The Diamond as Big as the Ritz," for instance, the Washington family appears to feel justified in violently opposing the government not only because they are immeasurably wealthy but also because they are in the "Wild West," where a higher premium is, mythologically speaking at least, placed on independence and rugged individualism. Similarly, in *The Great Gatsby,* part of Nick's crucial distinction from the other characters, and part of what makes him a more grounded and reliable narrator, lies in the fact that he is from the Midwest while they are all easterners. The more we look for regional characteristics and conflicts in Fitzgerald's fiction, the more we find, and this interest can certainly be traced back to his and his parents' marriages.

Other aspects of Fitzgerald's life are equally visible in his stories and novels. Although Fitzgerald never actually made enough money to sustain it, he and Zelda enjoyed a lavish lifestyle. And while Fitzgerald was devoted to his wife and they certainly enjoyed some happy times together, all told their relationship was destructive to both of them in many ways. They were both prone to excessive drinking, and their relationship was plagued by frequent and sometimes quite intense quarrels. Perhaps it is not surprising, then, that much of Fitzgerald's fiction seems to pose the question whether a lifestyle of leisure or excess can coexist with happiness and fulfilling relationships. In the short story "Babylon Revisited," for example, a marriage is torn apart by the couple's sudden prosperity and tendency to indulge their every desire. In *Tender Is the Night*, Dick and Nicole's marriage crumbles in part because of the influence of Nicole's money. Fitzgerald's own struggles with success illuminate his obsession with the American Dream—his need to understand what success, as defined by the myth of the American Dream, looks like and why people who achieve it are not always happy or fulfilled as a result. This is a theme addressed in many of Fitzgerald's works, such as "The Rich Boy," "Winter Dreams," and most powerfully, *The Great Gatsby*.

In addition to biographical background, it is valuable to obtain some historical context for the literary work you are studying. With Fitzgerald, this is particularly true as he is so well known for his ability to evoke the essence of a certain time and place. Much of Fitzgerald's writing was done in the tumultuous decades of the 1920s and 1930s, during which America was going through rapid change. In his fiction, Fitzgerald grapples with the ramifications of woman suffrage, global warfare, Prohibition, rapid changes in traditional gender roles, the rise of socialism, economic prosperity, and the stock market crash and resulting depression. Some background reading into the history of this period can prepare you to identify themes such as the social tension generated by evolving gender roles in "Bernice Bobs her Hair" or the definition of Americanness or American values in "Babylon Revisited" and to analyze these works in order to see precisely how they contribute to the cultural debates that were occurring at this moment in history.

Such background knowledge about Fitzgerald's life and times can help you identify and contextualize major issues or themes in his work, but you should be careful about using Fitzgerald's biography to interpret a literary text or vice versa. You probably would not, for example, explain Nicole and Dick's failed relationship simply by providing details about

Fitzgerald's own marriage. Similarly, your thesis should not put forth a claim about Fitzgerald's own marriage based on your analysis of Dick and Nicole. That is not to say that these kinds of arguments or analysis are never conducted, but they are always tricky and often tautological or otherwise logistically problematic.

What you can do, however, is use the biographical and historical information you obtain to help you pinpoint significant themes or issues. Reading about the regional differences in Fitzgerald's parents' marriage and in his own might inspire you to look for this idea in Fitzgerald's fiction, and you might find that this issue is a major theme of Fitzgerald's short story "The Ice Palace." You might then do some background reading on the cultural differences between the North and South and their perception of each other in the early decades of the 20th century to further ground yourself in the cultural atmosphere in which Fitzgerald lived and worked. However, no matter how much background reading you do, you can never really know Fitzgerald's innermost feelings or thoughts, so it is wise to keep your argument based on the literary text. You would probably not assert, for instance, that Fitzgerald believed relationships between northerners and southerners were doomed to failure, but you might, instead, argue that in the short story "The Ice Palace," Fitzgerald suggests that long after the Civil War, the North and South still hold so much enmity toward one another that it is difficult for individuals to bridge this gap.

In other words, use biographical and historical research not as a substitute for but as a complement to your own literary analysis. Such research can supply additional information and fill in some of the blanks in our understanding of Fitzgerald's works. For instance, it does not take long to realize that Fitzgerald explores the connection between financial wealth and happiness in story after story. Insightful and determined literary analysis of these stories will certainly help you decipher what conclusions Fitzgerald is drawing, but only biographical and historical work will help you determine why Fitzgerald was so obsessed with this question in the first place. Did it have anything to do with the fact that his father eventually had to rely financially on his mother's inheritance? Was it because of the completely unpredictable financial whims of the literary marketplace on which he depended? Is it connected to the years of plenty that America experienced after World War I followed by the dire poverty of the Great Depression? Once you have done the required research and formulated a theory as to why Fitzgerald was so interested in the connection between wealth and happiness, you can then revisit the works themselves with a fresh perspective on how they answer the question.

The need to separate the biographical from the fictional is certainly not unique to Fitzgerald studies. However, because Fitzgerald is so closely associated with a certain period of history and because his personality looms so large, you must take extra care simultaneously to learn as much as possible about the context of the literary work in order to conduct more informed, nuanced analyses and to keep the many layers—biography, history, literature—distinct in your mind and in your arguments.

TOPICS AND STRATEGIES

The sample topics provided below are designed to provide you some ideas for how you might approach writing an essay about a work of Fitzgerald's. Many of the samples will give you the titles of some possible works to focus on. Keep in mind the length of your essay when you are deciding on which works and how many of them you want to consider. You will want to make sure that you have adequate space to give thorough treatment to each work you talk about in your essay. You are certainly free to select works not mentioned in the sample topics as well. Bear in mind, too, that it it you choose multiple texts, it is good to have a rationale for grouping those texts in your essay. Ideally, you do not want the determining factor simply to be which texts you already have read. Instead, you might choose stories that were written at a certain period in history or stories that explore similar themes, for example.

Themes

One of the most common methods of approaching a piece of literature is to consider its themes, or major concerns. When we ask ourselves what a piece is really about, or what it wants to say, we are trying to discern its themes. Of course, it is not enough to identify the topics with which a work is concerned. You must then investigate the text to discover what unique message the writer is conveying about a particular theme. Many of Fitzgerald's works, for instance, concern the American Dream. In an essay, you would not simply identify this theme running through his works; you would describe precisely what Fitzgerald is saying about the American Dream in the text you are analyzing. You might argue, for example, that according to Fitzgerald's *The Great Gatsby*, the American Dream is certainly possible but that it often requires too many sacrifices to be worthwhile. Or you might conclude that *The Great Gatsby* celebrates the American Dream, illustrating that in America people can not only change their station and fortune but also can reinvent their very identities.

Sample Topics:

1. **The American Dream:** What does Fitzgerald's work say about the American Dream?

   Select the work or works that seem to say the most about the American Dream, such as *The Great Gatsby* or "The Diamond as Big as the Ritz." How is the American Dream defined in the work(s) you have chosen? Who achieves it? What exactly do they achieve and what must they give up in order to do so? Does the story or novel seem to be endorsing the American Dream as possible and worthwhile or condemning it for endorsing moral bankruptcy?

2. **Wealth:** In Fitzgerald's oeuvre, how are wealth and virtue connected?

   Some good works for this topic would be "May Day," "The Diamond as Big as the Ritz," "The Rich Boy," *The Great Gatsby,* and *Tender Is the Night.* What connections are made between money and morality in the work(s) you have chosen? Record the financial status of each character and note whether that character is portrayed as morally sound or corrupt. Can you identify any patterns? Do the patterns depend on how much money the character has? On how that character came into his or her money?

3. **Male bonding:** What does Fitzgerald's work say about relationships between men?

   You might focus on one or more of the following texts: "The Diamond as Big as the Ritz," "May Day," *The Great Gatsby,* and *This Side of Paradise.* Think about the relationships between men in the text(s) you have chosen. What are the relationships based on? What does each character gain from the relationship? Is the relationship hierarchical, or do the characters involved mutually influence each other? You might also compare these relationships to the relationships between women in the same text(s). Use your essay to make a claim that describes and evaluates male relationships in Fitzgerald's works.

Characters

If you are having difficulty devising a topic or method of critical approach to a piece of literature, it can be helpful to begin with an examination of its characters. List all of the characters and their traits, noting whether they develop during the course of the story or novel. Record what you know about the characters' relationships with one another as well. Then, you might look for any patterns: Is there something interesting to be said about Fitzgerald's portrayal of southern characters, or about women? You might choose to focus on a particular character who changes in an interesting way, analyzing his or her development and the reasons for and results of this evolution. Or there might be a particular relationship or group of relationships you can analyze and evaluate—romantic relationships or parent-child relationships, for example.

Sample Topics:

1. **Female characters and/or male characters:** Analyze and evaluate Fitzgerald's presentation of femininity, masculinity, or both.

   For this topic, you can choose just about any of Fitzgerald's works. "The Ice Palace" and "Winter Dreams," written during a high point in women's struggle for equal rights, would be good choices, as would any of Fitzgerald's novels, particularly *The Great Gatsby*. You might start by jotting down all the male and female characters in your chosen works and noting as much as you can about their characteristics. What are male characters and female characters like in this work? How are they similar and different? Some background reading on gender roles in the early 20th century would be useful so that you could gain a better sense of the actual world that Fitzgerald was responding to with his fictional one. Ultimately, you might write an essay that describes the various models of masculinity or femininity presented in a given text—what different roles are available for men and women—and then discuss what the work seems to think of these roles.

2. **Upper- and lower-class characters:** What commentary does Fitzgerald's work make about the class system in America?

Although many of Fitzgerald's works have something to say about class, the stories "May Day" and "The Diamond as Big as the Ritz" as well as the novels *This Side of Paradise, The Great Gatsby,* and *Tender Is the Night* would be particularly good choices. You might choose one of the novels or one or both of the short stories, depending on the length of your essay and the depth of your analysis. Begin by recording what you know about the characters in your chosen work(s). To what class does each character belong? What are their distinguishing characteristics? Their priorities? Can you identify any patterns? How do members of different classes interact? How does the narration treat upper-class and lower-class characters? Based on your notes, craft an essay that makes a claim about Fitzgerald's portrayal of class in America in the work(s) you have selected. Your claim might concern only the upper class or the lower class, or it might make a comparison between the two groups or analyze and evaluate their interactions.

3. **Parent-child relationships:** Analyze and evaluate Fitzgerald's portrayal of parent-child relationships.

Fitzgerald's work is filled with interesting parent-child relationships. You might write about *This Side of Paradise, The Great Gatsby, Tender Is the Night,* "Babylon Revisited," "Bernice Bobs Her Hair," or "The Diamond as Big as the Ritz." Record every parent-child relationship portrayed in the work(s) you have chosen and then analyze these relationships. How do the parents affect their child's development? Are most of the relationships you have examined positive or destructive? Can you determine what, according to Fitzgerald, constitutes a healthy or successful parent-child relationship?

History and Context

Fitzgerald's works are firmly rooted in early 20th-century America. Works such as *The Great Gatsby,* "The Ice Palace," and "Winter Dreams" depict the prosperous 1920s, and "Babylon Revisited," "Crazy Sunday," and *Tender Is the Night* portray a more somber American society in the aftermath of the 1929 stock market crash. Attaining some background knowledge about 1920s and 1930s America can prove extremely valuable to your understanding of these literary works and can help you arrive at an interesting idea for your essay. You should learn not only what major historical events were happening in the given period but also investigate what people believed. What ideas were important? Which were being challenged or revised? Once you have learned this, you can return to Fitzgerald's works with a sharper gaze in order to determine what the pieces are saying about the society in which Fitzgerald lived.

Sample Topics:

1. **The Roaring '20s:** The 1920s were a time of rapid social change and materialistic excess in America. What do Fitzgerald's works say about this period of American history? Are they critical or celebratory? Prophetic or lost in the moment?

   You should begin by doing some general background reading on this dynamic period of American history. Then choose one or more works written or set in that period, such as "The Diamond as Big as the Ritz," "Winter Dreams," "The Rich Boy," or *The Great Gatsby.* Then ask yourself how closely Fitzgerald's fictional portrayal matches the historical accounts you have read. It is a good idea to narrow your focus to a particular historical element once you have selected a text to work with. For example, if you decide to write about the historical context of *The Great Gatsby,* you might decide to focus on the women's rights movement, which was gaining considerable momentum in this decade after the passage of the Nineteenth Amendment ensuring women's right to vote. How is the social debate about women's roles reflected in the novel? Can you determine what Fitzgerald thought of women through his portrayal of characters such as Daisy and Jordan? Alternatively, you could decide to consider the American Dream, the "rags to riches" notion that America offers everyone the opportunity to move up the ladder of wealth, success, and status provided they work hard enough. How does the historical information about this idea compare to the way it is presented in *The Great Gatsby*?

2. **1930s America:** The 1930s provided a sobering contrast to the 1920s. American values shifted radically in the wake of the stock market crash and the Great Depression. How do Fitzgerald's works reflect and react to these shifts?

Do some background reading to determine what is distinctive about 1930s America. What makes this period in history different from the decades preceding and following it? What major social ideas were taking shape in this decade? Which were being challenged? How did Americans feel about themselves and their world at this point in history? Once you have gotten a sense of what the 1930s were like in America, read or reread one or more of Fitzgerald's works written and set in this decade, such as "Babylon Revisited," "Crazy Sunday," or *Tender Is the Night* and think about how the story or novel reflects what you have learned about the history of this period. What elements does Fitzgerald emphasize? What does he deemphasize? You will probably need to narrow your focus to a particular historical element once you have done some preliminary thinking and researching. You might examine in your essay, for example, Fitzgerald's portrayal of the film industry and Hollywood in "Crazy Sunday," or the effects of the stock market crash even on Americans living abroad as portrayed in "Babylon Revisited."

3. **The expatriate movement:** What does Fitzgerald's work say about the expatriate movement?

Begin by doing some background reading, learning as much as you can about American expatriates in the early 20th century. Why did they choose to leave America? What did America represent to them? Why did they relocate to the places they did? Did they still think of themselves as fundamentally American? Examine Fitzgerald's "Babylon Revisited" or *Tender Is the Night* to determine what he is saying about American expatriates. Does Fitzgerald's portrayal of their motives and lifestyles agree with the historical accounts you have read? Discuss the significance of any differences you discover between the historical accounts and Fitzgerald's fictional works. Do Fitzgerald's works give you insights not available in the historical accounts?

Philosophy and Ideas

Another way to approach a piece of literature is to think about what social ideas or philosophies it comments on or engages with in some way. Many of Fitzgerald's works concern the movement from innocence to experience, for example, an idea that has been pondered by many of the world's great thinkers and writers. Looking at Fitzgerald's works, particularly those such as *This Side of Paradise* that portray in great detail a character's journey from childhood to adulthood, ask yourself whether he expresses the Wordsworthian idea that childhood and the innocence that accompanies it are an ideal state from which we fall farther each day or whether Fitzgerald associates experience with wisdom and empathy. You can also turn your attention to more topical ideological or philosophical questions. To do this, some background reading on the period in which the piece was written and in which it is set is invaluable. For example, if you are studying Fitzgerald's "May Day," which explicitly references the ideological and philosophical debate about socialism, you might do some research into the socialist movement in early 20th-century America and then analyze the story to discover what Fitzgerald is saying about socialism and capitalism in this work.

Sample Topics:

1. **Innocence to experience:** What kind of commentary does Fitzgerald offer on the movement from innocence to experience?

While you could probably write an essay dealing with this topic on any of Fitzgerald's works, the novels *This Side of Paradise, The Great Gatsby,* and *Tender Is the Night* as well as the short stories "Bernice Bobs Her Hair" and "The Ice Palace" are particularly good choices. You could examine the movement that a character or characters make from innocence to experience, noting what sparks the change as well as what is gained and what is lost in the process. Ultimately, you should determine through your analysis what Fitzgerald is saying about innocence versus experience. Is one state preferable over the other? What are the virtues and pitfalls of each?

2. **Capitalism versus socialism/communism:** What does Fitzgerald's work say about the ideologies of capitalism and socialism?

You might begin with an examination of *The Great Gatsby* in order to discover what Fitzgerald is saying about capitalism and consumption. What attitude does the novel seem to take toward Gatsby's conspicuous consumption? Where do the raw materials used to serve Gatsby's needs come from? Where does the waste go when the lavish parties are over? An analysis of the short story "May Day" would enable you to examine this further and to investigate Fitzgerald's attitude toward socialism as well. In particular, you might look at the scenes in which the mob of soldiers threatens the protestor on the street and storms the office of the radical newspaper where Henry Bradin works.

Form and Genre

Thinking about the building blocks that Fitzgerald used to create the texts we study today can be very instructive. In fact, analyzing the form and genre of a piece can help you arrive at an interesting claim to make in your essay and provide you with evidence to support that claim. You might consider, for example, where Fitzgerald got his ideas: Is the story or novel you are studying based on biographical details from his own life? If so, how will learning these details help you arrive at a better understanding of the story's themes and meanings? You might also study how the story is put together. Is it in novel or story form? Is it divided into numbered or titled chapters? Where does each section take place? Where is the story's climax positioned in the piece? In addition, you will certainly want to consider the telling of the story. Who is the narrator? What do you know about him or her? How does the narrator affect your interpretation of the events he or she presents? In thinking about form and genre, keep in mind that the author, in this case Fitzgerald, is a careful craftsman who makes deliberate decisions about what stories to tell and precisely how to tell them; you are therefore justified in your effort to figure out how these decisions contribute to the meaning of a work. Your analysis of the story or novel's inspiration, structure, and/or narration can help you arrive at an interpretation to present in your essay.

Sample Topics:

1. **Narration:** Examine the narration and its effects on your interpretation of selected texts.

    It is a good idea to consider the narration in every text you read. Consider who is telling the story and for what reasons, and evaluate the reliability and trustworthiness of your narrator. Ask yourself how the narrator feels toward other characters in the piece and what he or she thinks of the events that transpire. Did the author intend for the narrator to function as the moral center of the story? Are his or her interpretations and evaluations made to seem proper and right? While an analysis of a work's narration will nearly always bear fruit, some particularly good texts to focus on are *The Great Gatsby* and "The Rich Boy."

2. **Biographical connections:** How do works based on Fitzgerald's own life or the lives of his acquaintances differ from the purely fictional? How might knowledge of these biographical connections help you interpret the works?

    Select a work of Fitzgerald's that is based on his own life or on the lives of those he knew; pertinent works include *Tender Is the Night,* "Crazy Sunday," "Bernice Bobs Her Hair," and "The Rich Boy." Investigate the connections between Fitzgerald's life and the work(s) you have selected. How did Fitzgerald change and mold reality into fiction? What does Fitzgerald change in the fictional accounts, and what does this tell us about his interpretations of the real events or people? How does your knowledge of the biographical links affect your interpretation of the work(s)?

3. **Organization:** How does the organization of a piece affect its meaning?

    You might select any of Fitzgerald's works for this particular topic. Think about how the piece is organized. Is it broken up into smaller pieces? How many, and how long is each piece? Are the pieces given names or numbers? It is often helpful to chart or map out the events of the story or novel, noting what happens in each section. Also notice in what order the events are presented. What would you consider the climax of the story or novel? Does it come in the middle of the piece or nearer the end? Think carefully about the other ways that Fitzgerald might have organized the piece and speculate on why he made the choices he did. How does your analysis of the organization help you come to a new understanding of the piece's meaning?

Symbols, Imagery, and Language

Works of literature are filled with symbols and images that can lead to meaningful discoveries about the themes and meanings of the piece. When reading, pay close attention to images that recur throughout a piece and to images that seem to be especially significant because of the attention the author devotes to them or their location near an important scene or character. Once you have identified potentially meaningful images and symbols, closely read the passages that include them. First, ask yourself what traditional associations these images or symbols carry, and then look closely at the particular way they function in the literary work you are studying. Is the author enhancing an image's traditional associations or perhaps tweaking them in some way? Once you have some ideas about the meaning of a particular image, think about ways to connect your new knowledge to the central ideas of the work. How does what you have discovered about a symbol or image help you interpret the story or novel? You can look at symbols and images within a single work or locate similar images in multiple works if you wish to consider Fitzgerald's work as a body instead of focusing on a single text. In addition to symbols and imagery, pay close attention to the author's language as you read. Keep in mind that the English language offers so many ways to say the same thing. Thinking about why Fitzgerald chose exactly the words that he did and not the other options available will often lead to meaningful discoveries about a work's theme that can help you construct or support a claim in your essay.

Sample Topics:

1. **Ads:** What does Fitzgerald say about our culture through the use of ads and the description of the advertising world?

Peruse Fitzgerald's work for images of advertisements. You might wish to look especially at *The Great Gatsby* and *This Side of Paradise*. What do these works seem to say about ads and the advertising world in general? What larger commentary do they make about the society that produces and consumes this kind of advertising? You might begin by analyzing any ads described in Fitzgerald's text, such as the billboard in *The Great Gatsby*. Then you might look at Amory's stint as a copywriter for an advertising company in *This Side of Paradise*. How does he feel about this job? What else is going on in his life during this time? Spend some time thinking about what advertising is designed to do and how it accomplishes its goals. How is it connected to consumerism and capitalism? Then, look back at your notes and consider what Fitzgerald is saying about American society through his portrayal of the elements of the advertising culture.

2. **Works of art:** What kind of commentary does Fitzgerald make about art and artists in his works?

You might begin by reading or rereading *The Great Gatsby*, paying particular attention to McKee and his photographs; or *Tender Is the Night*, focusing on McKisco and his fiction writing; or or "Crazy Sunday," concentrating on Joel Coles's movie making. What kind of art do these characters produce? How do they think of their art and their own roles as artists? How do other characters perceive them? What determines whether they are successful? In these works, is the creation of art a commercial act? If so, what does Fitzgerald seem to think of it? Does he make distinctions among different kinds of art or different kinds of artists? How do you think Fitzgerald perceives his own work and role as artist based on his portrayal of art in his literary works?

3. **Prose style:** How might an analysis of Fitzgerald's style of writing help you interpret his works?

Fitzgerald's style can be described as poetic or lyrical. He provides a great deal of detail and description. What does this suggest about the way Fitzgerald views the world? You might compare his writing to Hemingway's or Faulkner's to get a sense of the differences in style. One way to think about the importance of style is to imagine how the Fitzgerald piece you are working on would differ if it were written by another writer, such as Hemingway or Faulkner. How would the story or novel differ if it were presented in a different prose style? How is Fitzgerald's style significant to the meaning of his works?

Compare and Contrast Essays

Setting two elements side by side in order to determine their similarities and differences can be surprisingly illuminating. You might choose two elements that seem very similar to you and spend some time focusing on their distinguishing characteristics, or you might select two elements that seem very different and examine them closely for underlying similarities. You can choose elements within a single work, elements in two or more works by the same author, or even elements in works by different authors. You should not only identify differences and similarities but also choose the most meaningful ones and interpret them for your reader. This way, your essay will not amount to a list of interesting details but will instead use significant similarities and differences to make a point about the work(s) you are analyzing.

Sample Topics:

1. **Fitzgerald's work in the 1920s versus his work in the 1930s:** How did Fitzgerald's work change during the course of his career?

   Compare and contrast the work that Fitzgerald produced in the 1920s and the 1930s. What differences and similarities do you find? Consider the actual writing style as well the themes Fitzgerald explored. What can you attribute the differences to? Can you identify significant ways in which Fitzgerald's style evolved during this time? Alternatively, instead of using the decades as points of comparison, you might use a series of novels, such as *This Side of Paradise* (1920), *The Great Gatsby* (1925), and *Tender Is the Night* (1935), using an analysis of these novels to trace Fitzgerald's development through his career.

2. **Fitzgerald's work with that of another author:** Compare and contrast Fitzgerald's work with that of another author to note significant differences.

You might choose to compare and contrast Fitzgerald with Hemingway or Faulkner, for example, analyzing the significance of the similarities and differences you find. For a more manageable essay, you would probably need to narrow your focus, identifying a specific element to compare and contrast in the two authors' works. For example, you might select a story or two by Fitzgerald and Faulkner and craft an essay that compares and contrasts these two authors' treatment of the South, World War I, or the changing role of women in society.

3. **Elements across Fitzgerald's works:** Compare and contrast an element such as a theme or type of character across two or more of Fitzgerald's works.

Begin by selecting two or more works that have something in common. You might, for instance, have noticed that both *This Side of Paradise* and "May Day" deal with socialism in some form or other, or that *The Great Gatsby* and "The Ice Palace" seem to say similar things about the American Dream. Comparing and contrasting these elements across works will help you identify meaningful patterns and distinguishing characteristics. Similarly, you might analyze characters across novels. You might, for instance, compare and contrast the expatriate characters in *Tender Is the Night* and "Babylon Revisited," again looking for meaningful patterns or significant differences in these portrayals. You can also elect to compare and contrast elements within a single work. The novels, in particular, offer plenty of opportunities for single-work comparison and contrast: *The Great Gatsby*'s East Egg versus West Egg, for example, or Rosemary versus Nicole in *Tender Is the Night*.

BIBLIOGRAPHY AND ONLINE RESOURCES

Barks, Cathy W. The F. Scott Fitzgerald Society Web site. Updated Oct. 2006. Retrieved 8 Mar. 2007. <http://www.fitzgeraldsociety.org>.

Baughman, Judith, ed. *American Decades: 1920–1929.* Detroit: Manly/Gale, 1995.

Berg, A. Scott. *Max Perkins: Editor of Genius.* New York: Dutton, 1978.

Bloom, Harold, ed. *F. Scott Fitzgerald.* Bloom's Major Short Story Writers. Philadelphia: Chelsea House, 1999.

———. *F. Scott Fitzgerald.* Modern Critical Views. New York: Chelsea House, 1985.

Bruccoli, Matthew J. *Some Sort of Epic Grandeur: The Life of F. Scott Fitzgerald.* 2nd rev. ed. Columbia: University of South Carolina P, 2002.

Chambers, John B. *The Novels of F. Scott Fitzgerald.* New York: St. Martin's Press, 1989.

Cowley, Malcom, and Robert Cowley, eds. *Fitzgerald and the Jazz Age.* New York: Scribner's, 1966.

De Koster, Katie, ed. *Readings on F. Scott Fitzgerald.* Literary Companion Ser. San Diego, CA: Greenhaven, 1997.

Eble, Kenneth. *F. Scott Fitzgerald.* Twayne's United States Authors Series. Boston: Twayne, 1984.

Fahey, William A. *F. Scott Fitzgerald and the American Dream.* New York: Crowell, 1973.

F. Scott Fitzgerald Centenary Homepage. Updated Jan. 2002. Retrieved 8 Mar. 2007. <http://www.sc.edu/fitzgerald/>.

Goodwin, Donald W. "The Alcoholism of Fitzgerald." *Journal of the American Medical Association* 212 (6 April 1970): 86–90.

Kazin, Alfred. *F. Scott Fitzgerald, The Man and His Work.* New York: Collier, 1962.

Kuehl, John Richard. *Scott Fitzgerald: A Study of the Short Fiction.* Boston: Twayne, 1991.

Mizener, Arthur. *Scott Fitzgerald and His World.* New York: Putnam, 1972.

Prigozy, Ruth. *The Cambridge Companion to F. Scott Fitzgerald.* Cambridge: Cambridge UP, 2001.

Stavola, Thomas J. *Scott Fitzgerald: Crisis in an American Identity.* Totowa, NJ: Barnes & Noble, 1979.

Stern, Milton R. *The Golden Moment: The Novels of F. Scott Fitzgerald.* Urbana: U of Illinois P, 1970.

Trilling, Lionel. "F. Scott Fitzgerald." *The Liberal Imagination.* New York: Viking, 1950. 243–54.

Way, Brian. *F. Scott Fitzgerald and the Art of Social Fiction.* New York: St. Martin's Press, 1980.

THIS SIDE OF PARADISE

READING TO WRITE

*T*HIS *SIDE of Paradise,* despite being the work that originally put Fitzgerald on the literary map, is often overlooked in favor of his two later novels, *The Great Gatsby* and *Tender Is the Night.* Though it is not as sophisticated or finely crafted as the two later novels, *This Side of Paradise* portrays the development of a young aristocrat with great insight and feeling. Fitzgerald begins by describing Amory Blaine's parents and childhood and then depicts the boy's life at St. Regis Prep School and Princeton University, where perhaps the greatest of Amory's development occurs. When Amory discovers that Burne Holiday, an acquaintance of his at Princeton, has begun a movement to abolish the university clubs, which are responsible for sorting the young men into various stereotypical groups, he feels that

> [s]omeone else had discovered the path he might have followed. Burne Holiday was so evidently developing—and Amory had considered that he was doing the same. He had fallen into a deep cynicism over what had crossed his path, plotted the imperfectability of man and read Shaw and Chesterton enough to keep his mind from the edges of decadence—now suddenly all his mental processes of the last year and a half seemed stale and futile—a petty consummation of himself . . . and like a somber background lay that incident of the spring before, that filled half his nights with a dreary terror and made him unable to pray (135).

Some close attention to this passage can highlight several topics you might pursue in an essay about *This Side of Paradise* and also demonstrate that there are interesting and pertinent themes to be studied in this often underappreciated novel. The first thing you might notice here is Amory's regret and jealousy of Burne Holiday for his revolutionary zeal. It might be profitable to examine the remainder of the novel with an eye toward Burne Holiday, considering his life path as one that Amory has rejected. What ultimately happens to Burne? Does Fitzgerald present his life as better or more meaningful than Amory's? In addition, it might be useful to examine the text for other characters who represent life paths that Amory rejected.

The passage quoted above also demonstrates Amory's tendency to introspection. Here, he is confronting his own choices and perceptions of the world and coming to terms with the fact that he has not really been "developing" or growing as he thought he was. Amory condemns his recent thinking as "stale," devoid of fresh perspectives or ideas, and "futile," without the chance to make any kind of difference in the world the way that Burne's can. Amory had been "plot[ing] the imperfectability of man" instead of focusing on ways to improve him. Based on these observations, you might examine Amory's philosophizing from here through the remainder of the novel to see if he continues this line of thinking. Is this ultimately an epiphany for Amory? Does he move on to thought processes that are not "stale" and "futile"? Does he begin to "develop"? You might also use these observations as a springboard to begin thinking about Amory's conscious and deliberate construction of his identity, looking for other moments in which Amory ponders who he is and who he wants to be.

It is also in this passage that Amory realizes the significance of "that incident of the spring before," understanding that while he had consciously thought he had put the death of Dick Humbird behind him immediately after the incident, it had in fact been constantly in the background, influencing him every day. It might be fruitful to examine the rest of the text for evidence that the "incident" affected Amory and to investigate exactly how. You might also think about whether other events in Amory's life are haunting him without his knowledge.

Finally, Amory indicates that it is the "incident" that made him "unable to pray." This single phrase might prompt you to examine Amory's faith and belief in God through the course of the novel. Was Amory able to pray before the "incident"? What are his espoused beliefs? Are they consistent with his innermost thoughts? You might examine Amory's conversations with Monsignor Darcy and with Eleanor for further clues to Amory's spiritual condition.

A close reading of a single passage has opened up many exciting lines of inquiry you might pursue as you plan your essay on *This Side of Paradise.* Whichever you choose, you will likely need to identify other passages that seem to speak to your topic, analyzing them as well to uncover additional insights. This kind of careful reading is integral to literary analysis. After all, it is on a carefully built foundation of attention to detail and nuance that the best essays and most convincing arguments are built.

TOPICS AND STRATEGIES

This Side of Paradise is a novel so rich that it can be approached from almost countless angles. The sample topics below will give you an idea of the types of essays that might be written about this novel; they will get you thinking and help you generate your own topic. Alternatively, you might be intrigued by one of the sample topics and choose to focus your essay on the basic question it poses. However, rather than attempting to write an essay that answers each subquestion provided in the sample topic in a linear fashion, you should pursue those questions or relevant passages that seem most valuable or interesting to you, recording your thoughts as you work. Once you have generated some ideas and insights of your own, you are ready to leave the sample topic behind entirely and craft a thesis that will set out your particular perspective on the topic.

Themes

To begin thinking about the themes of *This Side of Paradise,* first consider what central ideas or concerns are present in the work. At the heart of it, what is this piece of literature really about? In this case, the work is pretty clearly about Amory Blaine and his journey from childhood to adulthood, but everyone makes this journey: What is it about Amory Blaine's journey that makes it worth our—and Fitzgerald's—time? What are the particular obstacles and challenges that Amory faces? What are his preoccupations? Amory spends a great deal of time thinking about his identity and the various factors that influence it; the construction of identity over time is a theme that you might investigate with an eye toward writing an essay. Additionally, Amory is somewhat reluctant to pass into adulthood because of his belief that as he grows older and acquires more experience, he loses virtue along with innocence; innocence versus experience is another theme worth investigating in the novel. Finally, as Amory gets older, his family fortune dwindles. By the end of the novel, Amory is faced with having to support himself and to confront the associations he has always made between poverty and corruption, wealth and virtue. These associations are another theme that might be fruitfully pursued in an essay on *This Side of Paradise.*

Sample Topics:

1. **Construction of identity:** According to the novel, how is identity constructed? What factors mold and shape us into the people we become?

   Amory himself charts his "reactions to his environment" this way: In his early years, he believes, there was "1. The fundamental Amory. / 2. Amory plus Beatrice. / 3. Amory plus Beatrice plus Minneapolis." Then, according to Amory, St. Regis's prep school had "pulled him to pieces and started him over again: 4. Amory plus St. Regis'. / 5. Amory plus St. Regis plus Princeton" (110). This last had gotten him as close as he would ever get to "success through conformity" (110). However, he had finally "chucked the whole thing" and returned to "6. The fundamental Amory," which he thought of as "idle, imaginative, and rebellious" (110). What do you make of Amory's explanation of his own development? Can a person really start all over again, as Amory claims to have done not once, but twice? In the terms of this novel, is identity something fundamental, or is it built by our experiences?

   To answer this question, examine Amory at each stage of his life. Try to decide what parts of Amory remain consistent and what parts change. Next to the changes, indicate whether they are sparked by an outside influence or something within Amory himself. Based on these notes, determine if there really is a "fundamental Amory." If there is a "true self," does the novel indicate that this a static identity, or can it develop as a person grows?

2. **Innocence versus experience:** How does the novel ultimately come down on the question of innocence versus experience?

Amory's mind makes a fairly strong association between innocence and goodness and between experience and corruption. You might begin by identifying and analyzing passages that comment on this connection. For example, when Amory is in trouble, he wishes for someone stupid to help him because "'stupid' and 'good' had somehow intermingled through previous association" (126). You should also look at the passages near the end of the novel in which Amory has a conversation with himself; in this conversation, he explains that a person has a certain number of "calories of virtue" that they give off as they move from innocence to experience. Once they have lost their innocence, they have no more calories of virtue and must begin to *"warm themselves"* in the aura of innocent others. Amory concludes, "I don't want to repeat my innocence. I want the pleasure of losing it again" (264). To write an essay on this topic, begin by analyzing the preceding passages. But you should also examine the novel to see whether Amory's conclusions are borne out. Find examples that either support or challenge his argument. Is Amory, in fact, "less good" at the end of the novel than he is at its start?

3. **Wealth and virtue:** What, according to the novel, is the connection between wealth and virtue? Corruption and poverty?

Near the end of the novel, after Amory's lawyer has let him know that there will be no more monthly allowances from his estate, Amory thinks to himself, "Misfortune is liable to make me a damn bad man" (266). What exactly does he mean here? In another instance, he exclaims, "I detest poor people. . . . I hate them for being poor. Poverty may have been beautiful once, but it's rotten now. It's the ugliest thing in the world. It's essentially cleaner to be corrupt and rich than it is to be innocent and poor" (262). Does this proclamation of Amory's prove true in the novel? You might begin with a list of characters, noting the financial status of each and whether the novel portrays them as good or evil, virtuous or corrupt. What about Amory himself? Is he, in fact, more corrupt as his fortunes dwindle?

4. **Masculinity:** What model of masculinity, if any, does the novel champion?

   According to Pearl James, "The war gave men a chance to be men in an honorific and absolute sense: it gave them the chance to do something that women could not do, which—in a world where women were increasingly independent socially, politically and economically—had very tangible appeal" (25). Think about how this quotation does or does not apply to Amory and his friends. Which traditionally masculine characteristics do each of the main characters possess? Does the novel offer any alternatives to the traditional definitions of masculinity?

Character

This Side of Paradise is populated by many remarkable characters. A study of any one of them or group of them would make an interesting essay. To create such an essay, you would first record all of the information you can glean about that character from the narrative. Note what the character says, thinks, and does and how other characters respond to him or her. Does the character change through the course of the novel? Is the change for better or worse? What prompts it? If you are studying a minor character, it is often useful to consider that character's function in the novel. Is he or she included to teach a lesson to the main character? To serve as a foil?

Sample Topics:

1. **Amory Blaine:** *This Side of Paradise* chronicles the life of Amory Blaine. Analyze and evaluate this character. Is this novel in the mode of the traditional quest narrative, in which the main character grows through the course of the novel from an inexperienced, confused young person into maturity, gaining through his experiences some sense of direction and purpose?

   You might begin an essay on this topic by tracing Amory's development through the novel. What stages can you identify?

Describe Amory at each of these stages and evaluate the qualities you identify. Does Amory seem to be growing in a positive way? Then, evaluate Amory at the novel's end. Decide whether he has reached a new level of maturity.

2. **Monsignor Darcy:** What is the significance of this character to the novel's themes?

   Begin by identifying key passages about Monsignor Darcy and his relationship with Amory. Does this man or his advice affect Amory in any significant way? Darcy calls Amory his "surrogate son" and often indicates that the two share important similarities. What are these similarities? Monsignor Darcy indicates that Amory will one day find faith. What is Amory's spiritual state at the novel's end?

3. **Tom D'Invilliers:** What is the function of this character in the narrative? Does Fitzgerald use him to comment on the role and status of the artist in society?

   Thomas D'Invilliers is initially known as "that awful highbrow" who wrote "passionate love-poems in the *Lit*" (63). In "Carnival," Amory and Tom discuss the transformation Tom has undergone into a more standard Princeton type, his journey into conformity, which Amory had fostered to help his friend succeed (94–95). In "Narcissus Off Duty," however, Amory mourns the loss of the more rebellious, independent streak in Tom, exclaiming to him, "Good Lord, Tom, you used to stand out against 'people.' Success has completely conventionalized you" (142). Trace Tom's development through the course of the novel along with Amory's perception of him. Based on your observations, try to determine why the author included Tom. Is his example intended to demonstrate something about conformity? To teach Amory a lesson?

4. **Female characters:** Analyze the main female characters in the novel: Isabelle, Clara, Rosalind, and Eleanor. What does the novel say about the role of women in society?

You might begin an essay on this topic by identifying and analyzing key passages that tell us about each woman: Isabelle, Clara, Rosalind, and Eleanor. Once you have done this, begin to compare and contrast them. What is different about these women and what is the same? Taking them as a whole, what generalizations can you make about the role of women in Amory's society?

5. **Burne Holiday:** What function does Burne Holiday serve in the novel? How is his character important to Amory's development?

In "Narcissus Off Duty," Amory remarks that "Burne Holiday was so evidently developing" (135). Amory notes that Burne now "grew more abstracted on the street . . . and once when Burne passed him four feet off, absolutely unseeingly, his mind a thousand miles away, Amory almost choked with the romantic joy of watching him" (142). When Burne determines to make a stand for peace and nonresistance, Amory labels him a "fanatic" and begins to think he is "just an unconscious pawn in the hands of anarchist publishers . . . but he haunts me" (158). You might begin by tracing Burne's development through the novel. Then record and analyze Amory's feelings about Burne and his development. Based on your notes, try to determine what purpose the character Burne Holiday serves in the novel. Does observing Burne Holiday inspire Amory to make changes of his own, for example?

History and Context

It is necessary to understand some background in order to comment insightfully on a piece of literature. You must acquaint yourself with the time and place in which the work is set and also consider the period in which the piece was penned in order to better gauge the author's perspective. You might consider historical events, political beliefs, social customs, and the like. With this kind of background knowledge, you are much better prepared to comment on whether the characters in a given work are representative of a certain group or whether they exhibit important and meaningful differences. Is Amory, for instance, typical in his nonchalant attitude toward the war? What does this attitude signify? In addition, with a little background knowledge, you will be much better prepared to comment on the author's intentions, to understand his response to or comments on a common idea or practice. The Mann Act is discussed in the novel, for instance, but a little background research on the law and gender roles in early 20th-century America can better prepare you to take in the nuances that Fitzgerald offers and thus to comment on his response to the Mann Act.

Sample Topics:

1. **War:** Although Amory goes off to war, the novel provides little detail about his experiences there. Why do you think this is so? What effect does this have on your interpretation of the novel?

   To write an essay on this topic, you should begin by reading about American society during World War I. An excellent general reference source for this kind of research is *American Decades: 1910—1919*; alternatively, Martin Marix Evans's *American Voices of World War I* gives insight into the everyday experiences of the American soldiers. After familiarizing yourself with the historical context of the war, examine what you know of Amory's experience with the war, and identify and analyze his comments about the war. For example, you might pay particular attention to Amory's comments on what he learned in the war: "I discovered that physical courage depends to a great extent on the physical shape a man is in" and that "men can stand anything if they get used to it" (217–18). You will need to discern whether the lack of detail about and focus on the war indicates that the experience was not paramount to Amory's development—and if this is true, what this means about Fitzgerald's take on the war—or whether you can infer a greater meaning in the absence from what little is there. Based on what you have learned about American society in the early 20th century and your analysis of the novel's treatment of the war, you can make a claim about how Fitzgerald is responding to contemporary social ideas on war in this novel.

2. **The Mann Act:** What kind of commentary is the novel making on the rules that govern the interaction between men and women in early 20th-century America?

When working on a question such as this one, keep in mind when the novel was written; it is too easy to fall into the trap of judging things like the Mann Act by today's standards. With this in mind, it might be a good idea to begin with some background reading on gender roles in early 20th-century America. The pertinent sections of Sheila Rowbotham's *A Century of Women: The History of Women in Britain and the United States in the Twentieth Century* will give you a good idea of the society's ideas about gender roles. Then do some research on the Mann Act, and locate references to it in the novel. Examine in particular book 2, chapter 4, titled "The Supercilious Sacrifice." Think about the way the novel portrays Jill and Alec, who are in violation of the law, as well the law enforcers. With whom does the novel encourage us to sympathize? Are there other instances in the novel in which Fitzgerald comments on the code of conduct expected between unmarried men and women?

3. **Effect of books:** According to the novel, how do books affect society?

You can tell a lot about a society by what books its citizens write and read. Do some research to determine who the major authors and thinkers were in the second decade of the 20th century. Then examine the role of reading in *This Side of Paradise.* Record the passages in which the author mentions what Amory (or another character) is reading. Use your knowledge of contemporary authors to analyze the characters' selections, and note the effects of their reading on the characters' perceptions and even their actions. Based on your notes, what do you think Fitzgerald is trying to say about the power of books?

Philosophy and Ideas

Thinking about philosophy and ideas in a piece of literature is similar to thinking about theme: You are asking, What is this piece really about? But you will need to think a little more broadly this time. What universal human concerns or significant social ideas does this work comment on? Because of the inherently broad scope of this sort of inquiry, it is necessary to narrow your focus once you have selected an idea or philosophy in the work that you would like to investigate. For example, in regard to philosophy, *This*

Side of Paradise seems to say something about destiny versus free will and about the nature versus nurture debate. To write about destiny versus free will, you might narrow your focus to Amory's beliefs, analyzing his perceptions on this complicated matter and then ascertaining whether the novel supports or challenges Amory's conclusions. To write about nature versus nurture, you might again zero in on Amory and focus your examination on the early part of the novel, which provides details about Amory's parents and his childhood environment, in order to determine which of these factors had the greatest impact on Amory's development. Finally, thinking in terms of the social ideas in the novel, you might decide to focus on class and dedicate your essay to determining what message the novel ultimately conveys about class distinctions in early 20th-century America.

Sample Topics:

1. **Destiny/fate:** What does the novel say about fate and destiny? Does it ultimately suggest that some outside force governs the world or that we make our own choices?

   Begin by identifying and analyzing passages that comment on destiny and free will. You might, for instance, look at Amory's decision to trust to his luck in passing his geometry exam (108–109). How is his luck connected to destiny and fate? Look also at his commentary upon failing the examination. Amory proclaims that destiny or fate was responsible; it was meant to happen. Analyze this sequence as well as others in the novel in which Amory or other characters comment on or seem to trust to fate and destiny. Based on your analysis, decide what the novel seems to be saying about fate and free will.

2. **Nature versus nurture:** According to the novel, what has a greater bearing on the kind of person one becomes—inheritance or environment?

   You might begin by recording what you know of Amory's parents, much of which is imparted in the first section of the novel, "Amory, Son of Beatrice." What was Amory's father like? What was Beatrice like? What qualities does Amory believe he inherited from each of his parents? Do these qualities remain with

Amory throughout his life? Then examine what Fitzgerald says about Amory's childhood, also described in "Amory, Son of Beatrice." Think about how this childhood affected Amory's personality and behavior and look for clues that belie his upbringing later in the novel. Then look back over your notes to determine whether the person Amory ultimately becomes reflects his inherited traits or his upbringing.

3. **Class:** What kind of commentary does the novel ultimately make on class distinctions in America?

You might begin by tracing Amory's evolving views on class. Locate and analyze passages that comment on Amory's perceptions of class barriers. At one point, for example, Fitzgerald says that he "resented social barriers as artificial distinctions made by the strong . . . to keep out the almost strong" (57). You might look also at Amory's responses to the movement to abolish the Princeton "clubs" into which upperclassmen are eventually sorted. Once you have determined how Amory's views develop, you should then determine what the novel seems to say about his final perceptions. Does he come to conclusions that the author seems to think are proper? Once you determine this, you can establish a claim about the novel's message regarding class.

Form and Genre

To write about form or genre, you have to think about the mechanics behind a piece of literature. Careful attention to the way a piece is crafted can lead to surprisingly rewarding insights about its themes and meanings. To begin thinking in this direction, you might consider how *This Side of Paradise* is different from and similar to other novels written in this period. You also might consider how the story is told. Who narrates it? How does the narrator influence readers' experience of the story? In what order are events presented? In addition, consider how the author arranged the material. Is the work divided into books, chapters, or sections? Are these titled or numbered? Are the sections long, or is the work broken up into shorter pieces? Why do you think the author made these decisions instead of opting for different strategies when writing this book? Once you have answered these questions, your task is then to discern which of these observations leads you to an interesting conclusion about the novel's meaning that you can present in an essay.

Sample Topics:

1. **"The Debutante" written as play script:** For the most part, dialogue in *This Side of Paradise* is presented in the traditional manner. What is the significance of Fitzgerald's decision to present "The Debutante" in the form of a play script?

   To craft an essay on this topic, you might begin by observing what part of Amory's life is conveyed as a play and think about what makes this point in Amory's development different. Is there any sense in which this part of his life is more of a "performance" than other parts?

2. **Narration:** How does the novel's narration affect your interpretation of its characters and events?

   Reread the novel, paying close attention to the manner in which it is told. What kind of narration is Fitzgerald using? See if you can identify instances in which the narrator's bias is revealed. For example, after saying that Amory, upon meeting the wives of other men, imagines them lamenting, "Oh, if only I could have gotten *you!*" the narrator remarks, "Oh, the enormous conceit of the man!" (156). What do this instance and others like it tell us about the narrator's viewpoint? Does it remain consistent or evolve through the course of the novel?

3. **Organization:** What is the significance of Fitzgerald's manner of arranging and dividing this novel?

   Begin by noting the manner in which the novel is organized, with book 1, the interlude, and book 2. Note also that the text within these sections is divided into chapters and then further divided into titled but unnumbered segments. Think about the significance of the titles, particularly of the books and the most significant subsections. It might be helpful to consider how this arrangement differs from other novels you have read.

4. **Epigraphs:** How do the epigraphs that preface *This Side of Paradise* influence your interpretation of the novel?

You should begin by looking closely at the epigraphs at the beginning of the novel. What do they mean, separately and taken together? Think about why Fitzgerald chose to put these particular quotations at the beginning of the novel. What do they suggest about the events to follow? How might they help you interpret the novel's meaning? You might also look for references to the authors of these quotations, Rupert Brooke and Oscar Wilde, elsewhere in the novel and do a bit of background reading on each of them.

Symbols, Imagery, and Language

Symbols and images are crafted by the author to carry meaning beyond what they would outside the context of the literary piece. Devoting your attention to these elements of a work can often bring to light important meanings or messages in the text, allowing you to discover and comment on the work's more subtle nuances. Additionally, paying attention to the very words that compose the piece of literature you are studying can be surprisingly and delightfully revealing. When you focus in on language, work on the assumption that Fitzgerald has carefully chosen each word on the page. Think about why he might have chosen those particular words instead of the many others with which he could have conveyed the same ideas. Of course, you will not be able to analyze every symbol or every word of a piece of literature, nor should you try to. Rather, your essay should focus on one set of related symbols or images or on a series of related passages. This type of essay requires a great deal of scrutiny of relatively small portions of text, but it can result in great discoveries.

Sample Topics:

1. **Image of Dick Humbird:** What does the image of Dick signify to Amory? What does this episode tell us about Amory's psychology?

Analyze the sections titled "The Devil," "In the Alley," and "At the Window" in which Amory is haunted by the specter of Dick Humbird, who was killed in a car accident on the way back to

Princeton in "Under the Arc-Light." To write an essay on this topic, do a close reading of each of the scenes in which Dick's ghost appears to Amory. Make a careful study of the ghostly image and its behavior, and consider Amory's behavior as well. What seems to provoke the image? How does it make Amory feel?

2. **Personality versus a personage:** What is the significance of these two terms in the novel?

Monsignor Darcy makes much of this distinction, first introduced in book 1, chapter 3, in a section titled "First Appearance of the Term 'Personage.'" Darcy describes a personality as "a psychical matter almost entirely" that "lowers the people it acts on" (115). A personage, however, "is never thought of apart from what he's done. He's a bar on which a thousand things have been hung— glittering things sometimes . . . but he uses those things with a cold mentality back of them" (115). You might begin with a close reading of Darcy's remarks, and then look for later references to these terms. Is this distinction between personality and personage ultimately a useful one for Amory? You might attempt to trace his understanding of them and their aid in the evolution of his character.

3. **Advertising:** What does the advertising industry symbolize in *This Side of Paradise?*

You might start by rereading the beginning of book 2, in which Amory works writing advertising copy. Think about why Fitzgerald chose this as Amory's one paying job. What does a copywriter do? Is Amory good at it? Why or why not? Think also about what else is going on in Amory's life when he takes this job. How might the symbolism of advertising be connected to Amory's desire to marry Rosalind and make a life with her?

Compare and Contrast Essays

It can be illuminating to examine themes or characters across novels. Focusing on Daisy in *The Great Gatsby* and Rosalind in *This Side of Paradise,* for instance, can enable you to comment more authoritatively on Fitzgerald's portrayal of women in his novels. Similarly, comparing Amory in *This Side of Paradise* and Dick in *Tender Is the Night* might lead you to conclusions about Fitzgerald's views on aristocracy and the tendency of wealth to corrupt. Of course, you can also compare and contrast elements in a single novel in order to bring those elements more sharply into focus. For example, you might compare and contrast Amory before and after the war in order to discuss how his wartime experiences affected him. You might also compare and contrast different characters in a single novel to emphasize their distinguishing characteristics. You might craft an essay, for example, that centers on the differences between Amory and Kerry or between Amory and Tom and comments on the significance of these differences, arguing that the novel champions a certain set of qualities over another.

Sample Topics:

1. **Daisy versus Rosalind:** Compare and contrast Daisy of *The Great Gatsby* and Rosalind of *This Side of Paradise.*

   You might begin your essay on this topic by making a list of the characteristics of Daisy and of Rosalind. Include what you can about their social status, their opinions on the status of women, the relationships they have, and the marriage choices they make. Note also whether Daisy and Rosalind are static characters or whether they develop in the course of the novel. What does this analysis reveal about Fitzgerald's portrayal of women in his novels?

2. **Amory versus Dick:** Compare and contrast Amory of *This Side of Paradise* with Dick of *Tender Is the Night.*

   A good way to begin is to record significant details about Amory and Dick. You might also identify key passages in the respective novels that illuminate their characters and analyze these. Record as much as you can about Amory's and Dick's attitudes about work, money, women, and class. Then compare and contrast what you know of Amory and Dick, looking for patterns. After you have studied your notes, you should be able to craft a thesis that says something about Fitzgerald's attitudes about work, money, women, or class.

3. **Prewar Amory versus postwar Amory:** Compare and contrast Amory's behavior and thoughts before and after the war.

Record what you know of Amory's character before he leaves for the war and after he returns. Pay particular attention to any changes evident in him. Based on your notes, you can write an essay that focuses on the effect of war on Amory, even though very little information is given about his wartime experiences.

BIBLIOGRAPHY FOR *THIS SIDE OF PARDISE*

Bloom, Harold, ed. *F. Scott Fitzgerald.* Modern Critical Views Ser. New York: Chelsea House, 1985.

Bruccoli, Matthew J. *Some Sort of Epic Grandeur: The Life of F. Scott Fitzgerald.* New York: Harcourt Brace Jovanovich, 1981.

Chambers, John B. *The Novels of F. Scott Fitzgerald.* New York: St. Martin's Press, 1989.

De Koster, Katie, ed. *Readings on F. Scott Fitzgerald.* Literary Companion Ser. San Diego, CA: Greenhaven Press, 1997.

Evans, Martin Marix. *American Voices of World War I.* Chicago: Fitzroy Dearborn, 2001.

Fitzgerald, F. Scott. *This Side of Paradise.* New York: Penguin, 1996.

James, Pearl. "History and Masculinity in F. Scott Fitzgerald's *This Side of Paradise.*" *Modern Fiction Studies* 51.1 (2005): 1–33.

Kazin, Alfred. *F. Scott Fitzgerald, The Man and His Work.* New York: Collier, 1962.

Kennedy, David M. *Over Here: The First World War and American Society.* Rev. ed. New York: Oxford UP, 2004.

Rowbotham, Sheila. *A Century of Women: The History of Women in Britain and the United States in the Twentieth Century.* New York: Penguin, 1999.

Tomkins, Vincent, ed. *American Decades: 1910—1919.* Detroit: Manly/Gale, 1996.

"BERNICE BOBS HER HAIR"

READING TO WRITE

THOUGH SELDOM ranked among Fitzgerald's very best short stories in terms of technical mastery, "Bernice Bobs Her Hair" is nevertheless a frequently anthologized, widely read, and very entertaining treatment of one of Fitzgerald's favorite topics: the ferocity of social competition. And while many of the social customs the story describes now seem foreign and almost absurdly dated, most readers today can still easily relate to the intense pressure that the characters feel to fit in with their contemporaries, even if "fitting in," ironically, means "competing with." Also familiar to us are the opposing versions of womanhood portrayed in the characters of Marjorie and Bernice; the debate over whether in order for a woman to be successful she must also be hard and cold is one that still rages today. These very general features of the story, which still speak to readers in the 21st century, provide any number of starting points for essays on "Bernice Bobs Her Hair."

Looking for ideas and themes in a work that are familiar in your own life is a great way to begin searching for an essay topic. Another useful technique, especially if you are having a difficult time getting started, is to look at specific passages that grab your attention for some reason, perhaps because the language is particularly striking, because something significant happens in the passage, or simply because the passage occupies a transitional point in the story. For instance, the following passage from "Bernice Bobs Her Hair" does not appear especially crucial to the plot; however, it is the first paragraph of the second section of the story and the first time that the two principal characters, Bernice and Marjorie, are alone and away from the social sphere:

> When Marjorie and Bernice reached home at half after midnight they said good night at the top of the stairs. Though cousins, they were not intimates. As a matter of fact Marjorie had no female intimates—she considered girls stupid. Bernice on the contrary all through this parent-arranged visit had rather longed to exchange those confidences flavored with giggles and tears that she considered an indispensable factor in all feminine intercourse. But in this respect she found Marjorie rather cold; felt somehow the same difficulty in talking to her that she had in talking to men. Marjorie never giggled, was never frightened, seldom embarrassed, and in fact had very few of the qualities which Bernice considered appropriately and blessedly feminine. (29)

This passage introduces competing ideals of femininity. Marjorie, representing a newer model for women, "considered girls stupid . . . never giggled, was never frightened, seldom embarrassed" and, to Bernice at least, comes off as "cold." Bernice presents another possible version of femininity, a more traditionally "girlish" one. She looks forward to late-night talks involving lots of giggling and tears—in other words, emotionally charged conversations. Bernice also has "difficulty" talking to men, and the narration implies that she exhibits the "appropriately and blessedly feminine" qualities of being frightened and embarrassed on occasion. Taking these possible versions of womanhood out of the context of the rest of the story, you will probably find that neither proves very satisfying. Marjorie's position of emotional unavailability sounds too rigid, but Bernice's yearning for giggles and her pride in being able to be frightened and embarrassed make her appear weak and silly. One thread that you might want to follow, starting at this passage and continuing through the rest of the story, is how these disparate femininities stack up when contrasted directly. Further, you might see if the story comes to any resolution on the point; for instance, does one version of femininity triumph, or is there an evolution of a third possibility?

Also palpable in this passage is a sense of loneliness. On a first reading of "Bernice Bobs Her Hair," with all of its dances and parties and various characters always interacting, it does not seem to be a story about loneliness. However, a close look at this paragraph by itself reveals Bernice's frustrated desire to have an intimate friendship juxtaposed with Marjorie's desire not to require such friendships—different but equally lonely positions. The narration subtly heightens the sense of loneliness by setting the scene of the two women parting at the top of the stairs, walking in different directions, each to her own room, in a dark and silent house after midnight.

Finally, when reading a passage closely like this, be certain to give equal attention to every word and phrase and to pay attention to anything that emerges from the background. For example, why does the narrator feel compelled to clarify that this is a "parent-arranged visit"? At this point in the story, that piece of information hardly seems relevant, but it must be there for some reason. Does this imply that Marjorie and Bernice would not be spending time together if outside forces had not thrown them together? Or is this perhaps a way to introduce another theme—that of generational differences—to the story? The inclusion of the phrase "parent-arranged" in this passage should at least raise your curiosity enough so that you pay attention to what roles the parents play in the rest of the story.

On first glance, this passage may have seemed unremarkable, but with a little attention it reveals several possible ideas for crafting an essay topic. From here, you will need to examine the rest of the story to develop further one or more of the ideas that this passage has introduced. Once you have settled on a particular topic, you most certainly will come back to this strategy, choosing pertinent passages and reading them very carefully, in order to gather evidence with which to support your argument.

TOPICS AND STRATEGIES

The following sections are intended to help you find and begin focusing on specific ideas for essay topics on "Bernice Bobs Her Hair." Use these as starting points for your own thinking. If one of them appeals strongly to you, start with it and delve more deeply into the questions it raises by looking for and closely examining relevant passages in the story until you feel ready to make a claim, or thesis, about the story. Alternatively, use these as a broad guide to finding a suitable topic and then employ the same strategies to create your own essay topic. By no means should you feel compelled to answer each question presented or feel limited by the questions included here. Instead, use these questions as guidelines to spark your own thinking. However much, or little, you do rely on these questions in your brainstorming, be sure not to organize your essay according to them, answering them one by one. The best organizational strategy for your essay will depend on the particular argument that you are making; it will become much clearer to you once you have produced an outline of your ideas.

Themes

When we talk of themes in literature, we simply mean the central ideas—the big ideas, if you will—in a work. The easiest way to work with themes is to start with broad features in the story. For instance, "Bernice Bobs Her Hair" tells the story of two cousins, one who is socially awkward and one who is wildly popular; much of the story revolves around the popular cousin helping the dull cousin learn to compete in the social arena. To show how this works, the story must present to us the social arena; from this, you can see how this is a story about competition in the social sphere. Once you have identified this broad concern of the story, you must narrow down your topic. For instance, you might examine the effects that social competition has on the characters, or how social competition plays an important but ironic role in maintaining social bonds. While looking at the characters' social interactions within the context of social competition, you might notice that despite all of the socializing that they are doing, they also exhibit signs of being very lonely. For instance, Bernice's euphoria over her sudden social success temporarily masks how isolated she feels, but at a word from Marjorie, all of her confidence collapses and she finds herself just as alone as she always was, suggesting that this is her natural state. This separate but related theme could lead you in entirely new directions in terms of essay ideas as you then explore what the story has to say about loneliness, even in the midst of a crowd. When you have discovered a particular theme that interests you, the next step is to determine what the story's stance is. You cannot write an essay simply saying that "Bernice Bobs Her Hair" deals with social competition. Your essay should argue what the story has to say about social competition. The best way to gather evidence for such an essay is to look for passages that deal with the theme and to do a close reading of those passages.

Sample Topics:

1. **Social competition:** What does the story ultimately say about social competition? Is it simply a destructive force, or can it be productive as well?

   To write an essay on this topic, begin by trying to determine how social competition works in the community of the story. What unwritten rules shape the young people's behavior in the social sphere? Marjorie and the narrator enumerate many of these rules, but you should look also for the more subtle rules, most often revealed when one of the characters violates one and receives a negative reaction from the community. Because you are looking at the social sphere in terms of competition, it is important to identify who "wins" and what it is that the winner achieves through his or her victory. Then explore what the story has to say about this competition. Does it condemn it? Do the young people learn important skills from this competitiveness?

2. **Loneliness:** Much Western literature of the 20th century suggests that loneliness is a fundamental characteristic of the human condition. What does "Bernice Bobs Her Hair" have to say about this? Does it propose any strategies for coping with loneliness?

   You will need to begin by sifting through all of the many moments of sociability in the story to pinpoint those moments where characters' loneliness is most evident. This does not necessarily require that the characters be alone; Warren, for instance, often seems to be lonely while in the midst of a great crowd of people simply because the one person he really wants to be with and to connect with, Marjorie, is not there. To write an essay dealing with this, find as many moments of loneliness as possible and compare them. What happens when people are lonely? What causes it, and what do they do about it? Does loneliness give the characters a chance to be reflective, or does it drive them to behave impulsively in order to escape the feeling of being alone?

3. **Intergenerational conflict:** How does Fitzgerald handle this age-old conflict in the story? Does the story seem to value one

generation's ideas over another's? Does it provide any resolutions to this conflict?

Such an essay would rely on evidence drawn not only from the occasions in which two generations interact directly but also from the way each generation comments privately on the other. For instance, Marjorie explains to a somewhat horrified Bernice, "our mothers were all very well in their way, but they know very little about their daughters' problems" (33). You will need to find as many instances of intergenerational conflict and commentary as possible to see what kind of big picture emerges. What does each generation think of the other? Does the story suggest that this conflict is necessary in order for the younger generation to find an identity, or are the young people more or less just like their parents? Is the world changing so rapidly that there truly are fundamental differences separating the generations?

4. **Social constraint/individual freedom:** Most of the action of the story is driven by the fierce pressures of social constraint, which severely obscure any sense of the characters' individual motivations. What does the story ultimately say about the forces of social convention? Is it possible to be an individual and comply with these social forces at the same time?

Similar to the first essay topic in this section, this one requires you to identify and clarify the set of rules that guide the young people in this short story. For instance, when Bernice asks her cousin, "Don't you think I know how to dress myself?" and Marjorie replies, "No," the implication, of course, is not that Bernice does not know literally how to put clothes on but that she does not wear the fashions that Marjorie's society demands of those who want to be a part of it (32). As long as Bernice wears what she wants to, she will be "punished" by being marginalized by the rest of Marjorie's community. What other examples of the conflict between social constraint and individual freedom does the story demonstrate? Does the story ever seem to condone or criticize one of these forces?

5. **Innocence to experience:** Countless works of literature tackle this theme, but each in its own way and with its own commentary on the process. What commentary does Fitzgerald provide? Has Bernice grown up by the end of the story? Were the most painful aspects of her transformation necessary in order for her to mature? Was it worth it?

This topic assumes that there is some sort of change in Bernice—or possibly one of the other main characters—over the course of the story. To begin working on this topic, try to identify the ways that Bernice can be characterized as innocent at the beginning of the story, and then contrast that with who she is by the end of the story? What has changed? Think about what lessons she has learned and where those lessons came from. Moving from a state of innocence to a state of experience implies losing some things while gaining others. Does the story suggest that Bernice lost more than she gained? Or is the knowledge she now possesses worth giving up innocence for?

Character

The most straightforward, and usually most productive, way to look at characters in a work of literature is simply to trace their development through the course of the work. In this story, for instance, how does Marjorie change as the story goes on? How does Bernice? In "Bernice Bobs Her Hair," Marjorie explicitly attempts to mold Bernice, with Bernice's permission and cooperation, indicating that this is a story intensely interested in character development. If, in the course of brainstorming, you decide that Bernice has indeed changed during the story, your next questions should be when, how, and why did she change. Of course, you do not have to limit this study only to the main characters; all of the various characters in the story exist for some reason and are therefore worth looking at. More than once, for instance, the story mentions Jim Strain and Ethel Demorest, but they never play a direct role in the plot or undergo any character development. What purpose do they serve? Are they a counterpoint to other characters? Do they offer another possible way of life that the story chooses not to explore? While not every minor character will reveal anything useful, some of them may indirectly shed some light on important ideas or on the main characters of the story.

This is particularly true when a minor character, such as Otis Ormonde, gets a notable amount of attention in the narration. Finally, as counterintuitive as it sounds, do not ignore characters who are not present. Sometimes, the characters just offstage—Bernice's mother, for instance—play an important role that can only be inferred through the characters who are present.

Sample Topics:

1. **Bernice's character development:** For this story to end the way that it does, Bernice has to do something that appears to be "out of character." What does this mean? Has she changed in some fundamental way, or is she acting unlike herself and will return to being the same old Bernice afterward?

   To make a reasonable claim about Bernice's character development, you would first need to establish what Bernice's character is at the beginning of the story and then at the end. In this way, you will see exactly how she has changed over the course of the story. The narration does not directly reveal who she is at any given time; you have to infer that from what you are shown. For instance, what kind of person does it take to cut off Marjorie's hair while she sleeps and then to throw it on Warren's front porch? Is Bernice that kind of person at the beginning of the story? What has changed? It may be useful also to consider whether Bernice might regret this behavior later. If she wants to go back to being her old self, can she? Why or why not?

2. **Marjorie's character development:** Who is Marjorie, and how does she change over the course of the story (if at all)? What does the way she changes, or not change, tell us?

   Marjorie is the other major character of this story and so deserves the same analysis as Bernice. What do we know about Marjorie? Is it surprising, given what we do know, that she helps Bernice at all? What are her motivations for doing so? Is it surprising that she turns on Bernice eventually? Why or why not? Does Marjorie grow or learn anything across the course of the story? Might she change in any way when she wakes up to find her hair gone? If you see her as primarily a static character, what does that mean for your interpretation of the story?

3. **Minor characters as types:** The story sums up many of the minor characters in just a phrase or two, indicating that they exist as stereotypes rather than as actual people. What does this type of characterization reveal about the society that the story is portraying?

This essay topic requires you to pay more attention to the background of the story. "Bernice Bobs Her Hair" is populated by characters who have no, or very few, direct appearances in the plot: Roberta Dillon, Martha Carey, G. Reese Stoddard, Sarah Hopkins, and so on. Yet they exist for a reason. Why does the narrator tell us that over G. Reese Stoddard's "bureau at home hangs a Harvard law degree" (26)? Or that "Martha is cheerful and awfully witty and an awfully slick girl" (31)? A good starting point for an essay on this topic would simply be to make a list of all of the minor characters and what the story reveals about them. Then address the question of why so many supporting roles exist for such a relatively short story such as this? If they are not portrayed as real people, then what do they stand for? And why does the story need them?

4. **Absent characters:** Sometimes, characters who never directly appear end up playing a large role in a story. Who are the absent characters in "Bernice Bobs Her Hair"? What roles do they play in the action of the story?

Much like the previous topic, this topic requires keen attention to the less obvious details of the story. While minor characters play a role in the story, so do some characters who never show up at all. An essay on this topic can examine the influence of absent characters who are mentioned, such as Bernice's mother, or even those who are not mentioned at all, such as the girls' fathers. For instance, you might tackle the issue of why fathers are so conspicuously absent from this story. By imagining how this story would be different if the fathers were present, you can begin to conceptualize how their absence affects the characters.

History and Context

The historical context of a work can sometimes provide the largest obstacles to an appreciation of it, particularly if the work contains a large number of topical references that you do not recognize. The flip side of this, however, is that if you are willing to look explicitly at the historical context and do a little research, whole new facets of the work can come alive. "Bernice Bobs Her Hair" was written and set during a tumultuous time in American history. The bloody and devastating World War I had just ended, the influenza pandemic of 1918 had killed half a million Americans, the U.S. Constitution had been amended to prohibit alcohol and was in the process of being amended to give women the right to vote, and the "Roaring '20s" were just beginning. While "Bernice Bobs Her Hair" does not make direct reference to all of these historical events, this is the environment in which the story was conceived and written, so it necessarily reflects this, however indirectly. By focusing directly on the historical and social context, you can better understand why the characters do and say some of the things they do and why some actions that may seem benign to us—such as a young woman getting a bobbed haircut—carry the consequences they do in the story.

Sample Topics:

1. **Women's suffrage movement:** "Bernice Bobs Her Hair" was published just three months before the final ratification of the Nineteenth Amendment guaranteed American women the right to vote. How is this story commenting on the movement for women's rights?

   To produce an essay on this topic, begin by researching the women's suffrage movement in the early 20th century in a source such as Doris Weatherford's *A History of the American Suffragist Movement.* Be sure to look not only at the prosuffrage arguments but also at the arguments of their opponents. Which of these arguments are reflected in "Bernice Bobs Her Hair"? Which characters are aligned with which arguments? What about the narration itself—what side does it seem to agree with? How do comments like Marjorie's—"If [a girl] looks like a million dollars she can talk about Russia, ping-pong, or the League of Nations and get away with it" (35)—connect with issues like women's suffrage? Would the young women of the story behave differently if the suffrage movement had not been so successful? Would the young men have acted differently?

2. **World War I / U.S. isolationism:** This story was written just after the conclusion of World War I, in which America, which had reluctantly abandoned its long-standing policy of isolationism, had lost more than 115,000 soldiers. How are the war and its aftereffects present in the story? Does the story comment at all on American policies or war in general?

Begin by researching the social effects of World War I in the United States in sources such as David M. Kennedy's *Over Here: The First World War and American Society.* What is important when researching for this topic is not so much the war itself as the lingering effects of the war. What was the general mood of America immediately after the war? What did Americans think about world politics? Did they want to isolate themselves from the rest of the world given the devastating consequences of participating in such a large-scale war? After gaining some familiarity with the general tenor of American society on these issues, look again at "Bernice Bobs Her Hair." How do you interpret lines such as "Bernice paused before she threw her handgrenade" (32)? Is the intensely insulated world of Marjorie's social scene indicative of a particular worldview?

3. **Hairstyles and fashions:** The climax of this story involves a haircut. Why is this an important event? What makes this particular haircut so scandalous? What social assumptions went along with a bobbed haircut on a young woman like Bernice?

Hairstyles and fashions always carry some sort of social meaning, but these meanings are attached to a particular point in time. To write an essay on this topic, research what women's fashions and haircuts meant in 1919–20. Some good places to start are *Women of the 20s* by George H. Douglas and Angela J. Latham's *Posing a Threat: Flappers, Chorus Girls, and Other Brazen Performers of the American 1920s.* What kind of woman wore her hair bobbed? Does Bernice's bobbed hair, even though she did not really want that style, end up fitting her personality after all? What is the significance of her giving Marjorie a similar hairstyle?

Form and Genre

Creative writers work with particular forms of writing that have been used, defined, and redefined by countless writers who preceded them, and the conventions of each form and genre strongly influence how the finished work will look and sound. The more readers and essay writers know about a particular form or genre, the more they can understand how the author is using that form in his or her own unique way. Understanding this will give you even more ways to approach and appreciate the work.

Sample Topics:

1. **The use of the surprise ending:** In many of his short stories, including "Bernice Bobs Her Hair," Fitzgerald employed the element of surprise to end the story. Evaluate how well this device works in this particular story. Is the surprise believable in the context of the rest of the story?

   To begin thinking about this topic, it might be useful to evaluate your own responses to the story. When you read the story for the first time, how surprised were you that Bernice cut off Marjorie's hair and threw it on Warren's porch? Why did that action come as a surprise? What would have been a more predictable ending for this story? Contrast what the predictable ending would have been to the actual ending. What is Fitzgerald saying about Bernice, or even about people in general, by offering the surprise ending?

2. **Scene division:** As in many of his stories, Fitzgerald divided "Bernice Bobs Her Hair" into numbered sections. What function do these divisions serve?

   Look carefully at where the scene breaks occur and contrast the endings and beginnings of consecutive scenes. What changes across the scene breaks? Try to imagine the story without the numbered sections—just paragraph breaks where the numbered breaks are—and consider how that would change your reading of the story.

3. **Narration and point of view:** For the most part, "Bernice Bobs Her Hair" is told from a third-person limited point of view with the narration limited primarily to Bernice's perspective. How does this affect your feelings about Bernice and about Marjorie?

Look at the story, paying especially close attention to the narration. At times, the narrator seems to be third-person omniscient. What is the general effect of an omniscient narration? Is the objectivity of such a narration more trustworthy than other types of narration? But this narration also is characterized by some limitation to Bernice's perspective, too. How does that affect your feelings about Bernice? About other characters?

Compare and Contrast Essays

Juxtaposing two or more elements from a story can offer entirely new perspectives. For example, it would not be difficult to write an essay arguing that Bernice is the "good" girl of the story who is taken advantage of and therefore deserves the reader's full sympathy. However, if you put Bernice's ideas of what it means to be a woman side-by-side with Marjorie's, you might find that while Marjorie is not a good model, Bernice's ideas are a little weak and unsatisfactory in comparison. You might then modify the idea somewhat: While you may still believe that Bernice is the more sympathetic character, you might now believe that she has room for improvement, and you can explore whether she is moving in the direction of becoming a more complete and self-sufficient woman by the story's end. In this case, using the techniques of comparing and contrasting would lead to a more sophisticated analysis of Bernice's character. Because we naturally tend to think in terms of binaries—men and women, young and old, fiction and nonfiction, right and wrong—topics for compare and contrast essays are virtually limitless.

Sample Topics:

1. **Compare and contrast gender roles in the realm of social competition:** The story offers a look into the different ways that the young men and young women of this society compete for position. How does the competition differ? Does one gender have a more difficult time than the other?

To pursue this topic, look at the scenes where men are competing for the attention of the women and contrast these to the scenes in which women are competing for the men's attention. Does one gender demonstrate more camaraderie even when competing? Is one gender characterized by ruthlessness in competition? What accounts for the differences between the rules of competition between the two genders?

2. **Compare and contrast Fitzgerald's fictional and nonfictional views on social popularity:** "Bernice Bobs Her Hair" was based on an actual letter that Fitzgerald wrote his younger sister to offer his advice on how to be popular. How does his letter compare to the story? What is different? What does this reveal about Fitzgerald's personal feelings about popularity?

The place to begin working on this essay topic is to read Fitzgerald's original correspondence to his sister, Annabel, available in *Correspondence of F. Scott Fitzgerald.* In many ways, Fitzgerald assumes the role of Marjorie in giving advice to his sister, who occupies the role of Bernice. How does the advice Fitzgerald gives differ from Marjorie's advice? How does its tone differ? Considering the outcome of "Bernice Bobs Her Hair," is Fitzgerald's advice to his sister ironic or hypocritical?

3. **Compare and contrast Bernice's and Marjorie's styles of verbal communication:** On more than one occasion, Bernice says something to Marjorie that she does not literally mean; instead, she expects Marjorie to interpret what she really means. Marjorie, on the other hand, says exactly what she means and insists on accepting what Bernice says at face value. What do these differing approaches to communication say about each of the young women? Is one style of communication presented as superior to the other?

An essay on this topic would examine and contrast the ways that the two main characters communicate and would attempt to decide which style of communication the narrative seems to value. Notice the different ways that Marjorie and Bernice express themselves. Even when speaking to her mother, Marjorie seems always to say exactly what is on her mind. She is more concerned with saying what she means than with the effects her words have on her listener. Bernice, on the other hand, expects a far subtler game to be played. She wants her listener to "read between the lines" and to feel the emotional content of what she is saying. What do these contrasting styles of communication tell us about the two young women? Who does a better job, in the world of the story, communicating? What does the story ultimately say about the value and meaning of communication?

BIBLIOGRAPHY FOR "BERNICE BOBS HER HAIR"

Douglas, George H. *Women of the 20s.* Dallas, TX: Saybrook, 1986.

Fitzgerald, F. Scott. "Bernice Bobs Her Hair." *The Short Stories of F. Scott Fitzgerald: A New Collection.* Ed. Matthew J. Bruccoli. New York: Scribner's, 1989. 25–47.

Kennedy, David M. *Over Here: The First World War and American Society.* Rev. ed. New York: Oxford UP, 2004.

Kuehl, John Richard. *Scott Fitzgerald: A Study of the Short Fiction.* Boston: Twayne, 1991.

Latham, Angela J. *Posing a Threat: Flappers, Chorus Girls, and Other Brazen Performers of the 1920s.* Hanover, NH: Wesleyan UP, 2000.

Prigozy, Ruth. *The Cambridge Companion to F. Scott Fitzgerald.* Cambridge: Cambridge UP, 2001.

Weatherford, Doris. *A History of the American Suffragist Movement.* Santa Barbara, CA: ABC-CLIO, 1998.

"THE ICE PALACE"

READING TO WRITE

WRITTEN WHILE the United States was in the process of adopting the Nineteenth Amendment, Fitzgerald's "The Ice Palace" clearly concerns itself with the changing role of women in American society. It is also fundamentally concerned, of course, with the cultures of the North and the South and their relationship to each other. The nexus of these broad concerns is Sally Carrol Happer, a young southern woman preparing to marry into a northern family. An investigation into Fitzgerald's portrayal of this character would be a good way to begin to uncover the story's many meanings.

You might begin with a look at Sally Carrol's relationship with her future mother-in-law, Mrs. Bellamy. Because of Sally Carrol's excitement about moving North—she tells her friends that she is doing so because she wants her "mind to grow" and that she wants "to live where things happen on a big scale" (51)—she might be expected to get along quite well with her northern mother-in-law and to adjust quickly and thrive in her new environment. Surprisingly, though, Sally Carrol finds that

> Mrs. Bellamy seemed to typify the town in being innately hostile to strangers. She called Sally Carrol "Sally," and could not be persuaded that the double name was anything more than a tedious, ridiculous nickname. To Sally Carrol this shortening of her name was like presenting her to the public half clothed. She loved "Sally Carrol"; she loathed "Sally." She knew also that Harry's mother disapproved of her bobbed hair; and she had never dared smoke down-stairs after that first day when Mrs. Bellamy had come into the library sniffing violently. (61)

Although it is tempting to see the North as a place more likely to be open to development of new, more independent roles for women, Sally Carrol finds that the markers of the "new woman" she has adopted, bobbed hair and a smoking habit, are met with disapproval by Mrs. Bellamy. This might prompt you to examine the story for more evidence that perhaps women in the North do not, in fact, enjoy greater freedom than those in the South. You might also consider whether there are other stereotypical associations that at first glance the story seems to perpetuate but, in fact, subverts.

If Sally Carrol heads North expecting to find greater possibilities for women, she may expect to feel a solidarity with other women that would extend past cultural boundaries. Not only does Mrs. Bellamy reject Sally Carrol's bobbed hair and smoking, however, she is also unwilling to look past cultural differences to prioritize a bond among women. Although to Sally Carrol the double name is fundamental to her identity, Mrs. Bellamy finds the name so "ridiculous" that it must be a "nickname." She insists on calling Sally Carrol what must be her "true" name, what she would be called if she had been raised in the North, simply "Sally." While nothing much seems to be at stake in this disagreement, Fitzgerald makes clear that a person's identity is connected to the traditions he or she grew up surrounded by. So steeped in their cultural traditions are the characters that it is equally difficult for Sally Carrol to accept the name Sally or for Mrs. Bellamy to address her future daughter-in-law as Sally Carrol. This cultural difference goes a long way toward preventing the women from establishing a positive relationship. It is unlikely that the women of the North and South will unite in a genuine, long-term bid for independence and equality, the story suggests, if they cannot even agree on what to call each other. You might examine the remainder of the story to determine whether geography always trumps gender or whether the reverse is ever true in Fitzgerald's world. Whichever you find to be the case, speculate on its significance.

A close look at a single passage can be most instructive and inspiring. You might begin your own thinking about "The Ice Palace" by selecting a passage that seems interesting to you in some way and subjecting it to a close examination. This activity may spark questions that will lead you to other passages you will wish to examine. Keep careful notes as you work, and before you know it you will be on your way to constructing a claim upon which to build a unique and successful essay.

TOPICS AND STRATEGIES

In writing an essay on "The Ice Palace," you may initially feel that although, or perhaps because, the story leaves you with so much to think about, you are unable to identify a good angle from which to approach your essay. The suggested topics below are designed to help you focus and sharpen your thoughts and ideas about the story into a claim upon which you can build an essay. Use them as helpful guides that ask you questions and point you to passages not to test your memory or elicit a certain rote essay from you but to stimulate your ideas and help you arrive at your own conclusions.

Themes

When you are thinking about writing an essay on the theme of a work of literature, begin by asking yourself what topics or subjects the story seems concerned with. "The Ice Palace" is clearly investigating what it means to be a northerner and what it means to be a southerner—self-perception and identity—and what these two groups of people think of each other. You might elect to write an essay on either of these themes. Once you have identified a theme you would like to investigate, reread the story, taking careful note of passages that seem to speak to your theme most directly. Then go back and analyze those passages to determine what the author is saying about the theme you have chosen. Your essay should not simply point out what the story is about, arguing only that "The Ice Palace" is a story about identity and self-perception of southerners and northerners, for example. This leaves you nothing to demonstrate or argue in your essay. Instead, you want your essay to identify and/or evaluate what the story says about your topic. You might argue, for example, that the story demonstrates that southerners identify themselves by looking toward the past, while northerners define themselves in terms of the present and future. Then your essay would have a job to do; it would need to demonstrate using evidence from the story that your claim is accurate and perhaps explain the significance of your claim. The next level would be to determine what the story says about these differences. In "The Ice Palace," is one form of self-identification presented as superior? Do the two approaches lead to unbridgeable differences between northerners and southerners?

Sample Topics:

1. **Self-perceptions of the North and South:** According to "The Ice Palace," how do northerners and southerners define and perceive themselves?

   Examine the scene in which Sally Carrol explains to her friends why she cannot marry a southerner and live in the South. What does her explanation tell us about the way southerners see themselves? Do her friends appear to agree with her? You might also look at the scene in which Sally Carrol takes Harry to the cemetery. What does this scene tell us about the way southerners define themselves and their culture? Look closely at the dinner party scene after Sally Carrol has just arrived. Pay particular attention to Harry's descriptions. Look also at Sally Carrol and Harry's visit to the ice palace. What does Harry's response to this monument tell us about the way he perceives himself and his culture?

2. **The North's and South's perceptions of each other:** According to the story, how do northerners and southerners perceive each other? Are these perceptions accurate? How do northerners' and southerners' perceptions of each other differ from the way these groups perceive themselves?

   Look closely at the scene in section 1 in which Sally Carrol explains to her friends why she wants to marry someone from the North and relocate there. What can you tell from this conversation about Sally Carrol's idea of the North? Is her vision of the North ultimately borne out as true? Look, too, at Harry's ideas of the South, particularly those he reveals to Sally Carrol in their quarrel. Are these ideas of Harry's supported in other ways in the course of the story? Look closely at Harry and Sally Carrol's interactions with each other as well as their respective communities' perceptions of their engagement. What do the two young people expect from each other based on their preconceived notions of what it means to be a southerner and a northerner? Do these expectations create problems? Why do you think Sally Carrol's friends are incredulous that she is engaged to a "Yankee"? What do Harry's northern folks think of his marrying a southerner?

Character

The meaning of a piece of literature often becomes clearer when you look closely at the characters who populate it. Identify the main characters and record what you know about them. Trace the development of each of the characters. Do any of them change in a surprising or interesting way? Does Sally Carrol, for example, learn anything in her adventure with Harry? Is she the same person at the end of the story as she was at the beginning? You might also think about whether there is an interesting relationship between two characters or sets of characters that you might explore, such as Harry and Sally Carrol's relationship or the relationship between Sally Carrol and Mrs. Bellamy. You should also consider the minor characters in a work of literature. Thinking about why the author created these characters might help you develop an interpretation of the work. In "The Ice Palace," for example, you might think about minor character Roger Patton and investigate his function in the story. You will also want to pay attention to the narrative's attitude toward the various characters. Does the story encourage you to view characters such as Sally Carrol, Harry, or Roger Patton in a negative or positive light?

Sample Topics:

1. **Sally Carrol Happer:** Analyze the main character of "Ice Palace," Sally Carrol Happer.

   Record what you know about Sally Carrol. What does she look like? How does she behave? What does she want out of life? Does Sally Carrol change through the course of the story? How? What prompts that change? Why does Sally Carrol feel as if she is "acting a part" when she tells Harry "Where you are is home for me" (57)? Try to determine whether the story portrays Sally Carrol and her development in a positive or negative light. Are readers supposed to admire and even perhaps emulate her? Why or why not?

2. **Harry Bellamy:** Analyze the character Harry Bellamy, Sally Carrol's Yankee fiancé.

   What do you know about Harry Bellamy? Record all the details you can glean about Harry, his background, and his opinions from the story. How do you think Harry feels about Sally Carrol?

Why do you think he insults southerners in front of Sally Carrol, knowing that this will offend her? Does Harry change through the course of the story or remain static? Why do you think Sally Carrol falls in love with him? Why does she refuse to marry him after all?

3. **Roger Patton:** What is Roger Patton's role in this story? What function does he serve?

Begin by recording everything you know about Roger Patton. Examine his behavior and the things he says to Sally Carrol. What do you make of his theory that "the Northern races are the tragic races—they don't indulge in the cheering luxury of tears" (60)? Why does Sally Carrol like Patton so much? Do you think it is significant that Roger Patton is the one who rescues Sally Carrol from the ice palace? How does this fit into the overall meaning of the story?

History and Context

It is helpful to consider when a piece of literature was written as well as its setting in order to place it thoroughly in context. "The Ice Palace," for example, was written when the United States was in the process of adopting the Nineteenth Amendment. Knowing this, you might focus on the role of women in the story to see if it responds in any way to the major discussion about women's rights that was at the forefront of public discourse at the time it was written. The story must also be considered in the context of war. Set in the post–World War I United States, the story also references the Civil War. Some background reading would help you to comment more astutely on Fitzgerald's use of the story to comment on perceptions of the Civil War in the early 20th-century United States or the role of women in the post–World War I era, for example.

Sample Topics:

1. **Women's suffrage movement:** David Ulrich notes that "The Ice Palace" was written "between the Senate's passing the Nineteenth Amendment and the Amendment's being ratified" (422). What do you think the story says about the changing role of women in society?

According to the critic David Ulrich, Fitzgerald's story "clearly suggests that Southern women who wanted to be 'useful' during the Civil War era faced obstacles similar to those confronting women in the post–World War I climate of the industrialized North. Social historians confirm Fitzgerald's insights" that war offers "women an artificial and short-lived opportunity to contribute to the work force" (422). Think about the women in "The Ice Palace," particularly Sally Carrol and Margery Lee. As far as you can gather from the evidence provided in the story, what similarities are there between the women of the World War I era and those of the Civil War era? What possibilities are open to women in Sally Carrol's world? Are they much different from those open to Margery Lee? How can you tell? Are there indications in the story that women's position in society has not in fact changed as much as it seems to have? You might write an essay that either supports or challenges Ulrich's assertion that "The Ice Palace" demonstrates that although there seems to be progress being made in terms of women's rights in the post–World War I era, this progress is doomed to be undone when society returns to peacetime.

2. **Civil War:** The Civil War looms large in "The Ice Palace." What kind of commentary is Fitzgerald making about the Civil War and its effects on subsequent generations in this story?

Reread the story, paying particular attention to references to the Civil War. When does it come up? Who seems to be concerned with it? Do the characters possess a realistic, objective vision of the Civil War? How do their perspectives on the Civil War affect their identities and their interactions with one another? Is the Civil War, a battle long past, ultimately a factor in the failure of Harry and Sally Carrol's relationship?

3. **World War I:** What does "The Ice Palace" ultimately say about the post–World War I United States?

You might begin by researching the cultural history of the early 20th-century United States; an excellent place to start would be the appropriate sections from David M. Kennedy's *Over Here: The*

First World War and American Society or Ralph K. Andrist's *The American Heritage History of the 20's and 30's.* Then reread "The Ice Palace" and compare Fitzgerald's portrayal of the post–World War I United States with the description you find in your background reading. What effects of the war are evident in the story? What elements of post–World War I society is Fitzgerald emphasizing? Which does he neglect? You might also consider that the story references not only World War I but also the Civil War. You might write an essay on Fitzgerald's portrayal of wartime societies. Can you identify any similarities between the Civil War era and the post–World War I era as they are portrayed in the story? Is Fitzgerald commenting on war in general in this story?

Philosophy and Ideas

To begin an essay on the philosophy and ideas engaged by a work of literature, you might start by casting a wide mental net. What broad social concerns or ideological debates might this literary work comment on? "The Ice Palace" immediately brings to mind the nature versus nurture debate. Also, a question that resonates both in Fitzgerald's story and in contemporary social discourse is, Just how closely are environment and identity connected? Keeping identity construction and environment in mind, you might turn to history and investigate what the story says about the way a group's identity is constructed by a shared memory of its past.

Sample Topics:

1. **Environment and identity:** According to the story, how much does the environment a person grows up in determine the type of person he or she becomes?

   You might begin by examining Sally Carrol at the start of the story and the way that she describes herself. What elements of the South are important to her? Then follow Sally Carrol through the rest of the story. How does she react to the North? How is it different from her hometown? How does it make her feel? Does she behave differently there? Based on your notes, try to determine how much of Sally Carrol's identity is based on the environment in which she was raised. One way to start thinking about this is to try to imagine Sally Carrol being raised in the North. In what ways would she be a different person? In what ways the same?

2. **Cultural memory:** What does the story say about cultural memory and its impact on individual identity?

   David W. Ulrich argues that Sally Carrol and Harry are shaped by cultural memory and that this cultural memory is in turn shaped by monuments such as the cemetery and the ice palace. According to Ulrich, cultures create public monuments to revise or sanitize their histories and thus create identities they are comfortable with. The cemetery and the ice palace help Sally Carrol and Harry "idealize their ancestors" (419). Analyze Sally Carrol's response to the cemetery and Harry's response to the ice palace. What evidence can you find that they are using these monuments to define their cultures and their own personal identities? You should also think about the effect cultural memory has on the two young people. Does Sally Carrol's attachment to the "Old South" serve her well, or does it impede her development into a fully realized person? What about Harry's devotion to the ice palace and the technological, progress-loving society it represents?

Form and Genre

Reading a piece of literature with a conscious eye to the artistic choices and strategies behind it can be quite illuminating. Looking at the way "The Ice Palace" is constructed, you will immediately notice that the story is divided into six sections with roman numerals at the heads and that the text begins and ends in much the same way, creating a sort of frame around the narrative. You could use either of these observations as a springboard to begin brainstorming for an essay. You might begin by asking why the author made the choices he did and consider what the effect would have been had he made other choices. The use of dialect for the speech of the southern characters is also a deliberate decision made by Fitzgerald, and you might think about the reasons for and ramifications of that decision. Although it might not initially appear so, examining the craft of a piece of literature can provide you with insight into its meanings and enable you to make arguments about its interpretation. For example, your study of the narrative frame might lead you to an argument that, according to "The Ice Palace," while time moves ever forward in a linear fashion in the North, the South is a place that keeps time with a sense of rhythm and cycles and spends as much time looking backward as forward.

Sample Topics:

1. **Frame:** Why do you think Fitzgerald chose to begin and end the story in much the same way?

   Examine the opening and closing scenes. What is similar in the scenes? Can you locate any significant differences? How does Fitzgerald's decision to frame the narrative with these similar scenes affect your interpretation of the story? Does it indicate that Sally Carrol has not been at all altered by her experience?

2. **Division of the story:** What is the significance of the way the story is divided into sections?

   Look closely at the way the story is divided. You might want to chart out what happens, what characters are present, and the setting in each section. Can you discover any meaningful patterns? Why do you think Fitzgerald opted to organize the story this way instead of simply not dividing it at all, dividing it into a different number of sections, or giving it chapter titles?

3. **Dialect:** Why do you think Fitzgerald opted to represent the speech of his southern characters with dialect? What effect does this have on your interpretation of the story?

   Examine the use of dialect in the story. Who uses it? In what situations? Does the use of dialect bring with it certain associations? Do you tend to see the characters who speak this way as less intelligent, for example? Does the rest of the story support those associations or challenge them?

Symbols, Imagery, and Language

Symbols and images abound in "The Ice Palace." The title itself suggests one important symbol, and as you read through the story looking for other objects that are invested with meaning, you are sure to discover the cemetery and the grave of Margery Lee as symbols for the South that counterbalance the ice palace of the North, as well as the sunlight, which seems to be a key indicator of Sally Carrol's emotional state. To write about any of these symbols or images, first record your instinctual association with them to get a sense of what they might traditionally stand for in our culture.

Then observe closely how these symbols figure in the story, analyzing the passages in which they appear. What associations do these symbols carry? How are they interpreted by the characters? Do the symbols mean the same thing to everyone who encounters them? You will need to decide what comment the author is making about the symbol or what he is using the symbol to say about something else. For example, you might write an essay about the meaning of cemeteries in southern culture as evidenced by the story, or you might write an essay arguing that through the symbol of the ice palace, Fitzgerald condemns northern society as cold, hard, and empty.

Sample Topics:

1. **Ice palace:** What does the ice palace represent in the story?

   Examine the descriptions of the ice palace provided in the story. What does it look like? Is it significant that it is a "palace" made of ice and not some other kind of building? What is its purpose? What happens there? Who goes to visit the palace? How does Sally Carrol respond to the ice palace? How does Harry? Why do you think the story is titled "The Ice Palace"? Why does Fitzgerald set the main event of the story, Sally Carrol's fall and realization that she cannot live in the North, in the ice palace?

2. **Cemetery:** What does the cemetery symbolize in the story for Sally Carrol and her community?

   Closely examine section II of "The Ice Palace," in which Sally Carrol takes Harry to "one of her favorite haunts, the cemetery" (52). Pay particular attention to the interaction between Sally Carrol and Harry. What can we discover about each of their feelings toward the cemetery? What does it mean for Sally Carrol? Why do you think she likes it, even though it "depresses some folks" (52)?

3. **Margery Lee:** What does Margery Lee symbolize in the story?

   Examine the scene in section II of the story in which Sally Carrol and Harry visit the cemetery and find a headstone with the name Margery Lee on it. How does Sally Carrol imagine Margery Lee? Why do you think she imagines her in the way she does? Why do you think Sally Carrol calls the date on Margery

Lee's tombstone, "1844–1873," "eloquent"? What is significant about this time frame? How old would Margery have been during the Civil War, and how is this significant?

4. **Sunlight:** How does sunlight figure symbolically in the story?

Reread the story looking for any references to the sun or sunlight. Can you locate any patterns? What is the sun like in the South versus the North, for example? Notice how descriptions of the sunlight are connected to Sally Carrol.

Compare and Contrast Essays

Compare and contrast essays work especially well with stories such as "The Ice Palace" that do a great deal of juxtaposition. In "The Ice Palace," which juxtaposes North and South, you almost cannot help but compare and contrast as you read. You might write an essay that compares and contrasts the North and South generally, but it might be better to focus on one or more elements of that larger comparison. You might, for instance, compare and contrast only the men, the women, the climate, the monuments, or even the speech of these two cultures. Once you have identified and described what is similar and different about the elements you have identified for comparison, examine how the story treats these elements. Does Fitzgerald seem to be suggesting the supremacy of one or the other?

Sample Topics:

1. **Northern men versus southern men:** How are men from the North and men from the South portrayed differently in "The Ice Palace"? What traits are associated with the men from each region? Is either set portrayed more favorably?

You might begin by looking at the way that Sally Carrol describes southern men as not "only money failures, but just sort of ineffectual and sad" (51). She attempts to explain herself to Clark: "I wouldn't change you for all the world. You're sweet the way you are. The things that'll make you fail I'll love always—the living in the past, the lazy days and nights you have, and all your carelessness and generosity" (51). Does the remainder of the story support Sally Carrol's opinion of southern men? Sally Carrol herself compares southern and northern men in terms of felines and canines. She says that most southern men are "feline," while all the northern men she has met are "canine" in disposition. Roger Patton defines canine as possessing "a certain conscious masculinity as opposed to subtlety" (59). What other associations do *feline* and *canine* carry? What does this distinction made by Sally Carrol say about her perceptions of southern and northern men?

2. **Northern women versus southern women:** How are women from the North and women from the South portrayed differently? What traits are associated with the women from each region? Is either set protrayed more favorably?

Examine Sally Carrol's perceptions of northern women. What do you make, for example, of the fact that Sally Carrol felt a "definite hostility" toward the women in Harry's family? Or the following opinion of Harry's sister: "Myra, her future sister-in-law, seemed the essence of spiritless conventionality. Her conversation was so utterly devoid of personality that Sally Carrol, who came from a country where a certain amount of charm and assurance could be taken for granted in the women, was inclined to despise her" (61)? Why do you think Mrs. Bellamy treats Sally Carrol the way she does? Does the story as a whole bear out Sally Carrol's idea that "[i]f those women aren't beautiful ... they're nothing. They just fade out when you look at them. They're glorified domestics. Men are the center of every mixed group" (61)? How does this estimation compare to southern women? Examine everything you can gather from the story about southern women. From your observations, does the story suggest that there are indeed significant differences between southern and northern women? If so, what exactly are these differences, and which group, if either, is presented in a more positive light?

3. **The Happer house versus the Bellamy house:** What do the descriptions of Sally Carrol's house and the Bellamy house say about the cultures in which they are situated?

Sally Carrol discovers that in the Bellamys' library, "[a]ll the chairs had little lace squares where one's head should rest, the couch was just comfortable," and "the books looked as if they had been read—some" (56). This reminds her of the "battered old library at home, with her father's huge medical books, and the oil-paintings of her three great-uncles, and the old couch that had been mended up for forty-five years and was still luxurious to dream in" (56). Compared with the library at home, the Bellamys' strikes Sally Carrol "as being neither attractive nor particularly otherwise. It was simply a room with a lot of fairly expensive things in it that all looked about fifteen years old" (56). Analyze these descriptions and use them to figure out what Sally Carrol thinks about her home and this new northern home of her fiancé. What sorts of things are valued in each place? Can you discern how Sally Carrol feels about the North and the South by these comparative observations she makes?

BIBLIOGRAPHY FOR "THE ICE PALACE"

Andrist, Ralph K., ed. *The American Heritage History of the 20's and 30's.* New York: American Heritage, 1987.

Bloom, Harold, ed. *F. Scott Fitzgerald.* Bloom's Major Short Story Writers. Philadelphia: Chelsea House, 1999.

———. *F. Scott Fitzgerald.* Modern Critical Views Ser. New York: Chelsea House, 1985.

Bruccoli, Matthew J. *Some Sort of Epic Grandeur: The Life of F. Scott Fitzgerald.* New York: Harcourt Brace Jovanovich, 1981.

Dolan, Marc. *Modern Lives: A Cultural Re-reading of "the Lost Generation."* West Lafayette, IN: Purdue UP, 1996.

Fitzgerald, F. Scott. "The Ice Palace." *The Short Stories of F. Scott Fitzgerald: A New Collection.* Ed. Matthew J. Bruccoli. New York: Scribner's, 1989. 48–69.

Hoffman, Frederick J. *The Twenties: American Writing in the Postwar Decade.* Rev. ed. New York: Collier, 1962.

Kennedy, David M. *Over Here: The First World War and American Society.* Rev. ed. New York: Oxford UP, 2004.

Ulrich, David W. "Memorials and Monuments: Historical Method and the (Re)construction of Memory in F. Scott Fitzgerald's 'The Ice Palace.'" *Studies in Short Fiction* 36 (1999): 417–36.

"MAY DAY"

READING TO WRITE

FITZGERALD'S NOVELETTE "May Day" depicts several events that occurred on May Day, 1919; although they seem to be disparate events, connections are revealed in surprising ways. The story begins by following Gordon Sterrett, a Yale alumnus who has fallen on hard times, as he attempts to borrow money from his one-time friend and Yale cohort Phillip Dean in order to pay off Jewel Hudson, a lower-class woman he has been seeing who is threatening to ruin him. Although Phillip refuses to lend Gordon the money on the grounds that it would inconvenience him, the two attend the Gamma Psi dance that evening, where Gordon hopes to meet a former girlfriend, Edith Bradin. Edith, upset at the drunken and desperate state in which she finds Gordon and annoyed at her own drunken escort, Peter Himmel, runs off to see her brother, Henry, who always works late on a socialist newspaper. Jewel shows up and leads Gordon away. When he awakens the next morning and finds himself married to Jewel, Gordon commits suicide.

While the Yale set has been preening and partying, two other characters are introduced, former soldiers named Gus Rose and Carrol Keys. These men set about to procure alcohol from Carrol's brother George, who works in the hotel that is hosting the Yale party. Ultimately, Gus and Carrol wind up leading a mob of soldiers that storms into the newspaper office where Henry and Edith are talking. Carrol falls from the balcony, and the May Day events result in not one but two deaths. With so much going on all at once, it can be difficult to figure out what exactly a piece like "May Day" is about and to identify a topic on which to base an essay, but the psychological motivations of its characters are one potential avenue. You might start your investigation into the novelette with an analysis of a paragraph that provides some interesting details about Gus and Carrol:

> The entire mental pabulum of these two men consisted of an offended
> nasal comment extended through the years upon the institution—army,
> business, or poorhouse—which kept them alive, and toward their imme-
> diate supervisor in that institution. Until that very morning the institu-
> tion had been the "government" and the immediate superior had been the
> "Cap'n"—from these two they had glided out and were now in the vaguely
> uncomfortable state before they should adopt their next bondage. They
> were uncertain, resentful, and somewhat ill at ease. This they hid by pre-
> tending an elaborate relief at being out of the army, and by assuring each
> other that military discipline should never again rule their stubborn, lib-
> erty-loving wills. Yet, as a matter of fact, they would have felt more at home
> in a prison than in this new-found and unquestionable freedom. (107)

This passage reveals that Gus and Carrol are not aware of their true motivations or desires. While they perceive themselves as men who have suf-
fered hard luck, according to the narration, in reality they are men who
cannot accept the responsibility of free will. They must have someone to
give them orders and someone to blame for their unhappiness. You might
look through the work for evidence to prove that Gus's and Carrol's inner
psychologies really are as the narrator describes. You might also attempt
to trace the ramifications of this insight into the men's unconscious motivations and identities. Can it help explain the riot that results in Carrol's
death? Do the two men intend to lead the riot, after all? The passage
also raises the question of how many other soldiers are driven by these
same motivations. How is this related to the soldiers' attitude toward the
socialist newspapermen? Is it only soldiers or the lower classes who are
afraid of free will, or do men like Phillip Dean and Peter Himmel share
some of this same psychology? Are they simply ruled by different institutions, or by social expectation, rather than direct command? Look again
at the story to see if there is any character who seems to embrace free
will and freedom and who is not ruled in some form or other by group
mentality. Finally, think about what all this means in terms of the overall
message of the story. What does it say about the very nature of human
beings and the way they navigate through the world?

This passage has provided some good questions to ask as you reread the
story and deepen your investigation. It would be a good idea to locate several more passages that seem to answer these questions and to carefully
analyze these passages in search of answers. After you have completed this

process, you can devise a thesis for your essay, one that might attempt to explain the reasons behind the May Day riot, to discuss the differences between the psyches of the Yale men and the soldiers, or even to speculate on what Fitzgerald thinks about the nature of human beings.

TOPICS AND STRATEGIES

The many sample topics listed below are designed to help you to generate ideas and arrive at a claim upon which to build your essay about Fitzgerald's "May Day." Although the sample topics are not necessarily a short cut, as you will still need to spend a significant amount of time analyzing passages and making notes before you can arrive at a claim and begin to draft your essay, they will make it easier for you to get started by helping you sharpen your focus onto a potentially fruitful topic and guiding your initial investigation and analysis in a promising direction. Use the prompts to guide your thinking and to spark your own ideas; do not feel compelled to address all of the questions or analyze each of the passages presented in the sample topics. The topics are not designed to elicit a specific response. Each writer who selects a particular topic will ideally wind up with a unique essay and a fresh and revealing take on Fitzgerald's "May Day."

Themes

When you address a work's themes, you are thinking about the major topics or subjects it covers. Literary works have multiple themes, and you might begin by simply identifying some of the major ones in the piece you are working on. "May Day," for example, is about many things, including social disparity, violence, and male bonding. Once you have identified the major themes, focus in on the one that seems most promising or interesting to you. Next, you will want to reread the work, noting any passages or scenes that seem related to your theme so that you can analyze these at length. Based on your analysis, you will be able to form a claim or thesis that states what the author is saying about the theme you have chosen. For example, your thesis should not say simply that male bonding is a major theme in "May Day." Instead, you might argue that Fitzgerald's "May Day" demonstrates that the lack of meaningful male bonding experiences in the post–World War I United States led to feelings of isolation and alienation and ultimately to violence. Although early in your writing process you narrowed your focus to a single theme, you may find that your thesis winds up touching on more than one of the themes you initially identified—in this case, male bonding and violence; this is natural and acceptable since many of the major themes of a work are connected to one another in some fashion.

Sample Topics:

1. **Social disparity:** What kind of commentary is the story making about social classes in America?

   Reread the story paying close attention to the various social classes represented in the story. Record everything the story tells you about each of these classes. Which characters belong to the upper classes and which to the lower? What do you know about these characters? How do they behave? What are the most significant differences between the two groups? Try to identify the tensions between classes, and trace how those tensions exert pressures on the characters and their actions.

2. **Violence and death:** What is the story ultimately saying about the role of violence in early 20th-century America?

   Record the details of each scene of violence and death in the story. What causes the outbreaks of violence? Who is harmed by them? What patterns can you discover? Is anything positive accomplished by the violence? What attitude does the narrative take toward these episodes?

3. **Male bonding:** According to critic Robert K. Martin, Fitzgerald's "May Day" is primarily about "the crisis of the male-bonding relationship" (99). Analyze and evaluate this assessment of the story.

   Identify all of the male relationships in the story. Record what details you can about these relationships, including relationships between two men, such as Dean and Gordon, as well as group relationships, such as the soldiers and the Yale alumni. What are these relationships built on? What do they do for those involved? Is there a focus on male relationships in the story? Does male bonding appear to be in crisis? Based on the story, what precipitates this crisis?

Character

Fitzgerald's "May Day" is populated with enough interesting characters to inspire many successful essays. When you are writing an essay about a character, make sure to trace his or her trajectory and to notice any changes in attitude or behavior. It is also important to determine how the narrative treats your character, whether it makes him or her appear sympathetic or villainous. You can often tell a great deal about the author's feelings about an idea or theme by the way he or she treats certain characters in the narrative.

Sample Topics:

1. **Phillip Dean:** Analyze and evaluate the character of Phillip Dean. What is the significance of this character to the themes of the story?

   You might begin by recording everything you know about Phillip Dean. Then, analyze the scenes that tell you the most about his character. You might pay particular attention to his interactions with his old Yale friend in trouble, Gordon Sterrett. What does Dean's treatment of Gordon tell us about Dean? Does Dean change at all through the course of the narrative? What is the larger function of his character in the story?

2. **Gordon Sterrett:** Analyze and evaluate the character of Gordon Sterrett. What is responsible for his downward spiral?

   Begin by recording everything you know about Gordon. Analyze his relationships with Phillip Dean, Edith Bradin, and Jewel Hudson. Trace his development through the course of the narrative. Can you identify what factors contribute to his downfall? What makes him different from other, more successful Yale graduates such as Phillip Dean? What do you make of Gordon's desire to become an artist?

3. **Edith Bradin:** Analyze the character of Edith Bradin.

   What do you make of Dean's description of her: "She's still sort of a pretty doll—you know what I mean: as if you touched her she'd smear" (99)? What does the narration tell us about Edith and her character traits and motivations? You might pay close attention to the scenes between Edith and Gordon and those between Edith and her brother Henry. What do these interactions reveal about Edith? Analyze her remark to Henry that it "seems sort of—of incongruous . . . me being at a party like that, and you over here working for a thing that'll make that sort of party impossible ever more, if your ideas work" (128).

4. **Jewel Hudson:** Analyze and evaluate the character of Jewel Hudson.

You might begin by recording everything you know about Jewel Hudson, including her background. How is she described by Gordon to Dean? What can you tell of the relationship between Gordon and Jewel? When she finally appears in the story, does Gordon's description of her seem accurate to you? What part does Jewel play in Gordon's suicide?

5. **Gus Rose and Carrol Keyes:** Analyze these characters and the group they represent.

What do you know about Gus and Carrol? Trace their actions through the course of the story. What motivates them? How do they become leaders of the mob that storms Henry's office? What do you think of Henry's assessment of them: "the soldiers don't know what they want, or what they hate, or what they like. They're used to acting in large bodies, and they seem to have to make demonstrations. So it happens to be against us" (128). Does the remainder of the narrative support Henry's assessment of Gus and Carrol?

History and Context

Spending a little time acquainting yourself with events and issues that contemporary readers would have known automatically can help you get a better grasp of a literary work like "May Day." For example, modern readers might be unfamiliar with the May Day riots of 1919 as well as the general atmosphere of the post–World War I United States. Learning this important contextual information will make you much better equipped to determine what Fitzgerald is saying about the post–World War I era or the May Day riots. This information will enable you not only to ascertain whether his portrayal matches those offered in historical accounts but also to speculate on the reasons behind any discrepancies you identify.

Sample Topics:

1. **May Day:** How does the history and tradition of May Day play into the story's meanings?

   What is the history of May Day? What does Henry mean when he explains to Edith: "There've been riots all over the city tonight. It's May Day, you see" (128)? Why is the Yale dance held on May Day? Is the meaning of May Day reflected in the story, or is it more of an ironic relationship? When researching the history of May Day, keep in mind that May Day has two somewhat connected but still distinct meanings. On the one hand, May Day is an ancient pagan holiday that has been preserved as a community celebration. Information on the customs and history of the ancient May Day holiday is widely available on the internet. For a more scholarly treatment, consult *A History of Pagan Europe* by Prudence Jones and Nigel Pennick. May Day also refers to International Workers' Day. To research the origins of this labor movement–based holiday, consult *Death in the Haymarket: A Story of Chicago, the First Labor Movement, and the Bombing That Divided Gilded Age America,* by James Green.

2. **May Day riots:** What kind of commentary is Fitzgerald making about the May Day riots of 1919?

   Begin with some research into the May Day riots of 1919, including their causes and ramifications. Once you have become familiar with the history, you can begin to evaluate Fitzgerald's presentation of the events. Think about the reasons behind the historical May Day riots, including socialist ideology, and compare the causes and results of the actual riots to those in the narrative. What does Fitzgerald change? What does he emphasize? Are the riots thematically important to the narrative, or are they simply there to move the plot forward?

3. **World War I:** How is the Allied victory presented in "May Day"?

Examine in particular the opening of the story. How is the post–World War I United States presented here? What are its distinguishing characteristics? Why do you think the opening sections are written in such stylized language? What does this have to do with the war victory? Is the story's opening echoed in later sections? What is the connection between the opening scene and the remainder of the story?

Philosophy and Ideas

To understand fully the meanings behind a work of literature, it is helpful to understand the major philosophies or social ideas it engages. In the case of "May Day," it would be particularly useful to have some background knowledge on the debate between capitalist modes of thought and the socialist/pacifist movement in the early 20th-century United States. Thus briefed, you can better ascertain Fitzgerald's response to this debate. A study of philosophy and ideas can be rewarding in just about any piece of literature; however, in a work such as "May Day," which makes direct reference to philosophies and ideas through the character of Henry Bradin—dedicated to a socialist newspaper—and the responses of other characters to Bradin's ideology, it is fairly certain that an analysis of the philosophies and ideas present in the work will be especially fruitful.

1. **Socialist/pacifist movements:** What kind of commentary is Fitzgerald making about socialism and pacifism in "May Day"?

You might begin with some background reading on the socialist and pacifist movements during this period. A good general starting point for this research would be the appropriate sections of *A Companion to 20th-Century America*, edited by Stephen J. Whitfield. What motivated the members of these movements? What were their goals? How were they perceived by more mainstream groups? Once you have gotten some background knowledge, examine the scene in section III in which Carrol Key and Gus Rose listen to a "little Jew" speaking against capitalism and war. Pay close attention also to the character Henry Bradin, Edith's brother, and analyze the scenes in which he is present, particularly the conversation he has with Edith and the mob storming of his office. Then, you may want to ascertain who is portrayed in a more positive light, Henry or the mob led by Carrol and Gus, as one measure of Fitzgerald's sympathies.

2. **Consumption/capitalism:** What kind of commentary is Fitzgerald making about consumption and capitalism?

Examine the opening sections of "May Day," paying particular attention to the behavior of the merchants:

> [T]he victorious war had brought plenty in its train, and the merchants had flocked thither . . . to taste of all the luscious feasts and witness the lavish entertainments prepared—and to buy for their women furs against the next winter and bags of golden mesh and varicolored slippers of silk and silver and rose satin and cloth of gold. So gaily and noisily were the peace and prosperity hymned by the scribes and poets of the conquering people that more and more spenders had gathered from the provinces to drink the wine of excitement, and faster and faster did the merchants dispose of their trinkets and slippers until they sent up a mighty cry for more trinkets and slippers in order that they might give in barter what was demanded of them. Some even of them flung up their hands helplessly, shouting "Alas! I have no more slippers! and alas! I have no more trinkets! May Heaven help me, for I know not what I shall do!" (98)

What does this passage say about postwar society? Why do you think this passage is written in such stylized—even stilted—language? How are this passage and its meanings connected to the rest of the story? What things are bought and sold throughout the narrative? What effect does money and consumption have on the characters? You might look especially at Gordon's request for money and the day he spends having lunch and shopping with Phillip Dean before being refused. Based on your notes in response to these questions, can you determine what message about capitalism and consumption Fitzgerald is sending here? You might also think about Fitzgerald's portrayal of capitalism in other works, such as *The Great Gatsby*.

Form and Genre

In writing an essay about a literary work, it is easy to gravitate toward its more abstract elements, such as symbols or themes; however, in many cases, approaching the story more like a painstakingly constructed piece of text can be just as productive. You might, for example, consider what outlet and audience the piece was written for, analyze the structure of the story, or take a close look at how the author chose to tell the story, including his choice of a narrator to tell the tale and the type of language employed in the telling. You might also consider whether the piece belongs to any literary movements or particular genres. For example, you might write an essay about "May Day" that attempts to explain why Fitzgerald chose to publish this piece in the venue he did, why the story includes elements of a fairy tale, or why "May Day" can or cannot be considered in the naturalistic tradition and to what end. Far from merely technical inquiries, these kinds of essays can reveal surprising insights about a literary work's central meanings.

Sample Topics:

1. **Publication in *The Smart Set:*** Fitzgerald published "May Day" in 1920 in *The Smart Set,* which paid him $200 for the manuscript. He did not attempt to publish the story in any of the higher-paying magazines first. What do you think motivated this decision?

   You might begin by doing some research into the magazine market in the early decades of the 20th century. You might even try to locate some old copies of these magazines to get a firsthand sense of what they were like. What sets a magazine like *The Smart Set* apart from, say, the *Post*? Who were the likely readers of these magazines? Do you think Fitzgerald was right to publish this particular story in *The Smart Set*? What kind of audience do you think he hoped to reach? Could there be other reasons besides audience for Fitzgerald's decision to publish "May Day" in a magazine like *The Smart Set* instead of a more mainstream, popular magazine?

2. **Organization and structure:** According to Anthony J. Mazzella, the principle of structure is the "pulsation of opposites . . . a step in one direction followed by a step in an opposite direction" (382). Do you agree with Mazzella's argument?

Map out the structure of "May Day," carefully noting what happens in each section, as well as where each scene is set. What patterns can you identify? You might write an essay that supports Mazzella's conclusion, illustrating this "pulsation of opposites" and speculating on its thematic resonance, or you might discern another organizational principle entirely that you demonstrate and analyze in your essay.

3. **Fairy tale form:** What elements of a fairy tale can you locate in "May Day"? How are they thematically significant?

According to Anthony Mazzella, the opening of "May Day" strongly suggests a fairy tale. He writes that "The fairy tale form is suggested by the passive voice of the narrator . . . the use of archaisms . . . the generality of reference . . . the artificiality of language and the central object of at least one well-known fairy tale—the slipper" as well as the "tone, that of pained as well as mocking exaggeration" (381). You might compare the opening of the novelette to the remainder of the text. Are there fairy tale elements throughout, or are they concentrated in the opening? You might also spend some time thinking about the function of traditional fairy tales. What does our society use them for? Why would Fitzgerald invoke the fairy tale in this piece of literature? Is he steering his reader toward a particular interpretation of the text?

4. **Naturalistic fiction:** Is "May Day" an example of naturalistic fiction? How do you know? Why is it important one way or the other?

Do some background reading on naturalism. Donald Pizer's *The Cambridge Companion to American Realism and Naturalism* would be a helpful source to consult. Then reread the story to judge whether it falls into that literary tradition. What forces propel the action in the story? Do the characters seem to have wills of their own that can affect their fates, or are they simply pawns moved about by forces beyond their control? You might write an essay that argues that "May Day" is or is not an example of naturalistic fiction and then discuss the ramifications of that argument. Why, for example, is it important to an understanding of the meaning of the story to know whether it is in the naturalistic tradition?

Symbols, Imagery, and Language

An analysis of the symbols and images in a work of literature often reveals insights into its meanings. As you begin to work with symbols, images, and language, it is helpful to remember that authors are superior craftspeople who spend a great deal of time revising and fine-tuning each work and that each image and choice of word or phrase is deliberate. Therefore, careful attention to images and language can lead to interesting claims about the meanings embedded in a particular text.

1. **Mr. In and Mr. Out:** How are these two characters significant to the story's themes?

   Closely examine section X, in which Peter and Dean become Mr. In and Mr. Out. What do they do in this scene? What do Peter and Dean achieve by adopting these roles? How is this episode connected to themes explored elsewhere in the novelette?

2. **May Day:** What is the symbolic meaning of the story's title?

   Begin by doing some research into all the different meanings of May Day, keeping in mind the two connected but distinct meanings of the holiday: the ancient pagan holiday that has been preserved as a community celebration and International Workers' Day. Information on the customs and history of the ancient May Day holiday is widely available on the internet. For a more scholarly treatment, consult *A History of Pagan Europe* by Prudence Jones and Nigel Pennick. To research the origins of the labor movement–based holiday, consult *Death in the Haymarket: A Story of Chicago, the First Labor Movement, and the Bombing That Divided Gilded Age America* by James Green. Then think about how each meaning is or is not reflected in the story. Would you say that one particular meaning is central to the story? Is there any irony in the title?

Compare and Contrast Essays

Comparing and contrasting elements of a piece of literature can help you identify salient features of particular events or characters as well as meaningful patterns or distinctions. For example, the two deaths that occur in "May Day," those of Carrol Keys and Gordon Sterrett, might help reveal what the novelette has to say about violence and death. Likewise, you might examine the relationships between Gordon and Edith and between Gordon and Jewel to comment on the role of women or the fate of romantic relationships in the novelette. Or you might compare sets of characters—Gus and Carrol representing the lower-class soldiers and Dean and Peter representing the upper-class Yale alumni—to make a claim about social class or male bonding in "May Day." Finally, comparisons can also be made across works. You might decide to examine, for instance, the theme of violence or male relationships across several of Fitzgerald's stories to see whether there are identifiable patterns or to chart a course of development through the writer's career.

Sample Topics:

1. **Gus and Carrol versus Dean and Peter:** Compare and contrast these two sets of characters.

   Begin by noting everything the novelette tells you about each of these characters, recording in particular what Gus and Carrol have in common and what Dean and Peter have in common. What makes each set of men friends? What ideas do they share? Then think about the similarities and differences between the two sets of friends. What makes Gus and Carrol similar to and different from Dean and Peter? Compare and contrast their relationships also. Is the bond between Gus and Carrol similar to or different from the one shared by Dean and Peter? Based on your observations and analysis, you might formulate a claim about social classes or male bonding in "May Day."

2. **Death of Gordon versus death of Carrol:** Compare and contrast these two events, and discuss their significance.

   You might begin by recording what you know of Gordon and Carrol, tracing the trajectories of their paths until each of their deaths. In what ways are these two characters similar, and in what significant ways are they different? What caused each of their deaths? How is each death treated in the narrative? Based on your analysis, what do you think the novelette is saying about life and death through the fates of these two characters?

3. **Edith versus Jewel:** Compare and contrast these two female characters, and discuss the significance of your findings.

Reread the story, paying close attention to Edith and Jewel, analyzing their background, their speech, their behavior, and their relationships with Gordon Sterrett. Pay attention also to how they are treated by other characters. In what ways are these two women similar, and in what ways are they different? Can you make any generalizations about women based on these two characters? Can you make any observations about the difference between upper- and lower-class women through this comparison?

BIBLIOGRAPHY FOR "MAY DAY"

Bloom, Harold, ed. *F. Scott Fitzgerald.* Bloom's Major Short Story Writers. Philadelphia: Chelsea House, 1999.

———. *F. Scott Fitzgerald.* Modern Critical Views Ser. New York: Chelsea House, 1985.

Fitzgerald, F. Scott. "May Day." *The Short Stories of F. Scott Fitzgerald: A New Collection.* Ed. Matthew J. Bruccoli. New York: Scribner's, 1989. 97–141.

Green, James. *Death in the Haymarket: A Story of Chicago, the First Labor Movement, and the Bombing That Divided Gilded Age America.* New York: Pantheon, 2006.

Jones, Prudence, and Nigel Pennick. *A History of Pagan Europe.* New York: Routledge, 2000.

Martin, Robert. "Sexual and Group Relationship in 'May Day': Fear and Longing." *Studies in Short Fiction* 15.1 (1978): 99–101.

Mazella, Anthony J. "The Tension of Opposites in Fitzgerald's 'May Day.'" *Studies in Short Fiction* 14.4 (1977): 379–85.

Pizer, Donald. *The Cambridge Companion to American Realism and Naturalism.* New York: Cambridge UP, 1995.

Whitfield, Stephen J. *A Companion to 20th-Century America.* Malden, MA: Blackwell, 2004.

"THE DIAMOND AS BIG AS THE RITZ"

READING TO WRITE

"THE DIAMOND as Big as the Ritz" is unique in Fitzgerald's oeuvre. While his other works are firmly grounded in the realistic tradition, this story is cut from an entirely different cloth altogether. It contains many elements of the fantastic and is reminiscent of some of Mark Twain's works in the way that it reads like a tall tale. Readers are asked, for example, to accept as truth that the Washington family does own, and live on top of, a diamond as big as the Ritz-Carlton hotel and that they shoot down any airplane that passes over them in order to protect this secret source of wealth. Although this story belongs to a different genre from that of most of Fitzgerald's other work, it deals with many of the same ideas and themes, including wealth, class, and social competition. In fact, the fantastic elements of the story allow Fitzgerald to explore these themes in more depth than he did in his more realistic pieces. For example, in this story, Fitzgerald imagines Braddock Washington, a man so rich that he would find it natural to try to make a bargain with God:

> There was no one else with whom he had ever needed to treat or bargain. He doubted only whether he had made his bribe big enough. God had His price, of course. God was made in man's image, so it had been said. He must have His price. And the price would be rare—no cathedral whose building consumed many years, no pyramid constructed by ten thousand workmen, would be like this cathedral, this pyramid. He paused here. That was his proposition. Everything would be up to specifications

and there was nothing vulgar in his assertion that it would be cheap at the price. He implied that Providence could take it or leave it. (212)

When Fitzgerald writes that Braddock thinks that Providence can either take or leave his offer, he reveals that Braddock values his money and his estate over his life. Braddock is willing to bargain for his property and lifestyle, offering some of it up for desperately needed divine assistance, but he is not willing to forfeit it all in exchange for his life. He would rather not live without it, as Fitzgerald makes clear by having Braddock kill himself and his family when he realizes that the estate cannot be saved.

It is clear from this passage not only how important Braddock's money is to him but also how much influence he assumes goes along with that money and the position it grants him. He is so wealthy that he has always had the upper hand; he has never been required to negotiate for anything he wants. Because, for all intents and purposes, he possesses an infinite source of money, he simply pays for anything and everything that he desires. Not surprisingly, given how he has lived his life thus far, Braddock believes that even God can be bought for the right price. Fitzgerald indicates here the immense power that money provides people who possess it as well as the self-importance and feeling of control it gives them. By exposing the ultimate futility of his immense sense of self-possession, the story calls into question all of Braddock Washington's beliefs.

These observations gathered from an analysis of a single passage can lead to some promising inquiries. You might, for example, investigate the rest of the story to determine whether as a whole it supports the idea that wealth equals control, or whether, with the destruction of the Washington estate, it ultimately undercuts that notion. And, if it does the latter, what does the story suggest is the source of real control, and what part does wealth play in it? Or you might attempt to discover whether John's experience with the Washingtons will teach him to view money in a different way. Will the vision of Braddock Washington unsuccessfully trying to bribe God and ultimately sacrificing himself rather than dealing with his losses change John's perception of wealth and luxury?

TOPICS AND STRATEGIES

There are many ways to approach writing an essay about "The Diamond as Big as the Ritz," as there are when writing about any work of literature.

The sample topics below are designed to help you decide what you might want to focus on in your essay and to help you derive a claim about the topic you have selected. Use the topics to help you focus on an aspect of the story and generate ideas. Do not worry about answering all of the questions in the sample topic in your essay; they are here simply to serve as jumping-off points for your own thinking. Once you have generated enough ideas to decide on a claim and have assembled evidence for that claim, you may find that your essay has taken on a direction of its own, and you can abandon the questions, pursuing instead your own ideas and analysis.

Themes

The themes of a work of literature are the broad concerns at the heart of it, what it is really about. A single work can have a number of themes running through it simultaneously, as this story does. For example, the story obviously engages the idea of the American Dream, as it presents a clear rags-to-riches story, but it is obviously not simply trumpeting one family's unbelievable success story. Instead, it goes on to examine how wealth, social responsibility, goodness, and even violence are interrelated. To begin working on the thematic level, identify a single theme that interests you. Once you have identified a theme, you must figure out what the story most wants to say about this theme. For instance, in writing an essay exploring the American Dream in "The Diamond as Big as the Ritz," you might start by observing that the story is about not just the pursuit of the American Dream but also its ultimate fulfillment and the destruction that apparently accompanies it. Depending on your research into the story and your own thoughts, you might then decide to focus on the ultimately destructive nature of the American Dream or on the way the Washington family corrupted the American Dream, leading to their downfall.

Sample Topics:

1. **The American Dream:** What kind of commentary is Fitzgerald making on the nature of the American Dream in this story?

   You might begin by jotting down your thoughts regarding the American Dream. What exactly is this phenomenon? How is it achieved? Who achieves it? Is it available to all Americans? In essence, decide what it means to have achieved the American

Dream and what society typically thinks of the person who has achieved it. Once you have recorded this information about our standard cultural perception of the American Dream, begin to analyze what the story says about it. Ask the same questions about how the dream is achieved and what qualities are necessary to achieve it, gaining your answers directly from the story. Does Fitzgerald's story support the traditional view of the American Dream, modify it, or challenge it somehow?

2. **Wealth and virtue:** What associations, if any, does "The Diamond as Big as the Ritz" make between money and goodness?

The general critical consensus about "The Diamond as Big as the Ritz" is that Fitzgerald intended to challenge the notion that wealth and virtue are connected, that if one has been successful enough to be wealthy, then one must be industrious, wise, and just and its reciprocal—that poor people must be inherently lazy and corrupt. Do you agree that the story seeks to sever the automatic associations between wealth and virtue? What evidence can you find for this? Does the story present instead the idea that money provides power and that power corrupts? What evidence can you find to support this idea? Does Fitzgerald modify it in any way?

3. **Class:** What kind of commentary does the story make on the different classes that exist within American society?

You might wish to look closely at section 6 of the story, which introduces the soldiers who have been captured and held in the pit. John "could tell from the coarse optimism and rugged vitality of the remarks and voices that they proceeded from the middle-class Americans of the more spirited type" (199). If these men are representative of the middle class, what does the story seem to think of this group? What do you make of the following exchange between Jasmine and Kismine: Jasmine says that "food tastes better outdoors," to which Kismine replies, "With that remark . . . Jasmine enters the middle class" (215)? What do we know about the upper class from John's relationships with some of the boys at St Midas's and their families? Are the Washingtons represen-

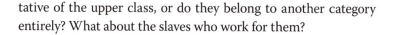

tative of the upper class, or do they belong to another category entirely? What about the slaves who work for them?

Character

One of the most fruitful approaches to writing an essay about a piece of literature is to analyze and evaluate the characters who populate it. It is often helpful to observe how the characters change or do not change through the course of the story and to analyze their motivations for change, both internal and external. Then determine whether the author is portraying the characters and their development as positive or negative. As you think about this, remember to consider the point of view through which the story is told and the reliability of the narrator. You can perform this kind of analysis on any character in a piece of literature, and the results often provide insight into the messages behind the work.

Sample Topics:

1. **John T. Unger:** Analyze the character John T. Unger and evaluate his role in the story.

   What do we know about John Unger? What happens to him in the course of the story? Would you say that he remains static through the events of the story, or does his character evolve? If you think he evolves, in what way? And what causes this to happen? Does John learn any lessons through his experience with Percy's family?

2. **Kismine and Jasmine:** Analyze the characters Kismine and Jasmine. What kind of commentary is Fitzgerald making on the role of women in the upper echelons of American capitalist society?

   Why does Fitzgerald include two sisters with similar names? How is each of the two sisters described? Does either of them change through the course of the story? What are their differences and similarities? How do they feel about money? Is either of them likely to succeed in life outside of their father's compound? Why do you think Kismine is so offended by John's observation that she is "much more sophisticated" than he had originally thought

(196)? Why is it significant that Jasmine's "favorite books had to do with poor girls who kept house for widowed fathers" (202)?

3. **Fitz-Norman Culpepper Washington:** Analyze and evaluate Fitz-Norman Culpepper Washington.

In section 4 of "The Diamond as Big as the Ritz," Percy tells John about his grandfather, Colonel Fitz-Norman Culpepper Washington. He plays no role in the present action of the story, and we only learn of him through this story that Percy tells John, so why is he included in the larger story? What kind of details does Percy provide? Based on his telling of this story, how do you think Percy feels about his grandfather? How does John respond to the story? Does Fitzgerald intend the character of Colonel Washington to represent a certain group or generation?

History and Context

It can be helpful and enlightening to read about the historical context of a piece of literature, including the time and place in which the piece is set as well as the time and place in which it was written. In the case of "The Diamond as Big as the Ritz," this may seem a little tricky, since the story seems to be in some ways timeless and placeless. However, it is set in the United States, even though Percy's father will not let the family property be surveyed and insists that the United States ends at his property line. Percy's family estate is in the West, John comes from the Midwest, and the boys go to school in New England. Although the Washingtons attempt in some ways to deny the progression of time and history, the narrator's mention of the ending of the World War suggests that the story takes place around the time in which it was written, approximately 1920 or so. You can then read up on early 20th-century ideas regarding economics, capitalism, and class structure in the United States, for example, to get a better sense of what Fitzgerald is saying about these things through the story.

Sample Topics:

1. **American capitalism:** What kind of commentary does "The Diamond as Big as the Ritz" make about America's brand of capitalism?

You might begin by doing some research on the history of American capitalism and its various stages of development. Meyer Weinberg's *A Short History of American Capitalism* is widely available on the internet; it provides a very readable and succinct, yet thorough, treatment of this subject and would be a good starting point. Writing specifically about capitalism in "The Diamond as Big as the Ritz," literary critic Brian Way observes, "Culpepper Washington represents the exploitative phase of American capitalism; his son Braddock belongs to the period of consolidation. He seals up the mine and concentrates his energies on safeguarding what he has. He is an expert in banking and investment, an evader of taxes, a corrupter of legislatures" (qtd. in *F. Scott Fitzgerald*, Bloom's Major Short Story Writers 45). Do you agree with Way's analysis? Does the story offer an accurate portrayal of the development of American capitalism? In what light does the story portray capitalism and its various stages? What elements of capitalism are emphasized? Which are deemphasized? To what end? Is Fitzgerald's portrayal in line with the usual ideas of American capitalism?

2. **Laws of economics:** What does "The Diamond as Big as the Ritz" say about free-market capitalism?

Percy explains that his family owned a diamond equal in "quantity to all the rest of the diamonds known to exist in the world. . . . if it were offered for sale not only would the bottom fall out of the market, but also, if the value should vary with its size in the usual arithmetical progression, there would not be enough gold in the world to buy a tenth part of it" (193). John sees Percy's family's situation as an "amazing predicament" because Fitz-Norman Culpepper Washington "was, in one sense, the richest man that ever lived—and yet was he worth anything at all? If his secret should transpire there was no telling to what measures the Government might resort in order to prevent a panic, in gold as well as in jewels. They might take over the claim immediately and institute a monopoly" (193).

What is Fitzgerald saying here about the nature of the U.S. free-market economy? Is he playing up its limitations? Its vulnerability? Its arbitrary nature?

3. **Contemporary response:** Fitzgerald had difficulty getting this story published. It was rejected by several magazines, including the *Post*. He ultimately had it published in *The Smart Set* and received only $300 for it, instead of his usual $1500 fee for a long story. Editors found it "baffling, blasphemous, or objectionably satiric about wealth" (Fitzgerald 182). Why do you think it was so ill-received when it was written, whereas it is currently regarded as a brilliant piece of literature?

Begin by familiarizing yourself with the history of the early 20th century as well as F. Scott Fitzgerald's biography (Arthur Mizener's *Scott Fitzgerald and His World* and Matthew J. Bruccoli's *Some Sort of Epic Grandeur: The Life of F. Scott Fitzgerald* would serve as excellent sources). Why might the story have been deemed "blasphemous"? Why might editors in the early part of the 20th century object to a satire about wealth? What has changed since then to make this story more acceptable?

Philosophy and Ideas

Taking into consideration what a piece of literature has to say about certain ideologies or philosophies—or considering how a work of literature embodies certain philosophies—can be especially illuminating. In writing an essay like this, first think about what universal or broad social ideas are present in the piece of literature. Then attempt to determine what the story or novel says about a particular idea or philosophy. For example, "The Diamond as Big as the Ritz" is obviously concerned with time and space, with dreams, and with the spending of money. Any of these larger ideas could be used as a starting point for an essay. To construct a claim upon which to base the essay, you might start by identifying key characters or passages that seem to be connected to the idea you want to write about. Then analyze these key elements, using them to help you figure out what message the author wants to convey about the larger idea you have chosen to work with.

Sample Topics:

1. **Time and space:** What does it mean that Percy's family's compound exists in a realm removed in a sense from conventional ideas of history and geography?

   When Percy and John arrive at the family estate, though they are in "the middle of the Montana Rockies," they are also on the "only five square miles of land in the country that's never been surveyed" (187). In fact, Percy's father says that "this is where the United States ends" (187). Section 4 recounts the story of Percy's grandfather, who managed his estate by using slaves "who had never realized that slavery was abolished" (193). Washington "read them a proclamation that he had composed, which announced that General Forrest had reorganized the shattered Southern armies and defeated the North in one pitched battle" (193). Why does Fitzgerald have the Washington family deny history and geography? What is required to manipulate other people's conceptions of time and space? What is there to be gained by doing so? Why do the Washington family ultimately lose their battle to create their own time and space?

2. **Dream versus reality:** What commentary does the story ultimately make about the nature of dreams and reality?

   What elements of the story possess a dreamlike quality? What do you make of the story's ending:

   > "What a dream it was," Kismine sighed, gazing up at the stars. "How strange it seems to be here with one dress and a penniless fiancé! Under the stars," she repeated. "I never noticed the stars before. I always thought of them as great big diamonds that belonged to some one. Now they frighten me. They make me feel that it was all a dream, all my youth." "It was a dream," said John quietly. "Everybody's youth is a dream, a form of chemical madness. . . . His was a great sin who first invented consciousness. Let us lose it for a few hours." So wrapping himself in his blanket he fell off to sleep. (216)

3. **Conspicuous consumption:** The Washington family compound is opulent and luxurious beyond compare, yet there is typically no one to see it except the immediate members of the family. Does this mean that the family spends money for their own enjoyment and does not engage in conspicuous consumption of the kind we find in, for example, Gatsby's parties in *The Great Gatsby*? What does the story say about conspicuous consumption?

Take a close look at the scenes that discuss the visitors who have been invited to the estate. Does the family do this, knowing the guests will be killed, because of their need for companionship, as Kismine would have us believe, or do they do it because they require acknowledgment and appreciation of their wealth? If the consumptive habits of the Washington family are not conspicuous, then what purpose do they serve? Why must they be so luxurious?

Form and Genre

To write about form and genre is to analyze a piece of literature based on its technical qualities and the way it compares to other works of the same kind. Paying attention to the genre the piece belongs to, for example, can provide clues about the meaning of the work. While most of Fitzgerald's work is clearly in the realistic tradition, "The Diamond as Big as the Ritz" is not. One of the first questions therefore becomes, What tradition does it belong to? Is the story an allegory, a tall tale, a fantasy? Does your interpretation of it change depending on how you classify it? For instance, if you decide it is a tall tale, do you then think of its primary purpose as entertainment, whereas classifying it as an allegory would mean that you expected it to impart a moral lesson? Also think about why Fitzgerald chose to depart from his usual form in this story. In addition, you may want to examine the way the story is constructed—in this case the story is divided into 11 sections titled only with roman numerals—to see whether its organization can give any clues to its meaning.

Sample Topics:

1. **Genre:** What genre does the story fall into, and why is this significant to its overall themes?

"The Diamond as Big as the Ritz" is unique in that it eschews the realistic tradition in which Fitzgerald typically wrote. How would you best describe this story? As an allegory? A tall tale? A fantasy? Upon what elements would you base that decision? Why is it important that this story is not written in the realistic tradition?

2. **Section divisions:** What is the significance of the manner in which Fitzgerald divided the story into 11 short sections?

Look closely at the way the story is divided. Why do you think Fitzgerald opted to organize it this way? You might want to chart out where each section is set along with the main characters and events of each section in order to identify patterns.

3. **Short story or novella:** Which category does "The Diamond as Big as the Ritz" belong to, and does this have any influence on your interpretation of it?

While originally sold and subsequently classified as a short story, "The Diamond as Big as the Ritz" can also be considered a novella, or short novel. Compared with short stories, novellas allow for more character development but are not required to have the many reversals and complicated plot structures of a full-length novel. One question worth asking is, Why does this story need to be novella-length? What happens in the story, or in the characters themselves, that requires more space than a typical short story? Why did Fitzgerald not write this as a shorter piece that may have been easier to sell to the magazines?

Symbols, Imagery, and Language

A promising way to approach writing an essay on a piece of literature is first to identify a symbol or image that you think is significant in some way. If a symbol or image is repeated throughout a piece of literature, or if the author devotes a substantial amount of space to the description of a particular image or symbol, you can be fairly certain that that symbol holds some meaning that will help you interpret the novel or story. Think about what traditional associations that symbol or image already and automatically carries with it. Then try to identify what specific associations the author is making with the symbol. For example, "The Diamond as Big as the Ritz" presents the village of Fish, which is inhabited by 12 men. Immediately, the Christian associations of these symbols are apparent. But what is Fitzgerald doing with these symbols and their traditional meanings? You might be tempted to think of the village as the antithesis to the materialistic, corrupt Washington family compound. However, you must take into account Fitzgerald's description of these men as "beyond religion." You might attempt in an essay to decipher Fitzgerald's use of these Christian symbols, figuring out what they mean in the universe of this particular story.

Sample Topics:

1. **Fish:** What is the symbolic significance of the town of Fish and its inhabitants? What can you learn by contrasting it to Percy's family's compound?

In section two of the "The Diamond as Big as the Ritz," Fitzgerald describes the village of "Fish, minute dismal, and forgotten. There were twelve men, so it was said, in the village of Fish, twelve somber and inexplicable souls who sucked a lean milk from the almost literally bare rock upon which a mysteriously populatory force had begotten them. They had become a race apart, these twelve men of Fish" (185). The 12 men gather every evening to see whether the train will stop at their station to deposit a figure who will then disappear into the sunset. Fitzgerald writes that these "men of Fish were beyond all religion—the barest and most savage tenets of even Christianity could gain no foothold on that barren rock—so there was no altar, no priest, no sacrifice; only each night at seven the silent concourse by the shanty depot, a congregation who lifted up a prayer of dim, anaemic wonder" (185). Why do you think Fitzgerald would call this village "Fish" and populate it with 12 men—certainly Christian imagery—and then say that these men are "beyond all religion"? How does the village of Fish compare to Percy's family's compound? What do you think Fitzgerald is trying to say about spirituality and the American Dream?

2. **Mining:** What kind of commentary is Fitzgerald making by having the Washington family make their money through mining?

According to literary scholar Brian Way, "Mining in many ways typifies the economic activity of the golden age: ruthless and often wastefully exploitative, it is the ultimate expression of personal greed and of indifference to the idea of a civilization" (qtd. in Bloom 45). What does Way mean here? Do you agree with his argument? What symbolic resonance does mining have, especially as an economic activity?

3. **Men in the pit:** What is the larger significance of the fact that Braddock Washington keeps men trapped in a pit?

   Have a close look at section 6, in which John learns that the Washingtons keep men who have discovered their estate locked in an underground pit so that they cannot reveal their secrets. Analyze the conversation between Mr. Washington and the men. What might it mean that the extremely wealthy Washingtons have these "middle-class Americans of the more spirited type" trapped? Is it significant that it is one of these men who ultimately brings about the destruction of the Washington estate?

Compare and Contrast Essays

Sometimes the best way to analyze something is to compare or contrast it with something else, thereby isolating its most salient characteristics. It is often useful to compare and contrast elements within a given literary work, but it can be even more productive to compare and contrast similar elements across multiple works of literature. For example, you might compare East versus West in "The Diamond as Big as the Ritz" to get a sense of the associations each of them carries in the story. To take another example, you might look at the idea of the American Dream or the consequences of being extremely wealthy across a number of F. Scott Fitzgerald's short stories and novels. Looking at one aspect across literary works not only allows you to collect more supporting evidence for your ideas and to showcase differences both large and subtle in Fitzgerald's conception of the American Dream or extreme wealth, it might also help you chart a progression in the author's ideas.

Sample Topics:

1. **East versus West:** What kind of dichotomy does Fitzgerald set up between the East and West in this story? Is either of them championed over the other?

   John is from a little town on the Mississippi, and Percy's home, as he makes clear to John, is "in the West." Why do both of their parents send them east to school? What are the characteristics of John's hometown, the West of Percy's origin, and New England? Which is most and least "civilized"? What values are connected with each place and with the West and the East generally?

2. **Percy versus John:** Compare and contrast Percy Washington and John Unger, paying particular attention to their attitudes toward money.

   Look closely at everything Fitzgerald says about Percy and John, including the homes they grew up in. John, like Percy, has been brought up to admire wealth. Fitzgerald writes, "The simple piety prevalent in Hades has the earnest worship of and respect for riches as the first article of its creed—had John felt otherwise than radiantly humble before them, his parents would have turned away in horror at the blasphemy" (186). Does John carry this "simple piety" with him through the course of the story, or does his attitude toward wealth evolve? What about Percy? Does he have the same "earnest worship of and respect for riches" as John does, or is his attitude toward wealth different because of the enormous riches of his family? Does the story ultimately give any sense of what Fitzgerald himself thinks of extreme wealth?

3. **The American Dream in "The Diamond as Big as the Ritz" versus _The Great Gatsby:_** What do these two works reveal about Fitzgerald's conception of the American Dream?

   Look carefully at the portrayal of the American Dream in each of these works. How are these portrayals similar and different?

What kind of person is able to achieve the dream? Is it ultimately fulfilling? Does comparing and contrasting these two works give a better picture of Fitzgerald's larger ideas about social climbing, wealth building, and success as defined by the American Dream?

BIBLIOGRAPHY AND ONLINE RESOURCES FOR "THE DIAMOND AS BIG AS THE RITZ"

Andrist, Ralph K., ed. *The American Heritage History of the 20's and 30's.* New York: American Heritage, 1987.

Bloom, Harold, ed. *F. Scott Fitzgerald.* Bloom's Major Short Story Writers. Broomall, PA: Chelsea House, 1999.

———. *F. Scott Fitzgerald.* Modern Critical Views Ser. New York: Chelsea House, 1985.

Bruccoli, Matthew J. *Some Sort of Epic Grandeur: The Life of F. Scott Fitzgerald.* 2nd rev. ed. U of South Carolina P, 2002.

De Koster, Katie, ed. *Readings on F. Scott Fitzgerald.* Literary Companions Ser. San Diego, CA: Greenhaven Press, 1997.

Fitzgerald, F. Scott. "The Diamond as Big as the Ritz." *The Short Stories of F. Scott Fitzgerald: A New Collection.* Ed. Matthew J. Bruccoli. New York: Scribner's, 1989. 182–216.

Hoffman, Frederick J. *The Twenties: American Writing in the Postwar Decade.* Rev. ed. New York: Collier, 1962.

Mizener, Arthur. *Scott Fitzgerald and His World.* New York: Putnam, 1972.

Parrish, Michael E. *Anxious Decades: America in Prosperity and Depression, 1920–1941.* New York: Norton, 1992.

Weinberg, Meyer. *A Short History of American Capitalism.* Updated 17 July 2006. 9 March 2007. <http://www.newhistory.org/>.

"WINTER DREAMS"

READING TO WRITE

ITZGERALD WROTE "Winter Dreams" as he was planning what would become the classic novel *The Great Gatsby*. Not surprisingly, the short story and the novel have many common elements. The plot of each centers on a young man who dreams of becoming a member of the wealthy upper class and connects that dream to the courtship of one of the most celebrated belles of the elite group to which he has aspirations of belonging. To win her would be evidence that he has indeed achieved unquestionable membership in society's upper echelons. Fitzgerald makes it clear that Daisy at least at one point loves Gatsby and pines for him even as she prepares to marry Tom Buchanan. Judy, however, never experiences a genuine attachment to Dexter. The narrator says that Judy keeps many young men on a string, giving them just enough attention so that they will keep courting her but never committing to any of them. Despite what Dexter learns to the contrary seven years later, as he is courting her it appears that Judy is

> not a girl who could be "won" in the kinetic sense—she was proof against cleverness, she was proof against charm; if any of these assailed her too strongly she would immediately resolve the affair to a physical basis, and under the magic of her physical splendor the strong as well as the brilliant played her game and not their own. She was entertained only by the gratification of her desires and by the direct exercise of her own charm. Perhaps from so much youthful love, so many youthful lovers, she had come, in self-defense, to nourish herself wholly from within. (227)

The passage portrays romance and courtship as a battle that men wage in order to "win" the most attractive woman by exerting their "cleverness" and "charm," "assailing" her with these qualities until she capitulates. In the case of Judy Jones, however, the courtship process is not progressing smoothly toward its logical end. Judy refuses to be won over by these suitors, and she has the luxury of doing so without risking their abandonment because of her great beauty. The "magic of [Judy's] physical splendor" causes the men to fear that if they drop out of the game, another of their lot will make off with a prize they will forever envy. Because of this trump card, Judy is able to make the men play "her game and not their own." In Judy's game, she herself is still the prize, but she is also in charge of the rules of play, capable of keeping all her suitors at bay and yet still involved in the game. Judy gains a great deal of power in this scenario, but it is power that she will instantly forfeit if she allows any man to win the game.

The narrator speculates that because of having so many men courting her, Judy has learned "in self-defense" to "nourish herself wholly from within," entertained by "the gratification of her desires and the direct exercise of her own charm." This makes sense considering that to keep herself empowered—in charge of the game of courtship—Judy must continue to position herself as the unattainable prize. To gain "nourishment" from any of the men who court her—to allow them to penetrate her defenses and to depend on them for emotional or psychological support—would mean giving up her position of power. So Judy finds fulfillment in the only safe way that she can, by using her beauty and charm to keep men attracted to her and entranced in her game. Judy, however, cannot keep this up forever. Her desirability as a candidate for a wife and mother declines as she ages. Indeed, Dexter learns seven years after his relationship with Judy Jones that she has married after all and is now a passive wife and mother who spends her days looking after her children and catering to a husband who does not treat her very well.

Although Judy may come across as heartless, cold, and even cruel in her behavior, particularly toward the main character, Dexter, an analysis of the quoted passage reveals some intriguing reasons for this behavior. This analysis might prompt you to examine further Judy's character and the paradoxical position of power she occupies or to investigate the role of women in Fitzgerald's fictional world by comparing Judy to Irene Scheerer, the woman to whom Dexter is briefly engaged, or even to

Daisy Buchanan of *The Great Gatsby*. You might also consider why Judy captivates Dexter so much and why he is so upset to learn of her fate. What does this reveal about him or about the nature of romantic love? Once you have decided on a particular line of inquiry to pursue, you can identify other relevant passages throughout the story and subject them to a careful analysis to see what they reveal. This process will almost certainly lead you to develop a claim that you assert in your essay as well as help you amass the evidence you will need to support that claim.

TOPICS AND STRATEGIES

The topics suggested below are provided to help you decide on an angle from which to approach "Winter Dreams" and to help you arrive at a claim to make in your essay. Do not feel restricted by the topics listed here or feel compelled to answer each of the subquestions provided under the sample topics. These are designed to spark your thinking and to guide you toward potentially fruitful lines of inquiry. One of the topics or subtopics might prompt you to discover an entirely new topic of your own, or you might decide to combine elements of two suggested topics to develop a line of thinking for your essay. In any case, remember that a great deal of thinking and planning needs to happen before you are ready to start crafting your essay. You might reach a dead end or two as you answer questions in an attempt to work toward a claim to make and support in your essay. Once you have established your claim, you will likely find that some of your analysis and brainstorming can be incorporated into your essay, but a great deal of it will now be abandoned. Do not be tempted to consider this wasted time or writing; it has served the important purpose of helping you discover what you want to say about the story.

Themes

If you plan to write an essay on one of the themes of "Winter Dreams," you should first ask yourself what major topics or concerns present themselves in the story. If you had to state in a couple of phrases what the story is about, what would you say? You might say that "Winter Dreams" is about disillusionment or the American Dream, and you might construct an essay on either of these themes. If you were interested in the theme of disillusionment, you would probably begin your brainstorming by rereading the story with a careful eye for any passages that seem connected to your theme. As you analyze these passages, you are trying to figure out what the story says about disillusionment. After much brainstorming and close reading of relevant passages, you might arrive at a thesis arguing, for instance, that Fitzgerald's "Winter Dreams" demonstrates that a certain amount of illusion is necessary for a person's happiness, or perhaps arguing that Fitzgerald's "Winter Dreams" indicates that disillusionment, while it might cause grief, actually frees people to fully embrace and enjoy the reality of their present lives.

Sample Topics:

1. **Illusion versus reality:** What kind of commentary does the story make about disillusionment?

   Begin by thinking about what illusions Dexter Green has in his childhood and early adulthood. Where do these illusions come from, and what sustains them? How is Dexter finally disillusioned? Is his false vision of the world crumbled all at once, or does he slowly lose it bit by bit? When Dexter discovers Judy's fate, the narrator tells us that "[h]e had thought that having nothing else to lose he was invulnerable at last—but he knew that he had just lost something more, as surely as if he had married Judy Jones and seen her fade away before his eyes" (235). Analyze this passage carefully as well as subsequent passages that detail Dexter's reaction to the news of Judy's married life. As you are planning your essay, think about whether it is always clear what is real and what is illusion in Dexter's perception of the world and whether Dexter is better off with or without his "winter dreams."

2. **The American Dream:** What kind of commentary does Fitzgerald make with this story about the nature of the American Dream?

   How do Dexter's "winter dreams" compare to the idea of the American Dream? In what ways are they the same and different? You might want to examine closely the opening passages of section II, in which the narrator states that Dexter "wanted not association with glittering things and glittering people—he wanted the glittering things themselves. Often he reached out for the best without knowing why he wanted it" (221). The narrator says that Dexter was "unconsciously dictated to by his winter dreams" (220). How do Dexter's dreams affect his decisions? Do Dexter's dreams come true? Think about whether the achievement of his dreams brings Dexter happiness. Based on this story, would you say that Fitzgerald considered the pursuit of the American Dream to be ennobling, destructive, or both?

3. **Romantic love:** "Winter Dreams" is centered on Dexter's failed romantic relationships with Judy and Irene. What kind of commentary does the story make about the nature of romantic love?

You might start by writing down everything you know about the romantic relationships in the story. What attracts Dexter to Judy? How does he describe his feelings for her? What about his relationship with Irene? Does Dexter learn anything about the nature of love and happiness from these two failed relationships? What does the reader take away from the story about the nature of romantic love?

Character

A good way to begin thinking about drafting an essay about "Winter Dreams"—or any other literary work, for that matter—is to consider the characters who populate it. It is natural to assess other people's motives, to try to figure out how their psyches operate. By applying that tendency to literary works, you can often gain a great deal of insight into their themes and meanings. Take Dexter Green, for example. Based on the information provided in the text, what kind of a person is he? How does he change during the course of the story? Once you have answered these questions, you can consider why the author presented this particular journey in this story.

Sample Topics:

1. **Dexter Green:** Analyze and evaluate the main character of "Winter Dreams," Dexter Green.

Begin by rereading the story, paying close attention to what the narrative reveals about Dexter. What do you know about his background, his goals, and the strategies he uses to achieve them? How does Dexter change through the course of the story? Is his disillusionment ultimately a positive or negative development? You will need to analyze the ending of the story, in particular, to help you make this determination.

2. **Irene Scheerer:** Analyze and evaluate the character of Irene Scheerer.

Reread the story, noting every mention of Irene. What do you know about her? What about her appeals to Dexter? You may want to examine in particular the narrator's remark that Dexter "knew that Irene would be no more than a curtain spread behind him, a hand moving among gleaming tea-cups, a voice calling to children" (231). What does this mean about Dexter? Does it signify anything about Irene? How does Dexter feel about abandoning a lifetime with Irene in exchange for what turns out to be a month with Judy Jones?

3. **Mr. Hendrick:** What is the function of this character in the story?

Record everything you know about Mr. Hendrick. Pay particular attention to his comments about Judy Jones on the golf course. Hedrick says to his golf partners, including Dexter, "All she needs is to be turned up and spanked for six months and then to be married off to an old-fashioned cavalry captain" (224). Analyze this and other remarks Hendrick makes about Judy. Do any other characters exhibit a similar point of view? As you are thinking about writing an essay on this topic, consider why Fitzgerald included this character in his fictional universe. What are his existence and his comments meant to highlight?

History and Context

Doing some background reading on early 20th-century American culture can be extremely valuable as you construct an essay on one of Fitzgerald's works. A good understanding of the culture that Fitzgerald wrote about and was himself a product of is integral to writing an essay about social issues. If you were interested in the role of women in society or distinctions between old money and new money, for example, you could not simply apply the social norms of 21st-century perspectives to evaluate what commentary Fitzgerald's work is making about these issues. Instead, you must understand what the current social atmosphere was like. What were the mainstream ideas about women and money? What new ideas were coming in to challenge them? With a firm grasp on the cultural atmosphere of the early 20th century, you are positioned to discern and evaluate Fitzgerald's commentary on these questions.

Sample Topics:

1. **The new woman of the 1920s:** What does the story say about the changing role of women in American society?

   You will need to do some research into women's rights in the first decades of the 20th century. You might begin with Jean V. Matthews's *The Rise of the New Woman: The Women's Movement in America, 1875–1930*. What conflicting ideas about women's roles in society were being entertained in this time period? How are these ideas reflected in "Winter Dreams," and where does Fitzgerald seem to fall in the debate? Reread the story, paying careful attention to all references to Judy Jones. Begin by analyzing, among other things, the passage that describes Judy as a little girl of 11 (218) and her revelation to Dexter that she is running away from a man because "he says I'm his ideal" (224). You should also have a close look at Judy's confession to Dexter that she is upset upon finding out that a man she cared about was actually "poor as a church-mouse" (226). What is really upsetting her here? What are Judy's motives for treating men the way that she does? Is the narrator's assessment of her accurate: "She was entertained only by the gratification of her desires and by the direct exercise of her own charm" (227)? What do you make of her lament to Dexter: "'I'm more beautiful than anybody else,' she said brokenly, 'why can't I be happy?'" (232)?

2. **Class distinctions:** What kind of commentary does the story make about class distinctions in the early 20th-century United States?

Do some background reading on early 20th-century American culture, paying particular attention to class distinctions and social hierarchies. You might start your reading with Ralph K. Andrist's *The American Heritage History of the 20's and 30's* or Judith Baughman's *American Decades: 1920–1929*. Once you get some background knowledge, return to "Winter Dreams" and begin recording what you know about Dexter's history. What information is given about his background and his youth? What do you make of the fact that the story begins with a distinction between Dexter and the other boys he works with: "Some of the caddies were poor as sin and lived in one-room houses with a neurasthenic cow in the front yard, but Dexter Green's father owned the second best grocery-store in Black Bear" (217)? How does Dexter imagine that his children's lives will be different from his own? In Dexter's mind, what is the difference between families who have had money for generations and his own situation, being relatively newly moneyed? You might analyze the passage in which Dexter compares himself to the other men who have loved Judy Jones: "He had seen that, in one sense, he was better than these men. He was newer and stronger. Yet in acknowledging to himself that he wished his children to be like them he was admitting that he was but the rough, strong stuff from which they eternally sprang" (225).

Philosophy and Ideas

Looking at some of the big questions implied by "Winter Dreams" is another useful way to work toward an essay topic. For instance, Dexter grapples with concepts of identity. When he first plays a round of golf at the Sherry Island Golf Club, where he used to caddy, he often has "the sense of being a trespasser" and tries to find something in the faces of the current caddies "that would lessen the gap which lay between his present and his past" (221). The story compounds Dexter's discomfort over how he came to be where he is by introducing several instances where invisible forces, fate perhaps, appear to control the characters' destinies more than they themselves do. Dexter's two chance meetings with Judy on the golf course—meetings that forever shape his life—are good examples. Running through both Dexter's and Judy's lives are questions about happiness; what role happiness plays in human life and how happiness can be achieved are the kinds of questions that philosophy has long grappled with.

Sample Topics:

1. **Identity:** According to "Winter Dreams," how is identity constructed? How much continuity is there in one's identity?

    If Dexter Green's identity rests heavily on his winter dreams, what has happened to him by story's end when the "dream was gone" (235)? Are the characters readily recognizable over the course of their lives? Are Judy Jones and Judy Simms the same person? How or how not? You should analyze these characters at various moments in their course of development and decide whether these characters possess certain traits that remain with them even as much about their lives changes. If so, what qualities are these, and how did the character come to possess them in the first place?

2. **The role of fate:** Judging from the story, how much control do people have over their own destinies?

    Much of Dexter's life is shaped by sheer coincidence. What if he had not been the one caddy on duty the morning he first met Judy and therefore quit caddying? What if he had not been golfing with Mr. T. A. Hedrick when Judy's ball struck him? What if he had not swum out to the raft the night Judy was out in the motorboat? What if Irene had not had a headache and canceled plans with Dexter? On the other hand, however, could not Dexter, at any of those moments, have decided to react differently? What about the narrator's assertion that Dexter was "unconsciously dictated to by his winter dreams" (220)? How much of a role do his dreams play in determining his fate? After a careful examination of the story, how much control would you say Dexter has over the course that his life takes? If you decide that Dexter, at least consciously, does not direct his own life, then what forces have the most influence on what happens to him?

3. **Happiness:** In the world of this story, what constitutes happiness? Does it seem to be a worthy goal? How can it be achieved?

    For Judy, happiness obviously should relate to beauty. "I'm more beautiful than anybody else," she cries to Dexter, "why can't I be happy?" (232). Dexter's concept of happiness involves wealth, to some degree, and ecstatic feelings like the ones that Judy arouses in him. Comparing a brief moment of ecstasy with Judy to the prospect of a life of marriage with Irene, Dexter muses that he had traded an "old penny's worth of happiness" for "this bushel of content" (230). Yet neither character seems particularly happy. What would it take for these characters to achieve happiness? Do any of the characters in the fictional world of "Winter Dreams" achieve this elusive quality? Does the story give us any clue to what true happiness is and how it might be achieved?

Form and Genre

Thinking about the actual construction of a piece of literature, including all of the artistic decisions that have gone into its creation, can be a valuable and rewarding exercise. Once you know that all of these decisions can be open to interpretation, you realize how rich studies of form and genre can be. After all, the author must decide not only what will happen in the story (plot) and who will be involved (characters); he or she must also decide how the story will be told—in what order, in what tense, in what degree of detail—and who will tell it. Each of these decisions will affect the story's meaning and can be fruitfully analyzed and interpreted by readers.

Sample Topics:

1. **Narration:** What effect does the narrator have on your inter-pretation of the story?

   Although the narrator of "Winter Dreams" is not named (as Nick is in *The Great Gatsby,* for example), a sense of his persona comes through in the telling of the story. Locate these instances in which the narrator's persona comes through, as in the opening of section II: "Now, of course, the quality and the season-ability of these winter dreams varied, but the stuff of them remained" (220). What kind of person is the narrator, as far as you can tell? Why does Fitzgerald choose to have this narrator's persona come through in the way that it does here?

2. **Time lapses:** Why is Dexter's life not given in a straight timeline?

Reread the story, taking care to note what parts of Dexter's life are revealed by the narrator and which are not. How does the narrator (and Fitzgerald) decide which events to include in this story? Analyze the narrator's remark that "[t]his story is not [Dexter's] biography, remember, although things creep into it which have nothing to do with those dreams he had when he was young. We are almost done with them and with him now. There is only one more incident to be related here, and it happens seven years farther on" (233). What elements in the story have nothing to do with Dexter's winter dreams, and why do they "creep in"?

3. **Organization:** Analyze and evaluate the organizational scheme of "Winter Dreams."

As you brainstorm for an essay on this topic, map out the story, carefully describing each of the six sections. Where is it set? What time frame does it cover? What happens in the section? You should also think about how the sections fit together. Why did Fitzgerald stop each section where he did? Why did he divide the story into six unnamed sections? Why do you think he opted to have six sections instead of, for example, five, which would give the story a clear middle section?

Symbols, Imagery, and Language

Paying attention to the symbols and images an author uses to convey meaning can be quite rewarding when studying a literary work. You should first locate those elements of the story that seem to carry more weight than their face value would suggest and then to analyze them. What larger meaning is the author attaching to these items? How does his use of them fit into the overall messages and themes of the piece? In "Winter Dreams," for example, you might notice the striking description of the Jones's home. An analysis of this description might reveal that in Dexter's mind, wealth is associated with unassailable purity. You would then consider how this symbol, complete with these associations, is used in the story. Why does Fitzgerald introduce this symbol with these meanings? How does this help you interpret other elements of the story?

Sample Topics:

1. **The Jones's home:** What symbolic meaning is attached to the Jones's home, and how is Fitzgerald using it in the story?

   Near the end of section III, Judy Jones's home is described. Dexter sees "the great white bulk of Mortimer Joneses house, somnolent, gorgeous, drenched with the splendor of the damp moonlight. Its solidity startled him. The strong walls, the steel of the girders, the breadth and beam and pomp of it were there only to bring out the contrast with the young beauty beside him" (232). What does the house represent? Why is it so "white" and "solid"? Once you have figured out what the house represents by analyzing the description that Fitzgerald provides, you should spend some time thinking about how the symbol functions in the context of the story. What, for instance, do you make of Dexter's claim that the house appeared as if designed to "bring out the contrast" with Judy?

2. **Seasons:** What symbolic meaning is connected to the seasons in "Winter Dreams"? Why are Dexter's dreams connected to winter?

   Pay close attention to the way the landscape is connected to Dexter's personality and moods, particularly in the opening passages of the story. Also think about the traditional symbolic meanings of the seasons, and then compare these to the way Fitzgerald is using them. In your essay, you might argue that Fitzgerald is using the seasons in a traditionally symbolic way or that he adapts or changes their symbolic meanings for his own purposes.

3. **Judy Jones:** In what way does Judy function more as a symbol than a character in her own right?

   Think about what Judy means to Dexter and to the other men who court her. What does she represent for them? What would it mean for one of them to win her hand in marriage? Why do you think Dexter is so disappointed on his first dinner date with Judy? You might also consider the significance of the narrator's claim that "No disillusion as to the world in which [Judy] had grown up could cure [Dexter's] illusion as to her desirability" (228).

Compare and Contrast Essays

Sometimes the best way to isolate the meaningful traits of a character or symbol is to set it beside a similar element in a different work. For instance, you might develop a more discerning picture of Dexter Green if you compare and contrast him to Jay Gatsby. You might use such a comparison simply in the brainstorming stage or focus on the comparison and contrast in an essay, determining and analyzing the most salient similarities and differences. Of course, you can also compare and contrast elements within a single work. For example, in "Winter Dreams," you might compare and contrast the two main female characters, Judy Jones and Irene Sheerer, looking for any meaningful patterns that would allow you to make a claim about Fitzgerald's portrayal of women and their roles in society.

Sample Topics:

1. **Jay Gatsby and Dexter Green:** "Winter Dreams" was written while Fitzgerald was planning *Gatsby*, and many comparisons can be made between the short story and the novel. One option would be to compare the main characters of each piece, Dexter Green and Jay Gatsby. What insights can you gain about these characters by setting them side by side?

   Record what you know about Dexter and Gatsby, including their backgrounds and their goals. Note also the development of these characters. How are their journeys alike and different? You might use your notes to attempt to draw a conclusion about Fitzgerald's perception of some element of the society in which he lived, the American Dream, perhaps, or romantic love.

2. **Judy Jones and Irene Scheerer:** Analyze and evaluate the two main female characters in Dexter's life.

   Record everything you know about Judy Jones and Irene Scheerer. How does Dexter feel about each of them, and why? What makes these two characters so different? Do they share any characteristics? Do either of them develop in any way through the course of the story? What conclusions can you draw about Fitzgerald's perception of women and their roles in society through your analysis of these two characters?

3. **Judy Jones of "Winter Dreams" and Marjorie of "Bernice Bobs Her Hair":** Compare and contrast these two women, both of whom are apparently "liberated" but suffer major setbacks, as well.

Reread these stories, taking care to note the characteristics of Judy and Marjorie. What are these women like? Describe their relationships with men and with other women. What attributes do they share? What are their respective fates? What patterns can you discover in your study of these two female characters? Can you use them to make an argument about Fitzgerald's perception of women, or certain types of women?

BIBLIOGRAPHY FOR "WINTER DREAMS"

Andrist, Ralph K., ed. *The American Heritage History of the 20's and 30's.* New York: American Heritage, 1987.

Baughman, Judith, ed. *American Decades: 1920–1929.* Detroit: Manly/Gale, 1995.

Bloom, Harold, ed. *F. Scott Fitzgerald.* Bloom's Major Short Story Writers. Philadelphia: Chelsea House, 1999.

———. *F. Scott Fitzgerald.* Modern Critical Views Ser. New York: Chelsea House, 1985.

Cowley, Malcom, and Robert Cowley, eds. *Fitzgerald and the Jazz Age.* New York: Scribner's, 1966.

Fahey, William A. *F. Scott Fitzgerald and the American Dream.* New York: Crowell, 1973.

Fitzgerald, F. Scott. "Winter Dreams." *The Short Stories of F. Scott Fitzgerald: A New Collection.* Ed. Matthew J. Bruccoli. New York: Scribner's, 1989. 217–36.

Matthews, Jean V. *The Rise of the New Woman: The Women's Movement in America, 1875–1930.* Chicago: Ivan R. Dee, 2003.

Pike, Gerald. "Four Voices in 'Winter Dreams.'" *Studies in Short Fiction* 23.3 (1986): 315–20.

Ulmann, Carrol, ed. "Winter Dreams." *Short Stories for Students.* Vol. 15. Detroit: Thomson Gale, 2005. 207–25.

THE GREAT GATSBY

READING TO WRITE

HERALDED AS one of American literature's foremost masterpieces, F. Scott Fitzgerald's *The Great Gatsby* tells in precise and beautiful language a story of self-creation, of achieving the American Dream, and of tragic love, a story that, though set in the 1920s, still captivates readers of all ages today. It is a novel so eloquent in language and rich in imagery and thematic resonance that it may leave the student writer feeling a bit overwhelmed. It is helpful to remember that you do not need to address every important aspect of *Gatsby*, that such a task is very nearly impossible. A promising way to hone in on a topic that is both meaningful and manageable is to begin by identifying a passage that seems key to the novel or relevant to a certain element of the novel that interests you. It is not necessary to know precisely what makes it important or how exactly it functions in the novel when you choose it. This will reveal itself in your analysis.

For example, one of the key questions in the novel for many readers is why Gatsby remains so obsessed with Daisy. After all, he successfully creates a new identity for himself and makes himself enormously wealthy. Why then, one wonders, can he not get over Daisy and find another woman with whom to share his success. The following passage seems to speak most directly to this question as it discusses the connection between Daisy and Gatsby's self-creation:

> His heart beat faster and faster as Daisy's white face came up to his own. He knew that when he kissed this girl, and forever wed his unutterable visions to her perishable breath, his mind would never romp again like the mind of God. So he waited, listening for a moment longer to the tuning fork that

had been struck upon a star. Then he kissed her. At his lips' touch she blossomed for him like a flower and the incarnation was complete. (117)

This passage is so interesting because it begins to reveal why Daisy is so important to Gatsby. Before he kisses her, his mind can romp "like the mind of God." He can be anything or anyone he wants to be. All of his options are open; his possibilities are limitless. As a living, breathing member of the world Gatsby wishes to join, it is Daisy who will help determine which possibilities will be closed off and which will come to life—Gatsby's "visions" will be wed to her "perishable breath." Thus, Daisy both validates and, through her expectations and her faith, creates the identity of Jay Gatsby. The final sentence of the passage states that "the incarnation was complete," and, at first glance, this seems to mean Daisy's incarnation into Gatsby's flower. The incarnation could also, however, be Gatsby's. This is the moment when Jay Gatsby comes to life and all the other versions of James Gatz fall away.

In an essay, you might explore further the idea that Gatsby is in a real way created by Daisy. What else, if anything, in the novel suggests this? What are the ramifications? On a related note, you might write an essay that traces the creation and destruction of "Jay Gatsby," examining all the steps and ingredients that go into his creation and how the persona is ultimately broken apart.

The passage above emphasizes the sacrifice that Gatsby makes when he creates himself anew as Jay Gatsby. It is a time of creation, of "incarnation," but with this comes mortality. Gatsby's heart begins to beat "faster and faster"; he is wed to Daisy's "perishable breath"; his mind can no longer romp like the mind of God. He becomes not only real, but finite, mortal. Why does Gatsby hesitate before he kisses Daisy, and why does he wait even a second to realize what he has been dreaming of? Is his quickly beating heart a sign not of excitement, but of fear? These questions might inspire you to write an essay on sacrifice and loss in the novel, in particular, how they are connected to achieving success, or the American Dream.

The passage might also inspire you think about the way Daisy, and female sexuality in general, is treated in the novel. Daisy's white face might represent innocence and purity. Fitzgerald writes that "she blossomed for [Gatsby] like a flower" (117). Why might Daisy's sexual response be likened to a blossoming flower, a flower that blossoms *for* Gatsby? You might examine the novel for other references to female sexuality and try to determine whether women are portrayed as desiring subjects or presented solely as the objects of male desire.

Choosing a passage that seems to be significant in some way can yield several promising lines of inquiry for an essay. It is important to pore over the passage, reading it multiple times, taking the time to focus on each word and phrase and consider its possible significance. In a work like *The Great Gatsby*, it would be difficult to choose a passage that would not yield some valuable insight under a close reading, so do not worry about picking the "right" passage to begin with. If one seems interesting to you, work with it for a while, and it will probably reward you with multiple insights and ideas. If it does not, you can always move on to another passage. One strategy is to choose several passages that have something in common to work with. Try doing a close reading of several passages that feature Daisy and Gatsby to get a better sense of their relationship, for example. Or you might analyze some passages that describe Nick and some that describe Tom in order to compare their characters. In any case, close and careful attention to language will help you develop and support a claim about some aspect of the novel.

TOPICS AND STRATEGIES

The suggested essay topics provided for you in this chapter are designed to help you to select an aspect of the novel to focus on and to help you work toward a claim you want to make about that subject. The sample topics offer questions to spur your thinking and point you to passages and scenes that may help you further develop your ideas. It is not necessary to answer all of the questions included in a sample topic or to examine each of the relevant passages mentioned. In fact, you may find that one question or a certain scene gets you thinking in a different direction entirely, and you may arrive at your own topic from there. Since the topics are designed to help you analyze an aspect of the novel and generate ideas about it, you probably do not want to organize your essay according to the questions, answering them one by one. Instead, use them to guide your thinking and prewriting process and then organize your essay in a way that best supports the claim you have decided to make.

Themes

When you begin to think about writing an essay on a novel such as *The Great Gatsby*, it is helpful to think first of the novel's major concerns. What subjects or issues does it deal with most intensely? In the case of

Gatsby, the theme of the American Dream immediately springs to mind, as Gatsby's is certainly a "rags to riches" kind of tale. The novel asks us to look closely at our perception of the American Dream and to consider what and who must be sacrificed in its pursuit. Another theme that the novel is obviously concerned with is identity and self-creation. Again, the novel makes us question whether we really can invent or reinvent ourselves and what we must give up if we choose to do so. Certainly, another of the novel's themes is money and its role in American society. Fitzgerald makes us examine what it signifies. Finally, a common thread that weaves itself through the novel's examination of the American Dream is self-creation, money, and loss. We are forced to question what these things we tend to hold up as ideals—the American Dream, self-creation, and money—actually cost us and what happens to us when we either cannot achieve them or, worse, when we achieve them and find them unfulfilling.

Sample Topics:

1. **The American Dream:** What kind of commentary is Fitzgerald making about the American Dream?

   According to critic David Trask, the novel is a critique of the American Dream, which "consisted of the belief (sometimes thought of as a promise) that people of talent in this land of opportunity and plenty could reasonably aspire to material success if they adhered to a fairly well-defined set of behavioral rules. . . . In addition, Americans easily assumed that spiritual satisfaction would accompany material success" (qtd. in Telgen 82). In your analysis, does the novel support the reality of the American Dream? Does it suggest that talented people can achieve success through hard work? What about the idea that spiritual satisfaction naturally accompanies material success? Does the novel support this idea or suggest that it is a mistaken notion? Does Gatsby achieve the American Dream? Is what he achieves worth the sacrifices he must make? Ultimately, do you agree with Trask that *The Great Gatsby* is a critique of the American Dream, or would you call it instead a celebration of the American Dream and its possibilities?

2. **Self-creation:** What is the novel saying about a person's ability to create his or her own identity?

Look closely at chapter 6 and examine the story of Gatsby's self-creation. How does Jay Gatsby come into being? Who was he originally? What is necessary for his transformation from James Gatz to Jay Gatsby? What is sacrificed? Does Gatsby gain what he wishes through this transformation? Nick says that Gatsby finally reveals the truth of his story because, once Tom tells Daisy how Gatsby earned his fortune, "'Jay Gatsby' had broken up like glass against Tom's hard malice and the long secret extravaganza was played out" (155). Examine this passage and what it says about the permanence of a created identity. According to the novel, is a self-created identity "authentic" or "real"? How would Nick answer this question?

3. **Money:** *The Great Gatsby* is set in a period in which many people became quite wealthy. How does money function in the novel? What can it buy? What can it not buy? Does it mean different things to different characters?

To write an essay on this topic, you might want to look at what Gatsby and Nick say about Daisy: "'Her voice is full of money,' [Gatsby] said suddenly. That was it. I'd never understood before. It was full of money—that was the inexhaustible charm that rose and fell in it, the jingle of it, the cymbal's song of it. . . . High in a white palace the king's daughter, the golden girl" (127). Examine the associations established here, and trace these associations throughout the novel.

4. **Loss:** In a novel that depicts a world of lavish extravagance, there is also a great deal of loss. Who suffers the greatest losses in the novel? What are they? Are they deserved?

Begin by making a list of the characters and recording what each character desires, what he gains, and what he loses. Include not only material things but sentiments such as love, hope, and idealism. Are there patterns to be found? What message is Fitzgerald trying to convey about loss in a world of plenty?

Character

Another way to get at the central ideas and meanings of a work is through a study of its characters. You can examine single characters, major or minor, and the roles they play in the novel, or you can study groups of characters, such as male or female characters. To study characters, analyze the descriptions given of them in the text and their actions, and consider whether the narration seems to align itself with the character or against him or her. It is often most useful to consider whether the characters evolve through the course of the story. Then attempt to figure out what caused the characters to change the way they did, and determine whether those changes were for better or worse. This strategy allows you to get at some of the messages embedded in the work by revealing what qualities and characteristics the author admires and which he condemns.

Sample Topics:

1. **Gatsby:** What kind of character is Gatsby? Does he function as a Christ figure in the novel? What parallels can be drawn between Gatsby's story and the story of Christ? If such a parallel can be established, what might Fitzgerald be conveying with this imagery?

   Examine closely what you know of Gatsby—his birth, his early life, and his transformation into Jay Gatsby. What does he stand for, and what is he sacrificed for? Finally, examine the effects he has on other people, particularly on Nick, who tells Gatsby's story.

2. **Nick Carraway/Tom Buchanan/Daisy Buchanan/Jordan Baker:** Analyze and evaluate one of the other major characters of the novel. Who is this character? What does he or she represent? How does he or she develop over the novel?

   All of the major characters of the novel can be analyzed in the same way that Gatsby himself can. To write on one of the major characters, begin by noting everything that you know about that character: descriptions, actions, reactions. Pay particularly close attention to the role the character plays in the overall plot. How does he or she influence other characters? One interesting approach, when possible, is to supplement your knowledge of the character with Fitzgerald's own estimation of that character. This information can often be found in a thorough biography, such as Matthew Bruccoli's *Some Sort of Epic Grandeur*. For instance, Bruccoli notes that in a letter to his publisher, Fitzgerald says that "the book contains no important woman character" (220). What does this mean in regard to Daisy? Why would Fitzgerald not consider her an "important woman character"? Do you? Likewise, Fitzgerald once considered that he ought to "have Tom Buchanan dominate the book" because, as he claims, "I suppose he's the best character I've ever done" (*Some Sort* 215–16). Why would Fitzgerald think of Tom as the "best character" he ever created?

3. **McKee as artist:** Judging by the character McKee, what does the novel have to say about art and artists?

Examine the description of McKee's character in chapter 2 of the novel and the examples of his art that appear in the text. There is a "dim enlargement of Mrs. Wilson's mother which hovered like ectoplasm on the wall" (34). McKee tells Nick that he has two studies of Long Island framed in his apartment called "Montauk Point—the Gulls" and "Montauk Point—the Sea" (36). He also has photographed his wife 127 times since they married. At the end of chapter 2, McKee is "sitting up between the sheets, clad in his underwear, with a great portfolio in his hand." He rattles off titles of his pieces for Nick: "Beauty and the Beast . . . Loneliness . . . Old Grocery House . . . Brook'n Bridge" (42). Think about what characterizes McKee's art. How does he choose his subjects? What does it mean that he has taken so many pictures of his wife? What do the titles of his photographs reveal? Why do you think McKee is described as a "pale feminine man," and why does he tell Nick not that he is an artist but that he is in the "artistic game" (34)? What is Fitzgerald saying about art through the creation of McKee's character?

4. **Male characters:** Examine the male characters in the novel, including Tom, Gatsby, Nick, and Wilson. What models of masculinity are presented here? Which, if any, does the novel champion?

To begin an essay on this topic, you might make a list of the male characters in the text and describe each of them in order to determine what qualities each of them represents. Are they creative or destructive? Passive or aggressive? Receptive or stubborn? Can two or more of the characters be grouped together under one model of masculinity? Once you have categorized the male characters, the next step would be to analyze what Fitzgerald is saying about the models of masculinity that have been identified. Can you determine the way of "being a man" for which Fitzgerald had the most respect?

5. **Female characters:** Critics have argued that Daisy is merely the object of male desire or a symbol of wealth and privilege. Is she a character with her own desires and sense of self-worth, or is this critical description of her more accurate? What is Fitzgerald saying about women's roles in society through the character Daisy? Examine other female characters in the book, including Jordan and Myrtle, as well. Do they all function as objects and symbols? If so, what does each of them symbolize?

   Analyze Daisy's reaction to the birth of her baby girl. She tells Nick, "I woke up out of the ether with an utterly abandoned feeling and asked the nurse right away if it was a boy or a girl. She told me it was a girl, and so I turned my head away and wept. 'All right,' I said, 'I'm glad it's a girl. And I hope she'll be a fool—that's the best thing a girl can be in this world, a beautiful little fool'" (21). Why would Daisy say something like this, and why would she repeat it to Nick? Is this a sentiment she truly believes, and if so, what has caused her to think this way? What does the novel as a whole seem to think of this idea?

History and Context

The Great Gatsby is set in 1920s America during the prosperous years that followed World War I. An understanding of this period and contemporary thought can shed some light on the novel's meanings. Knowing that women received voting rights in America in 1920, for example, might help you better understand the tension that seems to surround the role of women in *Gatsby*. Additionally, reading other seminal texts written during this time, such as T. S. Eliot's "The Waste Land" or works by James Joyce, Ernest Hemingway, and William Faulkner, can put Fitzgerald's vision of his era into a broader perspective and help you determine whether Fitzgerald's portrayal of the 1920s is excessively hopeful or tragic.

Sample Topics:

1. **"The Waste Land":** Read T. S. Eliot's "The Waste Land," published in 1922, and compare it to *The Great Gatsby*, published in 1925. How similar are Eliot's and Fitzgerald's visions of the 1920s?

Eliot's seminal poem, published in 1922, presents a vision of the post–World War I era as spiritually dead and morally corrupt. Does Fitzgerald also present a world bereft of spirituality, a world filled with corruption, as Eliot does? Or do the signs of hope and fulfillment in *The Great Gatsby* overcome the bleak sentiments? An examination of Fitzgerald's valley of ashes in the context of Eliot's poem might help in this line of inquiry.

2. **Roaring Twenties:** Evaluate Fitzgerald's portrayal of this period in American history.

The Great Gatsby has been called the "defining novel of the Twenties which have become trivialized and vulgarized by people who weren't there" (Bruccoli, preface ix). Does the novel trivialize and vulgarize the period in which it is set, or does it provide a more complicated, textured picture of the period? Read a history of the 1920s United States, such as Ralph K. Andrist's *The American Heritage History of the 20's and 30's* or Lynn Dumenil's *The Modern Temper: American Culture and Society in the 1920s*. How accurately does Fitzgerald portray the era? Which of its elements does he emphasize? Which does he downplay?

3. **Prohibition:** When America passed laws prohibiting the sale of alcohol, a great underworld of bootlegging developed and flourished. This created a United States that claimed to be concerned with order, morality, and self-restraint but supported a chaotic underworld. What does *The Great Gatsby* say about this paradoxical society?

How do various characters react to the idea that Gatsby is a bootlegger? What does the novel seem be saying about the ways that Gatsby made his money? Since Nick serves as the moral center of the novel, pay particular attention to his perception of Gatsby's activities.

4. **Racism/prejudice:** What is the novel's attitude toward racism and other kinds of prejudice?

According to Tom, everyone ought to read *The Rise of the Coloured Empires.* The idea, he says, is that "if we don't look out the white race will be—will be utterly submerged. It's all scientific stuff; it's been proved" (17). What are the likely ramifications of such ideas? Why do you think Fitzgerald puts these words and ideas into Tom's mouth? What do scientists say now about the biological or genetic basis of race? How do the other characters in the novel agree with these ideas? Do they subscribe to different prejudices based on factors other than skin color?

Philosophy and Ideas

There are many major ideas at play in *The Great Gatsby,* including notions of class and class conflict and the conception of the progression of time. It can be difficult to create a single claim about ideas that figure so largely in a work. In the case of *Gatsby,* it can be helpful to determine what Nick, as the narrator and moral center, comes to feel about a particular topic in order to discern what message the novel may be trying to convey about that topic. You might also find it helpful to select and analyze several relevant passages in order to develop a claim about a particular topic as well as evidence to support that claim.

Sample Topics:

1. **Class:** What sort of commentary is Fitzgerald making in this novel about class in America?

To begin thinking about this topic, you might first figure out which characters are associated with which class and then look at their fates. Who survives? Who is sacrificed? Does the novel give the idea that some people are expendable? You might consider whether class eventually trumps everything in the novel. Does it turn out to be more important than even love? How does Nick fit into all of this? To which class does he belong? What does he make of Tom and Daisy and their "rather distinguished secret society" (22)?

2. **Time:** Does the novel ultimately support a linear view of time or a more malleable, circular conception?

An essay on this topic will need to analyze the following famous exchange: "'I wouldn't ask too much of her,' [Nick] ventured. 'You can't repeat the past.' 'Can't repeat the past?' [Gatsby] cried incredulously. 'Why of course you can!'" (116). Does Gatsby continue to believe this until he dies, or does his belief begin to falter at some point? Also pay particular attention to the novel's final passage: "Gatsby believed in the green light, the orgastic future that year by year recedes before us. It eluded us then, but that's no matter—tomorrow we will run faster, stretch out our arms farther. . . . And one fine morning—So we beat on, boats against the current, borne back ceaselessly into the past" (189). What does the passage tell us about what Nick has learned about time and the human psyche from Gatsby?

3. **Conspicuous consumption:** What kind of commentary is the novel making about the habit of buying things and spending money so that others can appreciate the wealth of the spender?

Examine Gatsby's party scenes. Why does Gatsby throw such elaborate, lavish parties? What do they give him? Where does all the material needed for his guests' enjoyment come from? Where does the waste go when the party is over? You may wish to examine the scene in chapter 5 in which Gatsby shows Nick and Daisy all of his shirts:

> He took out a pile of shirts and began throwing them one by one before us, shirts of sheer linen and thick silk and fine flannel which lost their folds as they fell and covered the table in many colored disarray. While we admired he brought more and the soft rich heap mounted higher—shirts with stripes and scrolls and plaids in coral and apple green and lavender and faint orange with

monograms of Indian blue. Suddenly with a strained sound Daisy
bent her head into the shirts and began to cry stormily. (98)

Why does Gatsby feel compelled to show off his wardrobe this
way? What do you make of Daisy's emotional reaction?

Form and Genre

Sometimes it is helpful to study the way a work of literature is put together
to get at its meanings. You can look at the way it is constructed, whether
it is built like other novels, and what these similarities or differences
might mean. Look at how the story is told, in what tense, and through
what point of view. Look at who tells the story and whether that narrator
is reliable and objective. In short, looking at the novel as a novel, studying
the author's craft, can bring to the forefront interesting concerns.

Sample Topics:

1. **Nick as narrator:** What is the overall effect of Fitzgerald's use
of Nick as narrator of Gatsby's story?

To begin thinking about this essay topic, spend a few moments
imagining what Gatsby's story would be like if it were told by
someone else, by Tom Buchanan perhaps, or Myrtle. What kind
of person is Nick? What do we know about him and his values? Examine chapter 1 and the information that Nick gives us
about himself and his family. Trace his development throughout the novel. How and why does Nick change? In chapter 8,
Nick reveals that he is glad that he praised Gatsby, telling him
"You're worth the whole damn bunch of them put together"
(162). But he seems to be conflicted about his true feelings for
Gatsby. Nick says that he has learned to reserve judgment about
people. After getting to know Gatsby and being privy to all his
secrets, what does Nick ultimately think of him? What does he,
and readers by extension, take away from Gatsby's story?

2. ***The Great Gatsby* as masterpiece:** Why is this novel considered one of Western literature's best?

Shortly after the publication of *The Great Gatsby,* Fitzgerald
reacted to the novel's slow sales and mixed critical reviews in a
dejected letter to his publisher: "Now I shall write some cheap ones

[stories] until I've accumulated enough for my next novel. . . . If it will support me with no more intervals of trash I'll go on as a novelist. If not, I'm going to quit, come home, go to Hollywood and learn the movie business" (*Some Sort* 220). Clearly, *The Great Gatsby*'s initial reception was poor enough to rattle Fitzgerald's confidence in himself as a novelist. Why might Fitzgerald's novel have been so poorly received initially? Why is it currently considered one of the greatest 20th-century novels? Does it deserve this status?

3. **Chronology:** Why does Fitzgerald have Nick relate the events of the story in the order he does? Why does he reveal the true story of Gatsby's life at the moment he does? What effect does Fitzgerald achieve with these choices? How do they affect the readers' interpretation of events and characters?

Look closely at chapter 6, in which Nick explains his reasons for telling the story out of order: "He told me all this very much later, but I've put it down here with the idea of exploding those first wild rumors about his antecedents, which weren't even faintly true. Moreover he told it to me at a time of confusion, when I had reached the point of believing everything and nothing about him" (107). An analysis of the beginning of chapter 8 will also be helpful. Here, readers discover when Gatsby actually reveals the story of his origins to Nick: "It was this night he told me the strange story of his youth with Dan Cody—told it to me because 'Jay Gatsby' had broken up like glass against Tom's hard malice and the long secret extravaganza was played out" (155).

Symbols, Imagery, and Language

Another richly rewarding way to approach the construction of an argument and supporting essay on *The Great Gatsby* is to analyze its symbols and imagery. Meaningful symbols and powerful imagery can be found throughout the novel. Look for elements that seem to carry more meaning than their face value. Often, you can spot important symbols and images because they recur throughout the novel or because the narrative seems at first glance to devote too much attention to such a simple aspect of the characters' surroundings. Once you have found a promising symbol or image, the next step is to determine what it stands for and how it is used to further develop the novel's themes.

Sample Topics:

1. **Uncut pages of books in Gatsby's library:** What does the condition of these books symbolize in terms of the novel?

   Look closely at the description of Gatsby's library. What do the details tell you about him? What can you glean from the fact that all the books in Gatsby's library are real volumes, yet the pages remain uncut? What gives these books their value? What sort of value do they hold? How are these books different from those you might expect to find in the Buchanans' or the Wilsons' homes?

2. **The schedule for self-improvement in the back of Gatsby's childhood copy of *Hopalong Cassidy*:** How is this schedule significant to the book's larger themes?

   You might wish to read the original *Hopalong Cassidy* by Clarence E. Mulford in order to determine what effect this book might have had on young James Gatz. Is it significant that Gatsby writes his schedule in another book instead of in a notebook of his own? What is the significance of the schedule and each of its elements? What information can you glean about Gatsby's character and ambitions? What does Gatsby's father make of the schedule? What does his reaction tell us about Gatsby's character and early life?

3. **Eyes of T. J. Eckleburg:** What do the eyes on the billboard symbolize?

   Examine closely the beginning of chapter 3, which describes the valley of ashes and the eyes of Doctor T. J. Eckleburg, which are "blue and gigantic—their retinas are one yard high. They look out onto no face, but instead, from a pair of enormous yellow spectacles which pass over a nonexistent nose" (27). What are these eyes seeing? Who is being watched? How does sight function in the novel? Are there other images of watchful eyes in *Gatsby*? Is it significant that the eyes are an advertisement on a billboard? Also consider the fact that near the end of chapter 8, George Wilson refers to these eyes as the eyes of God.

4. **Green light at the end of Daisy's dock:** What does this image signify in the novel?

The first time Nick sees Gatsby, he says that "Gatsby stretched out his arms toward the dark water in a curious way, and far as I was from him I could have sworn that he was trembling. Involuntarily I glanced seaward—and distinguished nothing except a single green light, minute and far away, that might have been the end of the dock" (26). What do you make of Gatsby's stretched out arms and the fact that he is trembling? What does the green light symbolize for him? Nick comments again on the green light in chapter 5. After Gatsby has been reunited with Daisy, Nick tells us that "it was again a green light on a dock. His count of enchanted objects had diminished by one" (98). Do you agree with Nick's assessment? What do you make of the reference to the green light in the final passages of the novel?

Compare and Contrast Essays

Comparing and contrasting various elements of the novel can throw important distinguishing features into relief as well as emphasize common threads. Setting East Egg against West Egg, for instance, illuminates what makes each distinct and also what sets them both apart from other places, such as, for example, the valley of ashes. It is often rewarding to examine which element of the comparison is favored by the narration and for what reasons. For instance, you could set Tom's and Gatsby's parties side by side, list the qualities and characteristics of each, and use this analysis to determine how the novel intends to portray Tom and Gatsby. Although Tom comes from old money and Gatsby's money is quite new, a look at these scenes might reveal that it is Gatsby who displays the most "class."

Sample Topics:

1. **East Egg versus West Egg / new money versus old money:** What is Fitzgerald saying about the relationship between those from moneyed families and the newly rich? What are the essential differences between these two groups? Can they overlap at all?

Review the descriptions of East and West Egg given in chapter 1 and compare them. What does Nick mean when he refers to the "bizarre and not a little sinister contrast between them" (9)?

In addition, examine the scene in chapter 6 in which Nick first sees West Egg through Daisy's eyes. He had "grown to accept West Egg as a world complete in itself, with its own standards and its own great figures, second to nothing because it had no consciousness of being so, and now [he] was looking at it again, through Daisy's eyes" (110). What do Daisy and Tom think of West Egg? More important, what changes for Nick after this?

2. **East versus West:** Examine the dichotomy between the eastern and western United States that the novel sets up. What commentary on American society is Fitzgerald making here?

First ascertain what qualities and characteristics are associated in the novel with the East and West. A close look at chapter 9 will be helpful. What does Nick mean when he says, "I see now that this has been a story of the West, after all—Tom and Gatsby, Daisy and Jordan and I, were all Westerners, and perhaps we possessed some deficiency in common which made us subtly unadaptable to Eastern life" (184). What might this "deficiency" be? In what ways were all of these people "unadaptable to Eastern life"?

3. **Tom and Myrtle's dinner party versus Gatsby's parties:** What do these two parties demonstrate about the characters of Tom and Gatsby?

Look closely at these party scenes, Tom and Myrtle's in chapter 2 and Gatsby's in chapter 3. What is similar about them and what is different? Who attends the parties? How do the hosts behave? What do they expect to get out of these parties? Is Jordan Baker correct when she states that large parties like Gatsby's are actually more intimate than small gatherings? What exactly does she mean?

BIBLIOGRAPHY AND ONLINE RESOURCES FOR *THE GREAT GATSBY*

Andrist, Ralph K., ed. *The American Heritage History of the 20's and 30's.* New York: American Heritage, 1987.

Berman, Ronald. The Great Gatsby *and Modern Times.* Urbana: U of Illinois P, 1994.

Bloom, Harold, ed. *F. Scott Fitzgerald's* The Great Gatsby. Bloom's Notes: A Contemporary Literary Views Book. Broomall, PA: Chelsea House, 1999.

Bruccoli, Matthew J. Preface. *The Great Gatsby.* New York: Scribner, 1995.

———. *Some Sort of Epic Grandeur: The Life of F. Scott Fitzgerald.* New York: Harcourt Brace Jovanovich, 1981.

Callahan, John F. "F. Scott Fitzgerald's Evolving American Dream: The 'Pursuit of Happiness' in *Gatsby, Tender Is the Night,* and *The Last Tycoon.*" *Twentieth Century Literature* 42.3 (Fall 1996): 374–96.

Cowley, Malcom, and Robert Cowley, eds. *Fitzgerald and the Jazz Age.* New York: Scribner's, 1966.

De Koster, Katie, ed. "Chapter 2: *The Great Gatsby.*" *Readings on F. Scott Fitzgerald.* San Diego, CA: Greenhaven Press, 1997. 75–137.

Donaldson, Scott. "Possessions in *The Great Gatsby.*" *Southern Review* 37.2 (2001): 187–211.

Dumenil, Lynn. *The Modern Temper: American Culture and Society in the 1920s.* New York: Hill & Wang, 1995.

Fahey, William A. *F. Scott Fitzgerald and the American Dream.* New York: Crowell, 1973.

Fitzgerald, F. Scott. *The Great Gatsby.* New York: Scribner, 1995.

Forter, Greg. "Against Melancholia: Contemporary Mourning Theory, Fitzgerald's *The Great Gatsby,* and the Politics of Unfinished Grief." *Differences: A Journal of Feminist Cultural Studies* 14.2 (2003): 134–70.

F. Scott Fitzgerald Centenary Home Page. Updated Jan. 2002. Retrieved 12 Mar. 2007. <http:www.sc.edu/fitzgerald>.

Lathbury, Roger. *Literary Masterpieces:* The Great Gatsby. Detroit: Manly/Gale, 2000.

Lehan, Richard D. The Great Gatsby: *The Limits of Wonder.* Boston: Twayne, 1990.

Pendleton, Thomas A. *I'm Sorry about the Clock: Chronology, Composition, and Narrative Technique in* The Great Gatsby. Selinsgrove, PA: Susquehanna UP, 1993.

Telgen, Diane, ed. *"The Great Gatsby." Novels for Students.* Vol. 2. Detroit: Gale, 1997. 64–86.

"THE RICH BOY"

READING TO WRITE

"THE RICH Boy" is the story of Anson Hunter, a wealthy young man who enjoys an on-again, off-again relationship with a woman named Paula Legendre but puts off marrying her until she ultimately marries someone else. The opening passages reveal a bit about Anson's childhood; although he came from a very wealthy family, his father preferred to raise the children away from "fashionable" society, because he

> wanted to delay as long as possible his children's knowledge of that side of life. He was a man somewhat superior to his class, which composed New York society, and to his period, which was the snobbish and formalized vulgarity of the Gilded Age, and he wanted his sons to learn habits of concentration and have sound constitutions and grow up into right living and successful men. He and his wife kept an eye on them until the two older boys went away to school, but in huge establishments this is difficult—it was much simpler in the series of small and medium-sized houses in which my own youth was spent—I was never far out of the reach of my mother's voice, of the sense of her presence, her approval or disapproval. (318–19)

Perhaps the most striking element of the above passage is the contrast between the narrator's life and Anson's. The narrator points out that parental supervision is much easier in the smaller houses in which he grew up, which suggests that he grew up in a less privileged environment than did Anson. In addition, he seems to suggest that the way he was raised is more likely to result in the production of "right living and successful men" than the way Anson grew up. Based on these observations, you might examine the narration closely, looking for other clues about how the narrator perceives Anson and his privileged background. Then, you could determine what effect the narrator's biases have on the overall story.

You might also notice in this passage that according to the narrator and Anson's father, New York society in the Gilded Age was not likely to lead to "right living and successful men," as Mr. Hunter felt that he had to watch his children and their company carefully in order to cultivate these qualities in them. This observation might lead you to examine the remainder of the novelette, paying particular attention to whether it characterizes wealthy society in this time as morally bankrupt or corrupt. You should probably also look for signs of the success of Mr. Hunter's plan. Did keeping his sons away from "society" in their younger years make them different from other wealthy young men? Does Anson in fact grow up to be "right living and successful"? What are the factors that most affect Anson's character?

This single passage holds the keys to several potential essay topics. You might decide to pursue one of these or to select another passage that seems important or interesting to you and examine it for potential topics. Analyzing the language of a particular passage, or "close reading," is an excellent way not only to discover a topic to write about but also to work toward a claim to make about your topic. Once you have decided what you want to write about, you can select and close read several passages that are relevant to your topic, using your analysis to arrive at your thesis and to provide evidence with which to support that thesis.

TOPICS AND STRATEGIES

The sample topics presented below will give you a range of ideas to get you started on your essay about "The Rich Boy." Use them to help you generate ideas and arrive at a claim, or thesis, on which to base your essay. Feel free to blend two or more topics or branch off from one of these topics to develop one uniquely your own. The questions provided under each topic as well as the suggested passages to analyze are neither compulsory nor exhaustive. You should use the questions and passages to help you sharpen and extend your ideas and continue to develop your own questions and select passages for analysis that seem to you to speak to the topic you have decided to investigate.

Themes

The themes of a literary work are the topics or subjects with which the work is concerned. These will likely be broad, as in "The Rich Boy": the rich, commitment, and lost youth. The story obviously has something to say about each of these themes. To write an essay about a theme, you should identify pertinent scenes or passages and then closely analyze them to determine what you think the author is saying about that theme. After close and careful analysis of scenes and passages relevant to the theme of commitment, for example, you might write an essay that argues that Anson's wealth makes him too self-centered to be able to form a healthy, committed relationship. Or you might conclude that the novelette condemns all committed relationships as destructive to the individuals involved in them.

Sample Topics:

1. **The rich:** What kind of commentary does the story ultimately make about the rich?

    Analyze the narrator's comments about the rich in section I of the novelette:

    > They are different from you and me. They possess and enjoy early, and it does something to them, makes them soft where we are hard, and cynical where we are trustful, in a way that unless you were born rich, it is very difficult to understand. They think deep in their hearts, that they are better than we are because we had to discover the compensations and refuges of life for ourselves. Even when they enter deep into our world or sink below us, they still think that they are better than we are. They are different. The only way I can describe young Anson Hunter is to approach him as if he were a foreigner and cling stubbornly to my point of view. If I accept his for a moment I am lost—I have nothing to show but a preposterous movie. (318)

    Based on this passage, what kind of relationship does the narrator have with the rich? Why do you think he feels he must "cling stubbornly" to his point of view? What, precisely, is the danger of accepting, even momentarily, Anson's perspective? Why do you think this would result in nothing but a "preposterous movie"? Does the story presented by the narrator validate the claims he makes about the rich in the passage quoted above? Do you ultimately feel as though the narrator is objective and average enough that you can trust his opinions?

2. **Commitment:** Why do you think that Anson never marries Paula? In terms of the story, is this decision figured as a mistake? Does the narrator suggest that Anson forfeits his chance at happiness?

Reread the story, focusing on Anson and Paula's relationship. Why do they never get married, as they initially plan to? What is it about Anson that makes him reluctant to commit fully? How does Anson feel when Paula marries someone else? Examine Anson's relationships after Paula's marriage. How does he feel about commitment and marriage to women other than Paula? Examine also Anson's reaction to Paula's death. Does his response seem to be that of a man who truly loved her? Look at Anson's behavior at the very end of the novelette. Has he changed at all in his attitude toward commitment? Do you believe that Anson is happy or that he is likely to find happiness?

3. **Lost youth:** What kind of commentary is Fitzgerald making about lost youth in "The Rich Boy"?

Trace Anson's growth through the course of the story, and identify the pinnacle of his progress. At what point does he seem to be in top form? When does he begin to feel that all of his friends and acquaintances have moved past him? Why do you think he fails to mature as they do? Is Anson more inclined to mourn lost youth than other characters? What does the narrator think of Anson's lost youth?

Character

Fitzgerald's "The Rich Boy" is written with such a degree of psychological realism that the characters seem alive, so much so that any one of them would make a promising topic for an essay. There is certainly a great deal to say about the story's main character, Anson, but Paula, Dolly, and

Edna would make equally good topics. When writing about characters, consider everything you know about them, including what they say and how they behave as well as how other characters respond to them. Also trace the development of any character you are investigating to see what changes occur in the character's personality and perception and what prompts those changes. It is also helpful to try to determine how the narrator perceives the character you are studying and whether the character is intended to evoke sympathy or disapproval in readers. Finally, you might also consider relationships between characters as potentially rewarding essay topics. In "The Rich Boy," a number of individual relationships—Anson and Paula, Anson and Dolly, or Anson and Edna, for instance—might prove interesting to investigate in an essay.

Sample Topics:

1. **Anson Hunter:** Analyze and evaluate the main character of "The Rich Boy."

   Begin by recording everything you know about Anson. What kind of a person is he? What would you say are his main qualities? Why do you think that "Paula grew to think of him as two alternating personalities" (324). What does the narrator think of Anson? Does Anson change at all from the beginning of the story to the end? Is the change for better or worse? Why do you think the novelette is titled "The Rich Boy"? Is wealth a large determining factor of Anson's personality and behavior? Why does the narrator say that though "[m]ost of our lives end as a compromise—it was as a compromise that his life began" (320)? Does he fail to mature from a boy to a man? Is there any significance to his last name, "Hunter"?

2. **Paula:** Analyze and evaluate Paula Legendre's character. Does she change through the course of the story? Do you think she achieves happiness in her life?

   Begin by recording what you know of Paula. What is she like when she first meets Anson? What is their relationship like? Trace their relationship through its ups and downs. Why do you think she marries someone else? What does the fact that she divorced and remarried reveal about her? Does Paula seem happy in her new marriage? Analyze her final meeting with Anson and what she reveals to him, such as the fact that she "wanted to die" when she realized she was pregnant with her first child because her ex-husband was "like a stranger" to her (347). What does this say about Paula? Why do you think she reveals these things to Anson? How do the two feel about each other after all these years? Is Paula right when she says to Anson that although she had been infatuated with him, "we wouldn't have been happy. I'm not smart enough for you. I don't like things to be complicated like you do" (346)? Why do you think Fitzgerald chooses to have her die in childbirth?

3. **Dolly:** Analyze and evaluate Dolly's character.

Record everything you know about Dolly. What kind of family does she come from? What is her reputation? Why do you think she repeatedly falls in love with men who do not return her love? How does Anson feel about her? Trace the development of their relationship. How is Dolly affected by it? How is the end of their relationship characterized by the narrator? How is the reader encouraged to view it? Are you sympathetic with Dolly or with Anson? You might also compare Dolly to other women in the story, particularly Paula. What makes Dolly different? How do these differences come to matter?

4. **Edna and Anson:** Analyze and evaluate the character Edna. Why do you think Anson gets involved in Edna's affair? Is the reader supposed to feel that he is justified in doing so?

What do you know about Edna? About her husband Robert? Examine the scene in which Anson confronts Edna and Carey Sloane about their affair. Why does Anson feel that he has the right to control Edna's behavior? What does the narrative seem to say about this? What do you make of the following passage: "By seven they had taken the desperate step of telling him the truth—Robert Hunter's neglect, Edna's empty life, the casual dalliance that flamed up into passion—but like so many true stories it had the misfortune of being old, and its enfeebled body beat helplessly against the armor of Anson's will" (339)? Why is the story "old," and why does this fact make it unable to move Anson at all? Why do you think Fitzgerald had Carey Sloane commit suicide? How does this make you feel about Anson? How does it make Anson feel about himself? Can you make any generalizations about the roles of women and men in Fitzgerald's society based on Edna and Anson's relationship?

You might also choose to examine the relationship between Anson and Paula or the one between Anson and Dolly. You might trace the trajectory of either of these relationships, identifying what went wrong and what Anson's treatment of either of these women reveals about him.

History and Context

As a 21st-century reader of Fitzgerald, be mindful that you are reading literature written and set in the early 20th-century United States. You cannot simply apply modern perceptions of women's roles in society or divorce, for example, to "The Rich Boy." To determine and evaluate what Fitzgerald's work is saying about these subjects, you must place the work in context. Doing some background reading on women and marriage in the early 20th century, for example, would provide a sense of the social climate in which Fitzgerald was living and working. Thus grounded, you can examine "The Rich Boy" for evidence of Fitzgerald's own views on these topics.

Sample Topics:

1. **Divorce:** How is divorce characterized in "The Rich Boy"? What kind of commentary is Fitzgerald making about divorce?

Do some background reading on the history of divorce, particularly in the early 20th century, and get a sense of just who obtained divorces on what grounds, and what social meaning it carried with it. One source that examines these questions is Elaine Tyler May's *Great Expectations: Marriage and Divorce in Post-Victorian America*. Then examine the way that divorce is portrayed in "The Rich Boy." For instance, the narrator says that "Anson accepted without reservation the world of high finance and high extravagance, of divorce and dissipation, of snobbery and privilege" (319–20). What does this statement tell us about society's perception of divorce? What do you make of Paula's divorce? How does it appear to have affected her life? How do Edna and Carey Sloane react when Anson tells them that if Carey leaves town for six months and they stop seeing each other, then Anson will not object if Edna could "tell Robert Hunter that she wanted a divorce and go about it in the usual way" (339)? Do Edna and Carey take this as a possible course of action? Why or why not? Finally, you will want to compare Fitzgerald's portrayal of divorce in "The Rich Boy" to what you have learned about divorce in the early 20th-century United States to see whether Fitzgerald's story simply reflects the society he lived in or whether he was responding to that society through his story.

2. **War:** What effect does World War I have on Anson? How does your knowledge of the history of this period affect your interpretation of the novelette?

   Record what you know of Anson's experience in the military. To get a sense of what the typical soldier's experiences were, consult Martin Marix Evans's *American Voices of World War I*. Compared to the "average" soldier, does it appear that Anson was given preferential treatment because of his wealth and prestigious family? What is revealed about Anson's experience during the war? Does Anson seem at all changed by his wartime experiences? How is his relationship with Paula, for example, affected by it?

3. **Women:** How does Anson think about and treat women in "The Rich Boy"? Does his opinion accurately reflect the status of women in the early 20th century?

   You might begin with some background reading on the role of women in the United States in the early 20th century. For a good general overview, read the pertinent sections of Sheila Rowbotham's *A Century of Women: The History of Women in Britain and the United States in the Twentieth Century,* and refer to her bibliography for more-specific sources. Then reread the story focusing on the women and the way Anson treats them, beginning with Paula. How does Anson feel about marriage? Why does he wait so long to marry Paula that he loses his chance? Think also about the way Anson treats Dolly and what makes her different from Paula. What factors affect Anson's level of respect for a woman? The narrator seems surprised to note that "despite the trusting mothers, his attitude toward girls was not indiscriminately protective. It was up to the girl—if she showed an inclination toward looseness, she must take care of herself, even with him" (329). What does this reveal about Anson's perception of women? Finally, think about Anson's treatment of married women, including Edna. Consider why Anson's attitude toward young wives was "circumspect," why "he never abused the trust which their husbands . . . placed in him" (335).

Philosophy and Ideas

An interesting approach to writing about a piece of literature is to consider what kind of commentary it might be making about major philosophies or social ideas. First, identify which philosophies or ideas the piece of work you are investigating engages. Then figure out exactly how the literary work is responding to that philosophy or idea. For example, as "The Rich Boy" obviously comments on the human tendency to classify people by type, you might write an essay that sets out to determine what the story concludes—whether, according to Fitzgerald, it is possible to make any valuable generalizations about the "rich" or other groups of people.

Sample Topics:

1. **Individuals and types:** What kind of commentary is Fitzgerald making about the truth or usefulness of types?

   You might start by examining the opening of the story, particularly the following passage:

   > Begin with an individual, and before you know it you find that you have created a type; begin with a type, and you find that you have created—nothing. That is because we are all queer fish, queerer behind our faces and voices than we want anyone to know or than we know ourselves. When I hear a man proclaiming himself an "average, honest, open fellow," I feel pretty sure that he

has some definite and perhaps terrible abnormality which he has agreed to conceal. . . . There are no types, no plurals. (317–18)

If nothing definitive can be said about groups because we are all such "queer fish," then is it possible to make any generalizations at all based on Anson's story? Why did Fitzgerald title it "The Rich Boy" if in fact Anson is not supposed to be taken as a representative of "the rich"? Can you identify moments in which the narrator generalized, even though he has said that to do so is counterproductive?

2. **Time:** How does the novelette portray time, and how does that portrayal affect your interpretation of the story?

When Anson's drunken behavior gets him in trouble with Paula and her mother, they decide that the two should wait a proper amount of time for "Paula to brood over the incident" before joining Anson in Pensacola. Then, "[w]hen they came South three weeks later, neither Anson in his satisfaction nor Paula in her relief at the reunion realized that the psychological moment had passed forever" (324). What psychological moment is the narrator referring to here, and why can it not be returned to? When Anson goes to see Paula, afraid that he might lose her because of rumors that she has a "heavy beau," he considers asking her to marry him, but then, once his confidence returns, he decides to put it off. But Paula's "mood passed forever in the night," and she marries her beau. Again, the narrator asserts that as time passes opportunities are lost forever. Look for other instances in the text in which the narrator indicates that a certain moment has gone by and is now lost in the past. Think about the ramifications of this kind of view of time. Does it make the characters involved seem to have more or less control over their destinies? How might this be significant to your interpretation of the story?

Form and Genre

Learning the history behind the making of a piece of literature can sometimes spark questions that could lead to interesting insights and successful essays. For example, a little background research into "The Rich Boy" will reveal that the story is based on the life of one of Fitzgerald's school friends. You might stop here to consider how that knowledge affects your interpretation of the story. However, it is more interesting to discover that Fitzgerald altered the manuscript upon this friend's request. Besides speculating on why the friend wanted those particular sections removed, you might now ask what is the difference between the story with and without the excised parts. Background reading will also reveal that Fitzgerald was advised to stretch the story into a novel, and this might prompt you to examine the structure of the piece and to ask whether the novelette is indeed the most appropriate form for this material. And as with any piece, you must consider how the author chose to tell the story, including factors such as chronology and especially narration. Pay attention to who tells the story, how he or she tells it, and for what reason. Is the narrator reliable, and does he or she represent the author's point of view?

Sample Topics:

1. **Removed anecdotes:** Fitzgerald based "The Rich Boy" on the life of one of his school friends named Ludlow Fowler. He wrote to Fowler and admitted this, adding that "it is so disguised that no one except you and me and maybe two of the girls concerned would recognize, unless you give it away" (317). At Fowler's request, Fitzgerald removed two anecdotes from the manuscript when the novelette was included in *All the Sad Young Men*. The passages were restored in brackets in *The Short Stories of F. Scott Fitzgerald*.

   Analyze the following anecdote, which was removed from section IV of the manuscript:

   > There was a pretty debutante he knew in his car, and for two days they took their meals together. At first he told her a little about Paula and invented an esoteric incompatibility that was keeping them apart. The girl was of a wild, impulsive nature, and she was flattered by Anson's confidences. Like Kipling's soldier, he might have possessed himself of her before he reached New York, but luckily he was sober and kept control. (327–28)

   Examine the following anecdote, which was removed from a discussion of Anson's tendency to teach Sunday school after he had been out all night in section V of the novelette: "Once, by some mutual instinct, several children got up from the front row and moved to the last. He told this story frequently, and it was usually greeted with hilarious laughter" (329).

Why do you think Fowler would have wished these passages removed? What difference do these passages make to the overall story? Why do you think Fitzgerald agreed to remove the passages, and why did the editor of *The Short Stories of F. Scott Fitzgerald* choose to put them back, though in brackets?

2. **Narration:** Who is narrating the story of Anson's life? What do you know about the background of the narrator? What is revealed about his opinions? How do you think the presentation of the story is affected by the identity of the narrator?

You might begin by rereading the story, deliberately taking your focus off of Anson and concentrating on the character of the narrator instead. How does the narrator meet Anson? What does his comparison of his own childhood to Anson's reveal about him and his point of view? Instead of accepting what the narrator says at face value, think of him as a character in his own right, recording what details you can glean of his life and analyzing and evaluating what he says about himself and about Anson. You might spend some time thinking about how the story would be different if it were told by someone else, by Anson himself perhaps, by Paula, or one of Anson's Yale Club friends.

3. **Novelette:** Explore Fitzgerald's decision to keep "The Rich Boy" as a novelette rather than shorten it to a more acceptable short story length or add to it to make it a novel.

This rather long story or short novel is termed a novelette, and it was published in two parts in *Red Book* (in January and February 1926). One of Fitzgerald's friends, Ring Lardner, suggested that the piece should have been lengthened into a novel. Fitzgerald wrote to Maxwell Perkins that "it would have been absolutely impossible for me to have stretched 'The Rich Boy' into anything bigger than a novelette" (317). Evaluate Fitzgerald's decision to craft this piece into an eight-part novelette. What might have been cut to shorten it? Do you agree with Fitzgerald's opinion that it would have been "impossible" for him to lengthen "The Rich Boy" into a novel? Are there themes that remain unexplored?

Compare and Contrast Essays

Setting two elements of a work or two different works next to each other might result in a productive topic for an essay, or you might simply use the compare-contrast technique to throw important features of a particular subject into relief. For example, you might write an essay that compares and contrasts Anson's relationship with Paula and his relationship with Dolly. In such an essay, you might focus on what is similar about these relationships and use them to describe and evaluate Anson's perception of women and romantic love. Or, focusing on the differences, you might, for example, argue that the way Anson treats women depends a great deal on their family connections. You could also, however, spend some time thinking through these comparisons and contrasts and yet decide to write your essay on Anson and Dolly. Although you may not directly use your notes and analysis of Anson and Paula's relationship in your essay, odds are that they will have helped you identify important elements and key passages about Anson and Dolly that you may not have otherwise noticed.

Sample Topics:

1. **Anson's relationship with Paula versus Anson's relationship with Dolly:** Compare and contrast these two relationships. What do they ultimately reveal about Anson?

   Begin by recording everything you know about each of these women, including their family backgrounds and their relationships with Anson. Why do you think he selects these women as partners, and how does he feel toward each of them? How do the women feel about him? What causes the end of each of the relationships? Based on your notes, decide whether Anson has progressed at all in his ability to create and sustain a relationship. Does he make the same mistakes with Dolly as he does with Paula? Or new ones? What does Anson's relationship behavior say about him as a person?

2. **Nick, narrator of *The Great Gatsby*, versus the narrator of "The Rich Boy":** Compare and contrast the relationship between Nick and Gatsby and that between the narrator of "The Rich Boy" and Anson.

You might begin by comparing and contrasting Gatsby and Anson. Compare their behavior and their attitudes toward wealth and women. Based on this comparison, what do the rich have in common? Then compare and contrast Nick and the narrator of "The Rich Boy" and their attitudes toward Gatsby and Anson. Are these narrators to be trusted? If so, what do they tell us about Gatsby and Anson and the validity of their opinions? How do they really feel about their wealthy friends? Why do you think Fitzgerald includes characters like Nick and the narrator of "The Rich Boy" in works about the very rich?

3. **Anson Hunter of "The Rich Boy" versus Amory Blaine of *This Side of Paradise*:** Compare and contrast these two characters.

Both "The Rich Boy" and *This Side of Paradise* tell stories of wealthy young men and their journeys into adulthood. What is similar about Amory and Anson? What is different? Trace the development of each character. Does one evolve while the other remains static? What factors shape these characters and their development?

BIBLIOGRAPHY FOR "THE RICH BOY"

Bloom, Harold, ed. *F. Scott Fitzgerald*. Bloom's Major Short Story Writers. Philadelphia: Chelsea House, 1999.

———. *F. Scott Fitzgerald*. Modern Critical Views Ser. New York: Chelsea House, 1985.

Bruccoli, Matthew J. *Some Sort of Epic Grandeur: The Life of F. Scott Fitzgerald*. New York: Harcourt Brace Jovanovich, 1981.

Carter, Paul Allen. *The Twenties in America*. New York: Crowell, 1968.

Cowley, Malcom, and Robert Cowley, eds. *Fitzgerald and the Jazz Age*. New York: Scribner's, 1966.

De Koster, Katie, ed. *Readings on F. Scott Fitzgerald.* Literary Companion Ser. San Diego, CA: Greenhaven Press, 1997.

Douglas, George H. *Women of the 20s.* Dallas, TX: Saybrook, 1986.

Dumenil, Lynn. *The Modern Temper: American Culture and Society in the 1920s.* New York: Hill & Wang, 1995.

Evans, Martin Marix. *American Voices of World War I.* Chicago: Fitzroy Dearborn, 2001.

Fitzgerald, F. Scott. "The Rich Boy." *The Short Stories of F. Scott Fitzgerald: A New Collection.* Ed. Matthew J. Bruccoli. New York: Scribner's, 1989. 317–49.

May, Elaine Tyler. *Great Expectations: Marriage and Divorce in Post-Victorian America.* Chicago: U of Chicago P, 1980.

Rowbotham, Sheila. *A Century of Women: The History of Women in Britain and the United States in the Twentieth Century.* New York: Penguin, 1999.

"BABYLON REVISITED"

READING TO WRITE

FITZGERALD'S "BABYLON Revisited" re-creates, with an astonishing economy of detail, a very particular time and place in history, evoking for its readers the experience of living as an expatriate in Paris both before and after the stock market crash of 1929. More than that, the story touches a chord familiar to most readers in its portrayal of the desire to return to important moments in the past, be they pleasant or traumatic. These readily apparent features of the story—its compelling setting or the theme of returning to the past—could be starting points for many meaningful essays about "Babylon Revisited."

Another good way to decide on a topic for your essay and to begin to work toward creating a main point for your paper—a claim or thesis—is to take a close look at passages in the work that seem meaningful, puzzling, or relevant to a particular topic you are already interested in. The following passage, for example, stands out because of its poetic language and the glimpse it gives into the main character's thinking:

> So much for the effort and ingenuity of Montmarte. All the catering to vice and waste was on an utterly childish scale, and he suddenly realized the meaning of the word "dissipate"—to dissipate into thin air; to make nothing out of something. In the little hours of the night every move from place to place was an enormous human jump, an increase in paying for the privilege of slower and slower motion. (620)

When Charlie imagines the bar-hopping scene as an elaborate method of making "nothing out of something," it gives the idea that his own participation in that scene might have been driven by a personal need to get rid of something, although it is not clear what he had wanted to "dissipate." His description of the move from one venue to another as an "enormous human jump" gives a sense of the strain and the intense effort required for this "dissipation"; this raises the question of not only what he wanted to rid himself of but why he was willing to expend so much effort to do it. Something of an answer is provided in the further description of this "enormous human jump" as "an increase in paying for the privilege of slower and slower motion." For the average person, life is like a long, steady time line made up of a sequence of mostly mundane and occasionally important events. But, during his days of dissipation, Charlie was willing to pay exorbitant fees to escape the necessity of moving steadily along that time line, experiencing life moment by moment. He sought out places in which to lose himself in indulgence and inebriation, so much so that all time would run together, and, to his distorted vision, it would seem that his life was proceeding in "slower and slower motion." Thus, the "enormous human jump" refers not only to the great effort involved but also to Charlie's notion that because he slowed down the motion of his life in each bar, traveling to the next one amounted to hurling himself forward to another point on the time line of his life.

The slow motion that Charlie experienced in each new venue seemed a "privilege" because it protected him from the painful events that inevitably happen throughout an ordinary individual's life. Of course, in doing so, he protected himself from positive, meaningful things as well, just one of many ironies that are highlighted by the language of this passage. In fact, the juxtapositions and irony in this short paragraph are startling enough—such as the "enormous human jump" required to achieve "slower and slower motion"—that they should alert you to watch for irony and contradiction on a larger scale throughout the story.

A close look at this passage has provided several ideas you might pursue in an essay, including the motivations behind Charlie's behavior, both before and after the crash. You might begin to look elsewhere in the story for clues about Charlie's state of mind, about what would make him feel the need to collapse time, and about the guilt he feels, once he has gotten sober, for intentionally missing out on the important things in life. You might also consider the manner in which Charlie seems to be speaking in this passage not only for himself but for a group. You might peruse the story for evidence of the larger social conditions that feed into an attitude like the one Charlie expresses in this passage. Once you have an idea of the larger topic you want to pursue, close readings of more passages like this will provide specific evidence and examples to support an argument.

TOPICS AND STRATEGIES

The sections below are designed to provide you with suggestions for what elements of "Babylon Revisited" you might focus on in an essay. You might combine one or more of these suggestions, or one of them might inspire you to choose a topic not presented here at all. In any case, these topics and prompts can help spark your thinking. Use them to identify passages you want to examine more closely and to help you arrive at a claim you want to make about the story.

Themes

When you begin to think about the themes of "Babylon Revisited," you are asking, "what is this story really *about?* What does it want to say?" Just looking at the setting and the characters of the story can begin to give some clues. Considering that the characters are all Americans who have moved to Paris, the story probably has something to say about expatriatism. This choice to focus on American characters who are removed from their home country allows Fitzgerald to focus more sharply on what it means to be American, so this is a potential theme as well. You can also examine the motivations and goals of the characters to get at the story's themes. Charlie must overcome not only his alcoholism but also his guilt to achieve his goal of building a family by having his daughter Honoria come to live with him. Honoria, though, seems to be happy and secure as a part of Charlie's in-laws' family. Guilt and the definition of family can therefore be identified as two more of the story's themes. Finally, look at what Charlie regrets. In addition to his wife's death and losing Honoria, he feels guilty for the lavish wastefulness he perpetuated when he was wealthy and for his focus on enjoying himself and his money over his relationship with his wife and daughter. Thus, materialism and true happiness are major concerns of the story. Once you have identified a theme that seems important or interesting, try to determine what the story is saying about that topic. One useful way to accomplish this is to focus on particular passages that seem relevant to the theme and examine them closely. An intense look at the language

Fitzgerald employs—why does he choose one word or phrase over all the other possible combinations possible to convey his meaning?—will help.

Sample Topics:

1. **Expatriatism:** What kind of commentary does "Babylon Revisited" make about expatriatism?

   To craft an argument on this point, begin by examining the clues that the story gives readers as to why the American characters in the story are living in Paris (or Prague, as the case may be). How does this choice affect their lives? Does the story see this lifestyle as positive? A paper exploring this theme might take the perspective of explaining the reasons why a particular character or set of characters has expatriated or may look at the effects that expatriates have on their adopted countries and how those countries either welcome or shun them.

2. **American-ness:** What does the story present as key American values, and does it present those values as positive?

   An essay on this topic would need to identify which of the characters in the story represent American values and what exactly those values are. In what light does the story portray these values? Where does Charlie fit into this analysis? Is he strongly associated with American values? Would he like to be?

3. **Regret/guilt:** What is the novel's central message about regret and guilt? Can these be productive forces?

   Begin by examining Charlie's feelings of regret and self-recriminations. Also take a close look at Charlie's visions and thoughts of his deceased wife. What role does Charlie's regret play in his efforts to reclaim Honoria? Is it ultimately a strong motivator, or does it somehow sabotage his efforts?

4. **Materialism/happiness:** What does "Babylon Revisited" say about the ability of wealth to corrupt? Is it impossible to be both wealthy and happy?

To address this topic, examine what effects wealth had on Charlie and his friends. Charlie has gone from wealthy to bankrupt and back to having money, if not as much as before. How have his relationships with people changed through the course of his financial ups and downs? Look also at Lincoln and Marion, and compare their lives to Charlie's. Are they less focused on material things? Are they happier?

5. **Family:** Fitzgerald portrays a man trying explicitly to rebuild his family step-by-step. According to "Babylon Revisited," what makes a good family?

A paper dealing with this topic might examine the Peters family and try to determine whether the story presents them as a "good family." If so, what makes them so? This essay would also examine Charlie's ideas of what is necessary for a good family. Is it similar to life at the Peters's? You might also evaluate whether the story suggests that Charlie is capable of establishing a good family life with Honoria, predicting, based on the information the story provides, what life would be like for Charlie and Honoria if he succeeded in winning back custody of her.

Character

Another way to approach writing an essay about a story is through a consideration of its characters. You can examine individual characters and trace their development through the course of the story. One of Charlie's primary aims in this story is to convince Marion that he has changed as a person; he contrasts his present self with who he was when he tells her, "But now it's different. I'm functioning, I'm behaving damn well." Such explicit explorations of characters in a work allow you not only to trace character development but also to compare and contrast your assessment with the character's self-evaluations. Sometimes, as in "Babylon Revisited," a setting can be so important to the story that it functions in much the same way as a character does. This may be an interesting feature of a story to focus on in an essay. You might elect to study a character who is representative of a certain idea or philosophy, such as Honoria in "Babylon Revisited." You might also look at relationships between characters and their development. Try to figure out what point Fitzgerald is making by creating relationships such as the one between Charlie and Marion. You could also examine the way that Fitzgerald portrays certain groups of people, such as women or Americans or expatriates, or some combination. Always pay attention to what characters do, how they look, what they say, as well as what other characters say about them and how the narration treats them.

Sample Topics:

1. **Charlie's character:** Perhaps the central question of the story concerns the truth and degree of Charlie's transformation. Has Charlie truly changed as he claims?

    An essay on this topic would first establish Charlie's old personality, describing what he was like before he claims to have changed as well the new personality he claims to have created for himself. It might then examine Charlie's behavior in Paris, charting behavior that indicates a true reformation as well as behavior that indicates that Charlie is still the same irresponsible person of old.

2. **Paris as a character:** Charlie interacts with Paris almost as much as he does with any human character in the story. What role does the city play in the story?

    To make a claim about Paris as a character in the story, you would first need to consider closely the descriptions of the city that the story presents. How has Paris changed in the time since Charlie has been away? How has it changed in Charlie's eyes? What kinds of effects does Paris exert on Charlie or any other character? Could the events of the story happen in another place? What essential elements of the city enable the action?

3. **Relationship between Charlie and Marion:** The narrator says that Charlie and Marion have an antithetic relationship with each other right from the start. What is at the heart of their conflict?

    To write an essay like this, you will need to figure out what each of these characters represents. What are their values? Use this analysis to discover why the characters are in opposition to one another. Is Fitzgerald opposing two different lifestyles or philosophies? You might also consider whether the story indicates that one of these lifestyles or philosophies is superior to the other. Does one of these characters win out over the other in the course of the story? With whom do your sympathies lie?

4. **Honoria's function in the story:** What function does Honoria fulfill in the story?

   Examine what readers are told about Honoria as well as what the child says and does in the course of the story. How do Charlie's feelings about her influence him? Is Honoria a character in her own right, or does she function primarily as a symbol? What might she symbolize? What does Charlie's failure to get her back mean in terms of this symbolism?

5. **Characterization of women:** What does the story say about the role of women in society?

   Take a close look at the women in this story: Helen, Marion, Lorraine, and perhaps even Honoria. What do they have in common? How do they behave? Do they seem to be in control of their lives, of their relationships? Contrast the portrayal of men and women in the story. What kinds of things do the women say and do? What about the men? What kind of generalizations can be made from these observations? How are these different gender roles important to the action or the themes of the story?

History and Context

One of the most compelling features of "Babylon Revisited" is its evocation of an era, particularly of the "lost generation," who felt that the world had lost direction and meaning after World War I. Many of the American artists and writers of this generation, including Fitzgerald, gravitated to Paris in the years between the world wars; accordingly, Europe, and Paris in particular, appear frequently in American fiction from this period. Expatriating came easier to those who had some money, of course, and Americans were celebrating an economic boom during the 1920s. However, the long harsh years of the Great Depression, not only in America but worldwide, followed closely on the heels of the stock market collapse of 1929. "Babylon

Revisited" follows up on these trends as it portrays the great and sudden wealth accumulated by some Americans as well as the aftermath of its loss in the stock market crash. You could examine what message the story is sending about this era and the people who lived through it. It can also be productive to take a close look at things that have changed a great deal since the setting of the story. For instance, you might research theories of alcoholism and the role of women in society in the 1920s and 1930s in order to understand the context in which the story is set. Then you might make some useful observations or arguments about how Fitzgerald is mirroring or responding to contemporary ideas through the story.

Sample Topics:

1. **The importance of the Left Bank and Montmarte to the story:** How are these locations meaningful in terms of the story's themes?

   Begin by researching what the Left Bank was like in the 1920s and 1930s and comparing that information to the descriptions offered in "Babylon Revisited." One interesting source to begin with would be Ernest Hemingway's memoir, *A Moveable Feast,* which not only describes 1920s Paris in great detail but also describes F. Scott Fitzgerald in 1920s Paris. What elements does Fitzgerald emphasize? Criticize? How much, if at all, was this environment responsible for Charlie's "dissipation"? An essay on this subject might also discuss the significance of Montmarte, or "Mount of Martyrs," to the story. Helen is referred to as a martyr in the story, at least in her sister's imaginings. You might evaluate Helen's character and decide if she did behave as a martyr. Are there any true martyrs in the story?

2. **The lost generation as context for the story:** What commentary does "Babylon Revisited" make about the lost generation?

   You should first research the lost generation and F. Scott Fitzgerald's connections to it. Research in this area could start with any history book that covers this era in detail or could focus more on the idea of the lost generation, in sources such as *Modern Lives: A Cultural Re-reading of "the Lost Generation"* by Marc Dolan. With a firmer understanding of what the lost generation was like, you would then look for any references in the story that might be related to the lost generation and its values and concerns. Then you would be positioned to argue what commentary the story is making about the lost generation. An essay might also consider how this context helps readers refine their understanding of the story's themes.

3. **The stock market as context and metaphor:** What role does the stock market play in the plot and themes of this story?

Basic information about the stock market, including its early 20th-century history, would inform this essay. Maury Klein's *Rainbow's End: The Crash of 1929* details, in very readable prose, all of the factors that led to the big stock market crash that bankrupted real people like Charlie. You might then consider the relevance of these events to the plot and themes of the story. Consider, too, the repeated image of "swinging" and the "ups and downs" of Charlie's personal fortunes and feelings, and then consider their connections to the stock market. In this context, explain what exactly it is that Charlie has "sold short."

4. **Historical view of alcoholism and "Babylon Revisited":** Within the context of contemporary thought, what does the story say about alcoholism? With this in mind, what does Charlie's future likely hold?

Begin by researching the conception of alcoholism in the early part of the 20th century, and compare those ideas to the portrayal of the characters in the story. Is Charlie presented as an alcoholic? Is his strategy of indulging in one drink per day likely to help keep him from drinking too much? How does the understanding of alcoholism in the story relate to other bad habits that stand in the way of Charlie's regaining custody of Honoria?

Philosophy and Ideas

Another way to approach an essay on "Babylon Revisited" is to think about the major ideas at work in the story. The story addresses some basic human concerns such as free will, the desire to revisit the past, and the sense of fairness or justice. To write an essay about one of these topics, you might first figure out what the characters think about it. You might begin thinking about an essay on fairness, for example, by examining what Marion has to say about it in terms of the money wasted by her brother-in-law. Then you would proceed to evaluate whether the story as a whole supports that character's expressed viewpoint. Is that character trustworthy? Does the story seem to want you to be sympathetic to his or her ideas?

Sample Topics:

1. **Free will/wheel of fortune:** According to "Babylon Revisited," who or what is responsible for what happens to people?

   Do we control our own destinies? Does the universe operate on karmic principles, rewarding us for good deeds and punishing us for bad? Is there a divine plan, or does the story suggest that human destinies are dealt randomly? An essay on this topic might look closely at the images of swings and swinging in the story. You might also try to determine whether the characters in the story seem to get what they deserve—whether the universe, as presented in the story, seems orderly. Whose fault is it that Charlie does not get Honoria back?

2. **Desire for the past:** What does "Babylon Revisited" say about the human desire to look behind us even as we claim to be focused on the future?

   Why does the story begin and end in the Ritz bar? Why does Charlie leave his brother-in-law's address for Duncan Schaeffer? Why does he frequent the places of his past? What motivates Charlie's desire to revisit his past? What are the consequences of this desire? If you work on this topic, you will certainly need to contrast Charlie's past with his present and with how he imagines his future will be. Try to determine why—if most of his memories are painful—he does not let them go.

3. **Fairness/justice:** What kind of commentary does the story make about fairness?

Marion feels a sense of injustice in the fact that she and her husband have had to work hard to get by when Charlie and Helen were getting richer and richer while not working at all. Further, Charlie and Helen were incredibly irresponsible with their money. What does the story seem to say about this attitude of Marion's? Are "fair" and "right" the same thing? Consider what is happening with Honoria. Are Marion's actions fair? Just? Both? Why or why not?

4. **Perspective:** Through whose eyes is this story told, and how does it affect your interpretation of its events and characters?

How do you learn about the fateful night that Helen was locked out of the apartment? How do you learn about Helen and Charlie's relationship? Does the view of Helen and Charlie's characters and roles in their relationship change in the course of the story, depending on who is presenting the information? Who is more reliable? Think about how your feelings about Charlie might be different if some information had been given through Marion's perspective or Lorraine's. How much does perspective influence meaning?

Form and Genre

"Babylon Revisited" is considered by many to be one of the finest examples of the short story. An essay might set out to support this claim by describing the ideal features of a short story and identifying these features in "Babylon Revisited," or it might set out to disprove this perception and concentrate on the ways in which the story deviates from the ideal. Or it might address more specific elements of the construction of the story, such as those indicated in the sample topics below.

Sample Topics:

1. **"Babylon Revisited" and the ideal structure of the short story:** It has been argued that the structure of "Babylon Revisited" is flawed because it contains not one climax but two. Evaluate this claim.

This type of essay would need to trace the structure of "Babylon Revisited," identifying the two climaxes. Then you would need to evaluate the function of each climax. Finally, you should argue whether the story is marred or enhanced by the use of two climaxes instead of the more traditional single climax.

2. **Scene division:** What is the significance of the five-scene structure of the story?

    Are there any patterns discernable within the structure? Begin tracing patterns by making a timeline of the story, noting carefully when each scene begins and ends. Consider also the location of each scene. As you keep notes of time and locations, watch for the emergence of meaningful patterns that might give you greater insight into the way the story unfolds.

3. **Narration:** "Babylon Revisited," like many short stories, employs third-person limited narration, but it slips into omniscient narration in a few spots. What is the significance of this shift?

    To research this topic further, carefully reread the story to pinpoint when the narrator slips into omniscience. What do all of these instances share in common? What do they reveal that you otherwise might not know? Do these instances increase your sympathy for, or antagonism against, any characters?

4. **"Babylon Revisited" as fiction:** Short stories, by definition, are works of fiction. What effect do the autobiographical features of this story have on your interpretations of it?

    Begin by researching Fitzgerald's life. Given Fitzgerald's sometimes extravagant lifestyle, his own expatriatism, his wife's "nervous" disposition, and the fact that Fitzgerald's daughter was sometimes in the custody of relatives, many elements of his biography will seem familiar after reading "Babylon Revisited." Does Fitzgerald's reliance on these autobiographical details affect the meaning of the story? Does it give you a new tool for interpreting the story?

Compare and Contrast Essays

One good way to arrive at a claim about "Babylon Revisited" is to compare and/or contrast two of its elements. By looking at the story's presentation of, for example, Paris and America, you can ascertain whether Fitzgerald is portraying one culture or the values it represents in the context of the story as superior to the other's. You can also compare and contrast people, such as Charlie and Lorraine, to get at questions of character. Looking at their perceptions of the past they shared together can give a sense of how much, if any, Charlie has changed since he last saw Lorraine. Many fruitful comparisons can be made, including different elements of the past and the present to ascertain what change has occurred and whether the story presents that change as positive or negative, as well as different relationships to ascertain what the story says about the consequences of human interaction.

Sample Topics:

1. **Contrasting Paris and America:** Is one ultimately presented as better than the other in the story? What is the story saying about the values that each represents?

   An essay on this topic would examine the descriptions of Paris in the story. What does the city seem to represent? This essay would also examine the story's commentary on American-ness. Which characters seem to best represent America? What do you know about them? What kind of life does each environment, Paris and America, seem conducive to? After studying these things, try to determine whether the story puts forth one place and corresponding value set as superior to the other.

2. **Comparing and contrasting Charlie with Lorraine:** How much has Charlie truly changed?

   How much difference is there, really, between Charlie and Lorraine? How do they feel about each other? How does Charlie feel about the past, particularly the tricycle incident? How about Lorraine? What does she mean when she says that everyone feels old except her? This is another way to get at the question of whether

Charlie has truly transformed himself as he claims to have. It also gives you a way to examine Charlie's less altruistic motivations for changing. What is Lorraine's world like now that she and others in her set are broke?

3. **Contrasting the Paris of Charlie's past with the Paris of his present:** What does the story say about the changes that Paris has undergone? Are they a reaction to or a mirror of the changes in the expatriate mindset and circumstance?

To pursue this approach, you would examine what the story says about Paris, carefully noting the differences between the Paris of Charlie's past and the Paris of his present. What is responsible for these changes? How much has the city really changed, and how much of the change is in Charlie's perception? What do the changes mean for your understanding of Charlie's actions and motivations?

4. **Contrasting Helen and Charlie's marriage with Marion and Lincoln's:** How does Charlie and Helen's marriage differ from Marion and Lincoln's? What kind of commentary does Fitzgerald make on marriage and relationships?

What kind of marriage did Helen and Charlie have? Compare and contrast their marriage to the one shared by Marion and Lincoln. How does each couple appear to have resolved conflicts and made decisions? Is either of these a positive model of marriage? Try to imagine mixing the couples. What kind of marriage would Charlie and Marion have? Helen and Lincoln? Given those imaginary scenarios, how do you think the dynamics of the actual marriages came about?

BIBLIOGRAPHY FOR "BABYLON REVISITED"

Bloom, Harold, ed. *F. Scott Fitzgerald.* Bloom's Major Short Story Writers. Philadelphia: Chelsea House, 1999.

Bruccoli, Matthew J., and Robert W. Trodgon, eds. *American Expatriate Writers: Paris in the Twenties.* Dictionary of Literary Biography Documentary Series 15. Detroit: Bruccoli Clark Layman/Gale, 1997.

De Koster, Katie, ed. *Readings on F. Scott Fitzgerald.* Literary Companion Ser. San Diego, CA: Greenhaven Press, 1997.

Dolan, Marc. *Modern Lives: A Cultural Re-reading of "the Lost Generation."* West Lafayette, IN: Purdue UP, 1996.

Fitzgerald, F. Scott. "Babylon Revisited." *The Short Stories of F. Scott Fitzgerald: A New Collection.* Ed. Matthew J. Bruccoli. New York: Scribner's, 1989. 616–33.

Hansen, Arlen J. *Expatriate Paris: A Cultural and Literary Guide to Paris in the 1920s.* New York: Arcade, 1990.

Harrison, James M. "Fitzgerald's 'Babylon Revisited.'" *The Explicator* 16.4 (1958): 1, 3. Rpt. in *Short Story Criticism.* Vol. 31. Detroit: Gale, 1999.

Hemingway, Ernest. *A Moveable Feast.* New York: Scribner's, 1964.

Klein, Maury. *Rainbow's End: The Crash of 1929.* Pivotal Moments in American History. New York: Oxford UP, 2003.

Kuehl, John Richard. *Scott Fitzgerald: A Study of the Short Fiction.* Boston: Twayne, 1991.

Prigozy, Ruth. *The Cambridge Companion to F. Scott Fitzgerald.* Cambridge: Cambridge UP, 2001.

Wilson, Kathleen, and Marie Lazzari, eds. "Babylon Revisited." *Short Stories for Students.* Vol. 4. Detroit: Gale, 2005. 1–33.

"CRAZY SUNDAY"

READING TO WRITE

PUBLISHED IN 1932, Fitzgerald's short story "Crazy Sunday" is based on his experiences as a writer in Hollywood. In fact, the central event of the story comes right from Fitzgerald's own life. He, like Joel, had embarrassed himself at a party by performing a song he had written, which drew boos rather than the intended laughter from the other guests. Although editors at the *Post* rejected the story because of its ambiguous ending and lack of resolution, Fitzgerald refused to revise it, choosing instead to publish it in the *American Mercury*, which paid him only $200, a fee well below what he was typically paid for a magazine story. Since the story is so closely connected to Fitzgerald's own experiences and since he felt strongly enough about it not to revise it, it promises to give some interesting insights into his feelings about Hollywood, the movie business, and the place of the writer in that world. To begin, examine the description of one of the story's principal characters:

> Joel Coles was writing continuity. He was twenty-eight and not yet broken by Hollywood. He had had what were considered nice assignments since his arrival six months before and he submitted his scenes and sequences with enthusiasm. He referred to himself modestly as a hack but really did not think of it that way. His mother had been a successful actress; Joel had spent his childhood between London and New York trying to separate the real from the unreal or at least to keep one guess ahead. He was a handsome man with the pleasant cow-brown eyes that in 1913 had gazed out at Broadway audiences from his mother's face. (698–99)

This passage conveys the sense that being a writer for a movie studio can seem like a good gig, at least at first. Joel has been given "nice assignments" and is working "with enthusiasm." But the passage also implies that there are other writers, perhaps those who have been around longer, who get assignments that are less than "nice" and who do not, or who no longer, exhibit the "enthusiasm" shown by Joel. That Joel has "not yet [been] broken by Hollywood" certainly indicates that he can expect to be at some point in the future. Presumably Joel refers to himself as a "hack" because that is the accepted way to talk and think about writers working in Hollywood. The passage explicitly states, however, that Joel is only pretending to consider himself a hack out of modesty. Joel may think of his own work in loftier terms. Perhaps he believes that a writer can truly produce art, even in Hollywood, provided he is talented and enthusiastic enough.

To pursue these lines of thinking in an essay, you might reread the remainder of the story to determine whether Joel continues to be successful or whether he gets any closer to being "broken by Hollywood." Consider what it is about Hollywood that threatens to break him or those other writers indicated in the passage. The passage indicates that the fate of the artist in Hollywood is one of the main themes of the story; you might investigate that theme further by focusing on Miles, whom Joel considers a great artist, and Joel's relationship with him.

The passage also asserts that because Joel spent his childhood with a mother who was an actress, he is always "trying to separate the real from the unreal or at least to keep one guess ahead." This signals another theme in the story—appearance versus reality. You might begin to think about whether Joel has ultimately learned to separate the real from the unreal or whether, as an adult, he is still guessing. You might examine the story for evidence that the line between the real and the unreal is indeed blurred in Hollywood, as it was in Joel's childhood, and for the consequences of this blurring. In addition, you might consider the difference between the world of the theater, hinted at by the reference to the Broadway stage, and the world of the Hollywood movie studio.

A close look at one passage has provided several lines of thought you might pursue as you think about producing an essay on "Crazy Sunday." To continue this process, you might select one of these approaches, the artist in Hollywood, for example, and then reread the story to identify other passages that seem relevant to this topic and examine those as you did the original passage. A study of several key passages would allow you to generate enough ideas to formulate a claim upon which to base an essay.

TOPICS AND STRATEGIES

The sample topics provided in the sections below are designed to get you thinking about the line of inquiry you might like to pursue as you plan an essay about Fitzgerald's "Crazy Sunday." Each topic will provide you with questions and key passages to analyze that will help you generate ideas and work toward a thesis or claim for your essay. Once you have used these questions and passages to arrive at a claim, organize your essay in the manner that best supports your argument. Do not feel compelled to address all of the questions or passages included in the sample topics in your essay or to address them in the order in which they appear here. Additionally, you should feel free to use these prompts to help you derive an altogether different topic or to combine two or more of the ideas presented here.

Themes

The themes of a piece of literature are the universal or broad ideas it grapples with. Fitzgerald's "Crazy Sunday" deals with two critical emotional and psychological concerns: insecurity and pride. You would do well to take either of these as a starting point for an essay on the story's themes. An essay on either of these themes would set out to determine what the story has to say about insecurity or about pride. Is Fitzgerald conveying some kind of lesson, a warning, or simply making a shrewd observation about human nature? You might also attempt to determine whether the message the story conveys about insecurity or pride is connected to the Hollywood scene and, if so, in precisely what ways. Since alcohol also plays a major role in the story, a writer might decide to investigate what Fitzgerald's story says about alcohol and its effects on people such as Joel.

Sample Topics:

1. **Insecurity:** In "Crazy Sunday," all of the characters seem to be plagued by various degrees of insecurity. Critic Sheldon Grebstein observes that this story "contrasts the psychical beauty, charisma, or talent of its major characters—Joel, Stella, Miles—with the instability, weakness, or tendency toward self-destruction which seems to coincide, even be necessary, to their beauty and talent" (qtd. in Milne 86). Is Fitzgerald saying that insecurity and beauty/talent are fundamentally connected? Why or why not?

You might begin with the following statement that Joel makes to Stella at the party: "Everybody's afraid, aren't they? . . . Everybody watches for everyone else's blunders, or tries to make sure they're with people that'll do them credit" (700). What exactly does Joel mean here? Does this observation prove true through the course of the story?

2. **Appearance versus reality:** A lot of performing goes on in Hollywood, both on and off the set. What does the story ultimately say about appearance versus reality?

Reread the story, paying particular attention to places in which things are not what they seem and to passages that refer directly to the problem of distinguishing between the real and the unreal. For example, Joel's mother was an actress, and he had spent his childhood "trying to separate the real from the unreal, or at least to keep one guess ahead" (699). In addition, when he looks at Stella, Joel cannot "decide whether she was an imitation of an English lady or an English lady was an imitation of her. She hovered somewhere between the realest of realities and the most blatant of impersonations" (705). You might also focus on instances in which characters are concerned with appearance above substance. For example, you might consider that Joel, as Stella confided in him, "pretended to listen and instead thought how well she was got up" (705). What do these passages tell us about the movie business and those involved in it?

3. **The artist in Hollywood:** What kind of commentary does the story make about the fate of the artist in Hollywood?

Analyze the description of Joel at the beginning of the story. What does this description reveal about Joel? What does it reveal about the general reputation of writers in Hollywood? Locate and analyze descriptions of Miles. Pay particular attention to Joel's opinion of Miles after his death: "He was the only American-born director with both an interesting temperament and an artistic conscience. Meshed in an industry, he had paid with his ruined nerves for having no resilience, no healthy cynicism, no refuge—only a pitiful and precarious escape" (712). What does this say about Joel's ideas regarding the fate of the artist in Hollywood? Have they evolved in the course of the story?

4. **Women:** What kind of commentary is Fitzgerald making about women, particularly women in Hollywood society?

Look closely at Joel's opinions of women. At the party, he says to Stella, "After a pretty woman has had her first child, she's very vulnerable, because she wants to be reassured about her own charm. She's got to have some new man's unqualified devotion to prove to herself she hasn't lost anything" (700). Later, when Stella is upset about Miles's infidelity, the narrator says that "Joel did not quite believe in picture actresses' grief. They have other preoccupations—they are beautiful rose-gold figures blown full of life by writers and directors, and after hours they sit around and talk in whispers and giggle innuendoes, and the ends of many adventures flow through them" (704). In addition to these revealing passages, you should analyze Joel's behavior toward women. Once you have a handle on what Joel thinks of women in Hollywood, consider whether the story as a whole supports or challenges his ideas. Is Joel ultimately the kind of character whose opinions readers are supposed to respect and even emulate?

5. **Alcohol:** What kind of commentary does the story make about alcohol and its role in Hollywood society?

Analyze the role of alcohol in Joel's life, in particular. Exactly how much drinking does he habitually do? Does he have a good sense of how alcohol affects him? Why does he drink? What about other characters in the story? What kind of reputation do drinkers carry? Is it deserved? Does the story suggest that something about Hollywood society leads people to indulge in alcohol to a greater extent than people who belong to other groups? How might alcohol be connected to the insecurity and pride that the story also examines?

Character

One of the best ways to determine what a piece of literature is about and to derive a claim on which to build an essay is to study the characters who populate it. "Crazy Sunday" has a cast of interesting characters, primarily Stella, Joel, and Miles, and you might choose any one of these characters to focus on in an essay. In addition, there are minor characters such as Nat who represent certain groups that you might study. It is often fruitful to determine whether a character evolves during the course of the story, and you can often tell a great deal about the meaning of a piece of literature if you can determine which of its characters are intended to be perceived as moral centers and reliable transmitters of information.

Sample Topics:

1. **Joel:** Analyze Joel's character and argue whether he changes in a positive way through the course of the story.

   What is Joel like at the beginning of the story? How well does he know himself and his strengths and weaknesses? Look closely at the description of Joel that we are given at the beginning of the story:

   > Joel Coles was writing continuity. He was twenty-eight and not yet broken by Hollywood. He had had what were considered nice assignments since his arrival six months before and he submitted his scenes and sequences with enthusiasm. He referred to himself modestly as a hack but really did not think of it that way. His mother had been a successful actress; Joel had spent his childhood between London and New York trying to separate the real from the unreal, or at least to keep one guess ahead. (698–99)

   What does this passage reveal about Joel? How, if at all, does he change through the course of the story? Does he come to understand himself or Hollywood any better by the end of the story? Does he succeed in learning to separate the "real from the unreal"? How do you know?

2. **Miles:** What kind of character is Miles Calman? What does he represent in the story?

   Look carefully at the passages in which Miles is described. When Miles is first introduced, it is revealed that he "was the only director on the lot who did not work under a supervisor and was responsible to the money men alone" (699). In section 3, the narrator mentions that Miles had the "unhappiest eyes Joel ever saw" and that he had "never made a cheap picture though he had sometimes paid heavily for the luxury of making experimental flops. In spite of his excellent company, one could not be with him long without realizing that he was not a well man" (704). After Miles's death, Joel's opinion of him is further revealed: "In the awful silence of his death all was clear about him. He was the only American-born director with both an interesting temperament and an artistic conscience. Meshed in an industry, he had paid with his ruined nerves for having no resilience, no healthy cynicism, no refuge—only a pitiful and precarious escape" (712). Analyze these passages. What do they say about Miles?

Look also at Miles's actions and words; do they present the same picture as Joel's perceptions do? You might consider the scene in which Miles admits to Joel that he is afraid to leave him alone with Stella. When Joel tries to reassure Miles of Stella's fidelity, Miles says, "'But how can I ask anything of her after what's happened? How can I expect her—' He broke off and his face grew harder as he said, 'I'll tell you one thing, right or wrong and no matter what I've done, if I ever had anything on her I'd divorce her. I can't have my pride hurt—that would be the last straw'" (707). What does this say about Miles and his relationship with Stella? What does she represent to him?

3. **Stella:** What characteristics and qualities does Stella represent? In what ways is she intrinsically connected to Hollywood?

Analyze the following quotation: "She hovered somewhere between the realest of realities and the most blatant of impersonations" (705). What do you think this means? What information is given on Stella and her background? What is the significance of the description of Stella as having a "fresh boyish face" with a "tired eyelid that always drooped a little over one eye" (700)? What can you glean about Stella through her interactions with Miles and Joel? Are Joel's perceptions of her, particularly toward the end of the story, accurate?

4. **Nat:** What do Nat and Joel have in common? Does Nat function as a foil or an alter ego for Joel?

Examine the story's depiction of Nat and his interactions with Joel. Look in particular at the end of section 1, in which he is described as the "good-humored, heavy-drinking, highly paid Nat Keogh" (701). He tells Joel that he has hired a manager to keep him from losing so much money gambling, to which Joel replies, "You mean an agent" (701). "No," says Nat, "I've got that too. I mean a manager. I make over everything to my wife and then he and my wife get together and hand me out the money. I pay him five thousand a year to hand me out my money" (701). Look also at Nat's treatment of Joel the day after the party. What does Joel think of Nat? Does his opinion of Nat change over the course of the story? Does the reader's?

History and Context

To fully understand the nuances of a piece of literature, you might find it helpful to step back from it and to look at its context. In the case of "Crazy Sunday," you might better understand the characters and their motivations if you take some time to become familiar with the history of Hollywood movies, psychoanalysis, and Fitzgerald's biography. Then you will be better equipped to understand Fitzgerald's motivations and to describe and evaluate his observations of and responses to his contemporary world.

Sample Topics:

1. **Biographical connection:** Many critics have remarked on the biographical connection in "Crazy Sunday," noting that the story is based on an actual episode in Fitzgerald's life in which he performed a song about a dog at a party given by Irving Thalberg and Norma Shearer. Though Fitzgerald had embarrassed himself as well as the other guests at the party, Shearer sent him a telegram much like the one Stella sends Joel in "Crazy Sunday." Fitzgerald was fired at the end of the week, but obviously he used the experience as literary fodder (Eble 78). How might this biographical information help you see the story in a new light or understand it in a different way?

According to Kenneth Eble, Fitzgerald intended his readers to identify Joel Coles with a fellow writer at the party, Dwight Taylor, and "gave himself the role of the writer who tried to save him." However, "[n]o perceptive reader of Fitzgerald's stories is likely to be fooled, for the central character clearly betrays the conscience, guilt, moralizing, and defiance with which Fitzgerald viewed his drinking" (44). Do you agree with Eble's estimation of Fitzgerald's intentions? Do you agree that Fitzgerald is much more closely aligned with Joel than with Nat?

2. **Hollywood and the movie business:** According to Judith Baughman, "Although Fitzgerald was an unsuccessful screenwriter, he was not, as legend has it, a pathetic, abused victim of the movie industry. During two of his three stays in Hollywood, he was given choice writing assignments and was paid well for his work. That he failed as a screenwriter was largely the result of his fundamental distrust for the medium, which he regarded as a debased alternative to print." What can you determine about Fitzgerald's opinion of the movie business through an examination of "Crazy Sunday?" Does the story support Baughman's argument that Fitzgerald viewed the movies as a "debased alternative to print"? For some background, you might begin by reading Aaron Latham's *Crazy Sundays: F. Scott Fitzgerald in Hollywood.*

You might consider that Joel is described as "not yet broken by Hollywood" and that he refers to himself "modestly as a hack but really [does] not think of it that way" (698–99). You should also examine the opening of section 2, in which Joel describes the guests at the Hollywood party as "people of bravery and industry, superior to a bourgeoisie that outdid them in ignorance and loose living, risen to a position of the highest prominence in a nation that for a decade had only wanted to be entertained" (701). Compare and contrast the tone of this passage with the skit Joel performs at the party. What does the skit itself and the audience's reaction to it reveal about Hollywood society? Finally, you might look at the scene in which Joel and Nat eat lunch at the studio. Joel finds "a gloomy consolation in staring at the group at the next table, the sad, lovely Siamese twins, the mean dwarfs, the proud giant from the circus picture" (703). There are also the "yellow-stained faces of pretty women, their eyes all melancholy and startling with mascara, their ball gowns garish in full day" (703). Why do you think that Joel finds a "gloomy consolation" in this scene? What does this scene reveal about the essence of Hollywood?

3. **Psychoanalysis:** What kind of commentary does "Crazy Sunday" make about psychoanalysis?

You might start by reading the relevant parts of Stephen Mitchell and Margaret Black's *Freud and Beyond: A History of Modern Psychoanalytic Thought* to gain an understanding of the psychological theory and practice that was prevalent in the time in which the story is set. Then reread the story with a particular focus on any mention of psychoanalysis. You should, of course, pay special attention to the passage in which Stella describes Miles's therapy to Joel: "The psychoanalyst told Miles that he had a mother complex. In his first marriage he transferred his mother complex to his wife, you see—and then his sex turned to me. But when we married the thing repeated itself—he transferred his mother complex to me and all his libido turned toward this other woman" (705). For his part, Joel "knew that this probably wasn't gibberish—yet it sounded like gibberish. He knew Eva Goebel [the other woman]; she was a motherly person, older and probably wiser than Stella, who was a golden child" (705). Peruse the rest of the story for clues about Miles's relationships with women. Does the analyst's theory seem to be true? Is Miles's therapy helpful to him and to his marriage? Does therapy function as a cure or as a crutch in this story?

Form and Genre

Paying careful attention to the craftsmanship behind a piece of literature can often yield valuable insight into its meaning and help you arrive at an insightful interpretation. To begin thinking about an essay of this kind, you might reread the piece while keeping in mind that it is a deliberate construction and asking yourself why the author made the decisions he did when he was writing it, because an author has many decisions to make aside from developing the plot. He or she must choose which character will tell the story, the order in which it will be told, and even each precise word the narrator and the characters will speak. Treating each aspect of a piece of literature as a well-considered decision may help you arrive at an interesting claim on which to base your essay.

Sample Topics:

1. **Organization:** What is the major organizing principle of the story? How does the organization affect the story's meaning?

   You might begin by rereading the story with a particular focus on the way it is put together. Pay attention to Fitzgerald's division of the story into five numbered sections. Why do you think he divided it this way? According to Sheldon Grebstein, the structure of the story depends not on these five sections but on three crazy Sundays, each of which "serves as the occasion for the exposure and humiliation of each of the main characters" (87). What do you think of this argument? Do you agree with its implication that the story is not primarily Joel's, but equal parts Joel's, Miles's, and Stella's? You might create an essay that supports Grebstein's idea or challenges it.

2. **Ending:** Analyze and evaluate the ending of "Crazy Sunday."

   The magazine the *Post* turned down "Crazy Sunday" because of its "difficult" ending. The editors complained that the story "didn't get anywhere or prove anything" (Fitzgerald 698). Despite this criticism, Fitzgerald refused to change the ending. He ultimately sold the story for a mere $200 to the *American Mercury*. To write an essay on this topic, you will need to do a close reading of the final passages of the story. Looking closely at these passages, try to figure out if the criticism Fitzgerald received regarding the ending of the story is valid. Decide for yourself if the story does, in fact, prove something. Once you have made this determination, you should also consider whether this story is supposed to prove something and whether all stories should come to a clean resolution in order to be valuable.

3. **Point of view:** What effect does point of view have on the meaning of the story?

   Reread "Crazy Sunday," paying particular attention to the narration. From which character's perspective do you receive most of the information? How does this character affect your interpretation of the story? Is the narration reliable? Can you trust all of the information and interpretation you are given throughout the story? To help you decide, consider how the story would have been different if it were told strictly through Stella's perspective or perhaps Miles's.

Symbols, Imagery, and Language

A good way to begin thinking about an essay on Fitzgerald's "Crazy Sunday," or any literary work, is to look for recurring symbols and images. A close analysis of the scenes in which the symbol appears and an examination of the language in those scenes can be revealing. In "Crazy Sunday," you might decide to look at the images of eyes, the Calmans' house, or the recurring motif of the "crazy Sunday" in order to develop a claim to pursue in an essay.

Sample Topics:

1. **Eyes:** The image of eyes is repeated throughout the story. Of what significance are these images?

   Locate and analyze all of the references to eyes as well as seeing, looking, gazing, and so forth. Look at the descriptions of each character's eyes. What do they reveal about these characters? You might look especially at the following exchange between Joel and Stella: "'Your eyes are like your mother's,' she said. 'I used to have a scrap book full of pictures of her.' 'Your eyes are like your own and not a bit like any other eyes,' he answered" (709).

2. **The Calmans' house:** Analyze the description of Miles and Stella's home. What does their home tell us about them?

   Look closely at the passages that describe the Calman home. What kind of place is it? What is the significance of the following quotation: "Miles Calman's house was built for great emotional moments—there was an air of listening, as if the far silences of its vistas hid an audience" (699)? Does the kind of interior living space that people seek out reveal something about their own interior lives?

3. **Sunday:** What does Sunday symbolize in the story?

The opening lines of the story tell us that "IT WAS SUNDAY—not a day, but rather a gap between two other days." On these other days, people endured a "hundred miles a day by automobiles to and fro across a country, the struggles of rival ingenuities in the conference rooms, the ceaseless compromise, [and] the clash and strain of many personalities fighting for their lives." But on Sunday, "individual life start[ed] up again with a glow kindling in eyes that had been glazed with monotony the afternoon before. Slowly as the hours waned they came awake like 'Puppenfeen' in a toy shop: an intense colloquy in a corner, lovers disappearing to neck in a hall" (698).

Based on this opening passage, what is the difference between Sundays and the remainder of the week? Does the description given here at the beginning of the story fit in with the details provided later? If Sundays are days in which "individual life" starts up again, why are they called "Crazy" in the title?

BIBLIOGRAPHY AND ONLINE RESOURCES FOR "CRAZY SUNDAY"

Baughman, Judith S. "Fitzgerald and the Movies." F. Scott Fitzgerald Centenary Website. University of South Carolina. Updated Dec. 2003. Retrieved 12 Mar. 2007. <http://www.sc.edu/fitzgerald/movies.html>.

Bloom, Harold, ed. *F. Scott Fitzgerald*. Bloom's Major Short Story Writers. Broomall, PA: Chelsea House, 1999.

Eble, Kenneth. "Touches of Disaster: Alcoholism and Mental Illness in Fitzgerald's Short Stories." *The Short Stories of F. Scott Fitzgerald: New Approaches in Criticism*. Ed. Jackson R. Bryer. Madison: U of Wisconsin P, 1982. 44–45.

Fitzgerald, F. Scott. "Crazy Sunday." *The Short Stories of F. Scott Fitzgerald: A New Collection*. Ed. Matthew J. Bruccoli. New York: Scribner's, 1989. 698–713.

Latham, Aaron. *Crazy Sundays: F. Scott Fitzgerald in Hollywood*. New York: Viking, 1971.

Milne, Ira Mark, and Timothy Sisler, eds. "Crazy Sunday." *Short Stories for Students*. Vol. 21. Detroit: Gale, 2005. 73–99.

Mitchell, Stephen, and Margaret Black. *Freud and Beyond: A History of Modern Psychoanalytic Thought*. New York: Basic, 1995.

Prigozy, Ruth. *The Cambridge Companion to F. Scott Fitzgerald*. Cambridge: Cambridge UP, 2001.

TENDER IS THE NIGHT

READING TO WRITE

F. Scott Fitzgerald's *Tender Is the Night* is a rich and complicated novel about expatriate life in the 1920s, childhood trauma and its long-term effects, and the illusions and realities of romantic love. Given the complexity of this novel, parsing out the many ideas and characters presented and then attempting to construct an argument about which to write an essay might initially seem overwhelming. But there is good news here. First, much of the difficulty stems from the vast number of essay topic possibilities the novel presents. Second, an essay does not have to—indeed, it should not try to—address all of these possibilities. Your first important step in writing about *Tender Is the Night,* then, lies simply in selecting a particular aspect of the book on which to concentrate before attempting to generate ideas and make a claim, or thesis. A promising method of selecting a topic or formulating a good question to attempt to answer in an essay is close reading. To get started, select a passage that strikes you as interesting or particularly rich in some way and devote a good deal of time and attention to a close scrutiny of its language.

Examine the following passage, for example, which promises to provide insight into Dick's psychological motivations as it describes him consciously doing something that he knows will change him. Dick has decided to track down Rosemary at the film studio:

> He knew what he was now doing marked a turning point in his life—it was out of line with everything that had preceded it—even out of line with what effect he might hope to produce upon Rosemary. Rosemary saw him always as a model of correctness—his presence walking around this block was an intrusion. But Dick's necessity of behaving as he did

was a projection of some submerged reality: he was compelled to walk there, or stand there, his shirt-sleeve fitting his wrist and his coat sleeve encasing his shirt-sleeve like a sleeve valve, his collar molded plastically to his neck, his red hair cut exactly, his hand holding his small briefcase like a dandy—just as another man once found it necessary to stand in front of a church in Ferrara, in sackcloth and ashes. Dick was paying some tribute to things unforgotten, unshriven, unexpurgated. (91)

The passage announces that Dick knows he is doing something out of character for him. But what is even more interesting is Dick's knowledge that what he is doing is "even out of line with what effect he might hope to produce upon Rosemary." This "effect" he hopes to "produce upon Rosemary" is presumably a continued admiration and attraction. Dick finds himself behaving in a way that will destroy her vision of him as a "model of correctness," presumably one of the aspects of his character that most appeals to her. In essence, Dick is afraid that he will drive Rosemary away by seeking her out. Despite these misgivings, he still feels "compelled" to pursue her. Further, this compulsion is some kind of "tribute to things unforgotten, unshriven, unexpurgated." This passage presents intriguing clues that might spark further investigation into Dick's character. Is he self-destructive by nature? What are those things "unforgotten, unshriven, and unexpurgated" referred to in this passage? The phrase "submerged reality" indicates that Dick is in some kind of denial. What is this "reality" that he has buried? Who is the man in "sackcloth and ashes"? This passage can certainly provide enough questions to set you on the path to writing an essay that investigates Dick's psyche and explores the subconscious motivations behind his actions.

This passage might also lead you to think some more about the nature of Dick and Rosemary's relationship. It appears that Rosemary wants to have an affair with Dick, but to do so would negate the very things that attract her to him in the first place. The desire resonates with echoes from John Keats's "Ode to a Grecian Urn": The object of desire is desirable only so long as the chase continues. Examining this passage to generate possible topics for an essay, you might decide to look for passages or instances similar to this one and attempt to determine what the novel is saying about the nature of human desire. Do we only want those things we cannot have? To answer this question, look carefully at what ultimately happens when Rosemary and Dick consummate their relationship.

You might also examine this passage in light of the incest motif that Fitzgerald weaves throughout the novel. Rosemary is a young girl who looks on an older man, Dick, as a "model of correctness," as one might a father figure. Dick feels "compelled" to pursue Rosemary even though he senses that his presence in her private space is an "intrusion." He senses that he will destroy the relationship by crossing the boundaries of propriety, yet he cannot keep himself in check. Consider how this scenario is similar to the incest described by Nicole's father. Does it bear any similarity to Dick and Nicole's relationship? You might pursue these questions in an essay that examines the incest theme in the novel and puts forth a claim about the significance of this theme in the novel.

An examination of this single passage has yielded some insight into the novel's principal characters and their motivations and has also provided several angles you might wish to pursue in an essay about *Tender Is the Night.* To proceed, you might find it helpful to select one of these angles and then identify additional passages that seem to provide more clues about it. Close read these passages and use them to help you answer some of the questions you began with and to construct a claim upon which you can base your essay. Some of the analysis of the language in your key passages will now become the evidence you present to back the claim you have decided to make in your essay.

TOPICS AND STRATEGIES

The sample topics offered below present many different ways to approach writing an essay about Fitzgerald's *Tender Is the Night.* Each sample topic provides you with questions to think about and particular scenes or passages that may help you answer them. Use these to generate your own ideas about the topic and, ultimately, to help you arrive at a claim to make about the novel that will become the cornerstone of your essay. Remember that you do not have to address all of the questions in a sample topic, nor should you restrict your thinking to the particular questions and passages provided. You might choose to focus intensely on one or two of the questions provided in a sample topic, or you might discover other passages in the novel that you find more pertinent to the topic than the ones suggested here.

Themes

To create an essay about one of the novel's themes, begin by asking what universal or broad ideas the novel is concerned with. Once you have identified a promising theme, you then proceed to determine what unique or interesting point the novel is making about this theme. It is often helpful to identify particular characters, scenes, or passages connected with the theme. A close analysis of these key elements can reveal a great deal about the novel as a whole. *Tender Is the Night* is definitely concerned with money, for example. To construct an essay about money as one of the themes of the novel, however, you would first need to narrow your focus a bit. You might concentrate on investigating the ways that money and power are connected in the novel. You might focus on old and new money, concentrating on the difference between the Warrens and their money versus the Hoyts and their money. You might even focus on the effect of Nicole's money on Dick's career, considering whether excess wealth makes it impossible or at least more difficult for a person to be productive. Once you have selected an angle from which to come at the larger theme, identify key passages to analyze that will help you arrive at a claim on which to base your essay and provide evidence for that claim.

Sample Topics:

1. **Expatriates:** What kind of commentary does the novel make about expatriates?

   Think about the reasons that Dick and Nicole are expatriates. What drove them away from the United States? What do they and other characters in the novel think of the United States and its citizens? Contrast the expatriates to the American "tourists" who are in Europe but have not expatriated. Do Americans lose their "American-ness" once they have been away from their native country for a certain period of time? Why do you think Dick goes back to the United States after he and Nicole split up?

2. **Forgiveness:** What kind of commentary does *Tender Is the Night* make about the human capacity for forgiveness? In book 2, chapter xxiii, as Dick is waiting for Baby Warren to get him out of jail after he has gotten into a fight with a cab driver and

assaulted a detective, Fitzgerald writes, "No mature Aryan is able to profit by a humiliation; when he forgives it has become part of his life, he has identified himself with the thing which has humiliated him" (233). Is this purely Dick's point of view or a philosophy that the novel as a whole appears to endorse?

Think of the various ways that the characters in the novel are injured and the ways that they respond to their injuries and the people who inflicted them. In the world of the novel, must all victims ultimately identify with the perpetrators of the crime in order to forgive? What exactly is meant here by *forgiveness?* Does it imply or necessitate reconciliation? Does the novel put forth more than one model of forgiveness?

3. **Money:** What role does money play in the novel? In what ways is it attached to power, security, and control? In what ways does it support or, alternatively, undermine identity?

Look closely at Rosemary, Nicole, and Baby Warren. What does their money enable them to do? What, if any, obligations do they incur by virtue of their wealth? What is the difference between Rosemary's wealth and the Warrens'? You might analyze book 1, chapter xxii, in which Rosemary and Nicole go shopping together. In addition, consider the effect that money has on Nicole and Dick's relationship. The narrator indicates that the Warren family "bought" Dick for Nicole. What does this mean exactly? Does Dick consider himself bought? What does the novel seem to think of this idea that money can buy all things, including doting spouses?

4. **Incest:** How does the central incident of incest, that of Nicole's father, reverberate through the remainder of the novel? What kind of commentary does Fitzgerald make with this theme?

What happens to Nicole as a result of the incest? How is her relationship with Dick similar to and different from her relationship with her father? Examine what is revealed about the film *Daddy's Girl,* for which Rosemary Hoyt is famous. How does the image of Rosemary as "Daddy's Girl" affect Dick? In what way can their relationship be said to be incestuous? Are there any other instances of men romantically or sexually involved with girls who regard them as paternal figures? What message does the novel seem to convey about these relationships? How do they affect everyone involved? What do they say about the larger society?

Character

Character can be an especially fruitful angle to consider when you are attempting to create a claim or thesis on which to base your essay. You might select a minor character, like Abe North or Tommy Barban, for instance, in *Tender Is the Night,* and write about his overall function in the novel. You might select a major character, such as Dick, Nicole, or Rosemary, and consider whether he or she evolves through the course of the novel, the causes of whatever changes occur, and whether any character development is construed as positive or negative in the universe of the novel. It is often interesting to consider not just individual characters but groups of similar characters and relationships among various characters. For instance, you might elect to study how female characters or expatriates are portrayed in the novel. In terms of relationships, you might focus on the novel's presentation of the relationship between parents and children or the relationship between romantic partners in order to determine what the novel seems to be saying about the various kinds of love between people and its effects on those people.

Sample Topics:

1. **Dick's character development:** Trace the evolution of Dick's character. What message or commentary can you derive from the course Fitzgerald draws for his life?

   To write this essay, first record your general impressions of Dick's character at various points in the novel. You might select a few key passages that either describe Dick's character or represent pivotal moments in his development. As you trace Dick's evolution, make sure to account for the fact that Dick's story is not told in strict chronological order. Look closely at what is known about his early life and his father, his experiences during the war, and his life with Nicole in its various stages. Does Dick continue to grow stronger and wiser throughout his life? If not, can you identify a moment or incident that seems to signal his decline? Finally, consider what meaning you can draw from the pattern you have discovered. Is Fitzgerald, for example, saying that we all must come to terms with our inevitable decline? Or does Dick make mistakes that account for his downfall?

Using this same approach, you might write an essay on any of the other major characters. You could look at Nicole or Rosemary, for example, and describe and evaluate her character development.

2. **Parent-child relationships:** What kind of commentary does the novel make about the relationships between parents and children?

Begin by listing and describing the parent-child relationships presented in the novel. What characterizes the relationships between Rosemary and her mother, Dick and his father, Nicole and her father, Nicole and her children? Based on these relationships, what are parent-child relationships like? Do they help or harm those involved? Can you determine what a healthy parent-child relationship looks like according to Fitzgerald? Alternatively, you might focus on one or two of the parent-child relationships instead of looking at them as a whole. You could, for example, look closely at Nicole's relationship with her parents and her relationship with her own children to study how her relationship with her parents is reflected in her own parenting style. Or you might focus on Nicole's relationship with her father and Rosemary's relationship with her mother in order to examine the effects of intense parent-child bonds.

3. **Baby Warren:** What is the significance of this character to the novel's larger themes?

Look closely at the description of Baby provided in book 2, chapter xiii. What do you know about her? What do you make of her decision not to marry? How does she use her money? Is she truly concerned about her sister's well-being? Why might Fitzgerald create a character such as Baby? Does she serve as a foil to any other character? Is she intended to serve as a symbol of all the women in the novel who try to "control" Dick? What do you make of Fitzgerald's description of her as a "compendium of all the discontented women who had loved Byron a hundred years before" (152)?

4. **Tommy Barban:** Why does Fitzgerald employ a minor character like Tommy in such a crucial role by the novel's end?

Tommy Barban is certainly among the cast of minor characters; large sections of the narrative do not even mention him. However, he plays a critical role in how the narrative ends. In a way, he steps into the role of the main character, which was Dick's role. Why does Fitzgerald have a minor player make such an impact? What does this reveal about Nicole's needs and desires? What does the fact that Tommy supplants Dick say about Dick's condition by the novel's end?

History and Context

It is important to consider the context in which a book was written for a full appreciation and understanding of it, especially when the world has changed as much as it has since the writing of *Tender Is the Night.* Some good research can prevent you from making incorrect assumptions or erroneous judgments that can all too easily happen if you were to apply contemporary thinking to works set in very different times. In many cases, a close look at the context—which provides a richer sense of the work in relationship to the ideology of its time—can result in an interesting claim on which to base an essay. Familiarizing yourself with psychological theory or the role of women in the early 20th century, for instance, can give you a sense of how the novel reflects or responds to contemporary thought.

Sample Topics:

1. **Contemporary psychological theory:** Is Fitzgerald's portrayal of the world of psychoanalysts and their patients, primarily Nicole, consistent with the reality of early 20th-century psychoanalysis? What elements, if any, does he alter? Which does he emphasize or deemphasize? To what end?

Working on this topic will require research into the psychoanalytic techniques, primarily Freudian, of the early 20th century. For an accessible but comprehensive treatment of the subject, consult

On Freud by Michael Trupp. For more advanced research, try *Freud and Beyond* by Stephen A. Mitchell and Margaret J. Black. After grounding yourself in the theory and practice that was standard at the time the novel is set, return to the world of the novel and think about how psychoanalysis is presented and used by the characters and the narrator. Does this novel invite us to psychoanalyze the characters? How accurately do the characters psychoanalyze one another? Is Fitzgerald's portrayal of Nicole's illness and recovery consistent with contemporary psychoanalysis? How have ideas about incest and its effects on survivors and their families changed since the early 20th century?

2. **War/violence:** This novel is set in Europe one decade after World War I, and many of the characters have had direct experience with the war. What is the effect of the war on society as depicted in *Tender Is the Night*? What does the novel say about violence, on scales both large and small?

Locate the scenes of violence in the novel. Who perpetrates the violence? Who are the victims? Is anything achieved through violence? What is lost? You might look specifically at Tommy Barban, paying particular attention to book 1, chapter vi, and book 2, chapter xvii. What does he represent, and what does the novel seem to think of him? Is he likeable, sympathetic? Look also at Dick's commentary on the "tragic hill of Thiepval" in book 1, chapter xiii. Examine his speech to Rosemary: "my entire beautiful lovely safe world blew itself up here with a great gust of high explosive love" (57). How is the war connected to love for Dick? What does the novel seem to think of Dick's attitude?

3. **Role of women in society:** What does the novel say about the role of women in early 20th-century Western society?

To get an idea of how women were treated and how they lived their lives in the early 20th century, read the pertinent sections of Sheila Rowbotham's *A Century of Women: The History of Women in Britain and the United States in the Twentieth Century*. Be sure to consult her extensive bibliography if you wish to do more targeted research as well. Then evaluate Fitzgerald's portrayal of women in *Tender Is the Night*. What do you think he means when he describes Nicole, Mary North, and Rosemary as different from other American women in that they "were all happy to exist in a man's world—they preserved their individuality through men and not by opposition to them. They would all three have made alternatively good courtesans or good wives not by the accident of birth but through the greater accident of finding their man or not finding him" (53). According to this passage, what are "ordinary" American women like? Examine this passage and the remainder of the novel as well to determine what makes these three women different. Does the novel portray this difference as a positive or negative one?

4. **The cinema:** Why does Fitzgerald cast Rosemary as a movie star? What impact does that have on how the other characters perceive her?

In its short history prior to the 1930s, the cinema was a modern curiosity, a technical challenge, and a burgeoning art form. In the 1930s, however, it matured into a business and a cultural force not unlike its status today. Research this pivotal moment in the history of cinema; Tino Balio's *Grand Design: Hollywood as a Modern Business Enterprise, 1930–1939* provides an excellent account of Hollywood's suddenly powerful status and would be a good source. Having researched the place movies occupied at this time period, think about Rosemary and the place she occupies. How does she compare to the real-life movie stars of this period? What conclusions would a contemporary audience of the novel have immediately jumped to knowing that she was a movie actress? How is her financial well-being connected to her popularity? How does this differentiate her from the other characters? How does this influence her behavior, her freedom, and the company she keeps? Does becoming a movie star mean that Rosemary enjoys more control over her destiny or less?

5. **Biographical connections:** How do the parallels between Fitzgerald's life and the novel affect your interpretation of *Tender Is the Night*?

Read a biography of Fitzgerald, such as Matthew J. Bruccoli's *Some Sort of Epic Grandeur*, paying particular attention to his life in the years during which he was writing *Tender Is the Night*. What parallels can be drawn between Nicole and Fitzgerald's wife, Zelda? Between Fitzgerald himself and Dick Diver? What new insight into the novel's meaning can you gain by understanding these connections?

Form and Genre

While it is often tempting to ignore the more technical or formal aspects of a work of literature, these basic building blocks can provide a great deal of insight into the work if you pause to consider them properly. A writer takes great pains to decide on such things as who will tell the story, in what order it will be told, how the work will be divided into books, chapters, or sections, and what it will be called. If you take time to examine these decisions and their implications, you can gain a better understanding of the artist's goals and the way the piece comes together as a whole to achieve the effects that it does.

Sample Topics:

1. **Point of view:** How does point of view affect your interpretation of characters and events?

   Through whose point of view is the story told? Is it consistent, or are different characters' points of view presented throughout the novel? Are you allowed to see into the thoughts and emotions of the characters? One way to start thinking about this topic is to imagine the novel being told through a different point of view. What, for instance, would this novel be like if it were told by Dick? By Nicole? While you should not write an essay describing how you imagine these versions of the novel, doing this imaginative exercise will provide you some insight into how the point of view influences the narrative.

2. **Title:** What is the significance of the novel's title? How might it color an interpretation of the novel's events?

   Fitzgerald takes the title of the novel from Keats's "Ode to a Nightingale":

Already with thee! tender is the night . . .
. . . But here there is no light,
Save what from heaven is with the breezes blown
Through verdurous glooms and winding mossy ways

Read the entire poem and think about its meaning. How might these lines help you understand the novel's themes? Who might the nightingale of the novel be?

3. **Chronology:** What effect does Fitzgerald achieve by telling the story in the order he does?

According to literary critic Mark White, contemporary critics frowned upon Fitzgerald's use of flashback in book 2, arguing that the book was poorly organized (quoted in Smith 253). This criticism caused Fitzgerald to wonder whether he should have told the story in strict chronological order. Malcolm Cowley revised the novel 10 years after Fitzgerald's death, putting a great deal of books 2 and 3 at the beginning of the novel and subtitling it "The Author's Final Version." This "final version" was not well received and did not become the standard version of the novel. Mark White explains why, arguing that "[f]ar from being 'a mistake,' the [original] structure of *Tender Is the Night* works well to deliver the evolution of Rosemary's views of Dick, and without that structure, much of what Hemingway called the 'magic' of the book would have been lost completely." What effect is achieved by opening the novel with Rosemary's view of Dick and Nicole? Is it necessary to the success of the book as a whole?

Symbols, Imagery, and Language

Just as a musical composer builds meanings out of individual notes and instruments, a writer creates meaning out of individual images, symbols, and language. Very often readers become so caught up in the broader movements of the plot and characters that they fail to see what is going on at a much smaller, but just as important, level. Consciously paying attention to striking or repetitive images, symbols that reappear throughout a story or novel, and the way that language is used can open up many possibilities for essay topics. Your task is to interpret how the writer is using the symbols, imagery, and language and to demonstrate to your audience how paying attention to these facets of the novel enhances the understanding of it.

Sample Topics:

1. **Dick on the aquaplane:** Take a close look at the scene in book 3, chapter vii, in which Dick attempts to lift another man onto his shoulders while riding a board pulled by a speed boat. After trying and failing three times, he is forced to give up. What is symbolized here?

   First think about what Dick's athletic prowess symbolizes in the novel. You might locate key scenes in which this is emphasized. What might the public failure of that prowess mean in the novel? What changes for Dick after this scene? For Rosemary? For Nicole? What is the connection between this scene and Nicole's affair with Tommy Barban?

2. **Acting:** What is the significance of the novel's many references to acting?

   Look closely at all of the references to acting in the novel. You might begin with a look at book 1, chapter ii, in which Rosemary and Mrs. McKisco discuss who is and is not "in the plot" (7). Look also at book 1, chapter xxiv, in which Rosemary says to Dick, "We're such actors—you and I" (105). Why does she choose this moment to make this pronouncement? What does she mean? Finally, you might examine the scene in book 3, chapter vii, in which Rosemary asks Dick and Nicole what they thought of her recent movies, and Dick responds with a definition of the difference between "acting" and "burlesquing" (288). Why does he respond to Rosemary's question in this way? What does his answer mean in the larger context of the novel? Once you have examined these scenes and any others that mention acting, you can begin to decide what the novel is trying to say. Are some people more invested in "acting" than others, or is every human being's very identity made up of performances put on for other people?

3. **The English language:** *Tender Is the Night* is written in elaborate, lyrical English, yet it proclaims the ineffectual nature of the English language. What kind of commentary does the novel make about the power, or lack thereof, of language?

Look for instances in the novel in which language is mentioned directly. For example, you might consider the significance of the fact that Nicole "knew few words and believed in none and in the world she was rather silent" (26). You might examine the scene in which Nicole tells Tommy to speak English to her because "in French you can be heroic and gallant with dignity, and you know it. But in English you can't be heroic and gallant without being a little absurd, and you know that too" (270). What do you think Nicole means here? You might also look at the passage in book 3, chapter v, that states that "There was little [Dick and Nicole] dared talk about in these days; seldom did they find the right word when it counted, it arrived always a moment too late when one could not reach the other any more" (267). What is the novel's overall take on the power of language?

4. **"Do you mind if I pull down the curtain?":** In book 1, chapter xx, Collis Clay tells Dick a story about Rosemary going into a compartment on a train with a friend of his and pulling down the curtains. Clay tells Dick that there was "some heavy stuff going on" when the conductor knocked on the door. Dick imagines the exchange between Rosemary and her beau: "—Do you mind if I pull down the curtain? / —Please do. It's too light in here" (88). What is the significance of this imagined exchange and the fact that, from this point on, the phrase "Do you mind if I pull down the curtain?" haunts Dick through the remainder of the novel?

Look at the exchange between Dick and Collis Clay in book 1, chapter xx. What is Collis's reason for telling the story? How does Dick interpret it? At what moments does the phrase "Do you mind if I pull down the curtain?" recur to him? What does the fact that this phrase recurs in Dick's mind say about his own psychology and his attachment to Rosemary?

Compare and Contrast Essays

Another way to construct a claim about a piece of literature is to set two elements side by side to compare and contrast them. You might set two elements in the same novel side by side—two characters, perhaps, or the relationships between two sets of characters—or you might compare similar elements across novels. Fitzgerald's two best completed novels, *The Great Gatsby* and *Tender Is the Night*, provide excellent opportunities for comparing and contrasting. You might study, for example, the artist figure or the heroine of each novel in order to identify patterns or trace changes in Fitzgerald's thinking.

Sample Topics:

1. **Artists figures—McKisco in *Tender Is the Night* versus McKee in *The Great Gatsby*:** Judging from these two characters, what does Fitzgerald see as the role of the artist in modern society?

   To write an essay on this topic, you should examine the description of McKee's character in chapter 2 of *The Great Gatsby* and the examples of his art that appear in the text, such as the "dim enlargement of Mrs. Wilson's mother which hovered like ectoplasm on the wall" (34). Think about what characterizes McKee's art. What is Fitzgerald saying about art through the creation of McKee's character? Then examine the character of McKisco in *Tender Is the Night*. What kind of writing does McKisco do? How does he behave? Why does the duel give his writing career such a boost? Compare your notes on these two artist figures. What conclusions can you draw about Fitzgerald's view of artists?

2. **Dick's relationship with Rosemary versus Nicole's relationship with Tommy Barban:** What do these relationships reveal about Dick and Nicole and the nature of their relationship with each other?

   Take a close look at these two extramarital relationships. What attracts Dick to Rosemary and Nicole to Tommy? What do Rosemary and Tommy expect to gain from these relationships? Would you consider either of these relationships healthy? Why or why not? What do they reveal about the emotional needs of Dick and

Nicole? Can you determine based on their new relationships how each of them has changed through the course of their marriage? Does Nicole's ability to establish a relationship with Tommy truly indicate that she is cured, as the novel indicates? Why or why not?

3. **Old money versus new money:** Where does the wealth of various characters come from, and what are the effects of the sources of their money on their behavior and their interactions with one another?

   While money itself carries meaning within the novel, so too does the source of one's money and one's attendant social status. From what sources do the various characters derive their wealth? What social status accompanies this wealth? How do Rosemary and Nicole think differently about money? When Mary North becomes the Contessa di Minghetti, how does she change her behavior? What does she obviously think it means? And what does it mean that she and Dick effect a sort of reconciliation later on?

4. **Nicole from *Tender Is the Night* and Daisy from *The Great Gatsby:*** What do Fitzgerald's two great heroines tell us about his idea of women?

   Compare Nicole Diver and Daisy Buchanan. In what ways are they similar? Chart the development of each of them. Do they progress, remain static, or deteriorate? What effect do they have on other characters in the novels, especially those who love them? How do money and status figure into both of their lives? What is different about these two characters? Nine years separated the publication of these two novels; can you chart a change in Fitzgerald's portrayal of women from Daisy to Nicole?

BIBLIOGRAPHY AND ONLINE RESOURCES FOR *TENDER IS THE NIGHT*

Balio, Tino. *Grand Design: Hollywood as a Modern Business Enterprise, 1930–1939.* Berkeley: U of California P, 1995.

Baughman, Judith S. "Fitzgerald and the Movies." F. Scott Fitzgerald Centenary Website. University of South Carolina. Updated Dec. 2003. Retrieved 12 Mar. 2007. <http://www.sc.edu/fitzgerald/movies.html>.

Bruccoli, Matthew. *The Composition of* Tender Is the Night. Pittsburgh: U of Pittsburgh P, 1963.

———. *Some Sort of Epic Grandeur: The Life of F. Scott Fitzgerald.* 2nd rev. ed. U of South Carolina P, 2002.

Bruccoli, Matthew J., and Judith S. Baughman. *Reader's Companion to F. Scott Fitzgerald:* Tender Is the Night. Columbia, SC: U of South Carolina P, 1996.

Callahan, John F. "F. Scott Fitzgerald's Evolving American Dream: The 'Pursuit of Happiness' in *Gatsby, Tender Is the Night,* and *The Last Tycoon.*" *Twentieth Century Literature* 42.3 (Fall 1996): 374–96.

De Koster, Katie, ed. "Chapter 3: *Tender Is the Night.*" *Readings on F. Scott Fitzgerald.* San Diego, CA: Greenhaven Press, 1997. 138–72.

Fitzgerald, F. Scott. *Tender Is the Night.* New York: Scribner, 1982.

Latham, Aaron. *Crazy Sundays: F. Scott Fitzgerald in Hollywood.* New York: Viking, 1971.

Mitchell, Stephen, and Margaret Black. *Freud and Beyond: A History of Modern Psychoanalytic Thought.* New York: Basic, 1995.

Smith, Jennifer, ed. *Tender Is the Night. Novels for Students.* Vol. 19. Detroit: Gale, 2004. 240–71.

Stern, Milton R. Tender Is the Night: *The Broken Universe.* New York: Twayne, 1994.

Trupp, Michael. *On Freud.* Belmont, CA: Wadsworth, 2000.

INDEX